D1274616

Praise for
Blacklegs, Card Sharps, and Confidence Men

"*Blacklegs, Card Sharps, and Confidence Men* is the most significant collection of riverlore published in decades. Thomas Ruys Smith's wide-ranging anthology includes selections from high and low culture, demonstrating the evolution of gambling from a widely feared part of the early river trade to a romanticized American cultural icon. This collection is essential to understanding the history of gambling in America and solidifies Smith's reputation as the leading cultural historian of American river life."

—THOMAS C. BUCHANAN, author of *Black Life on the Mississippi:*
Slaves, Free Blacks, and the Western Steamboat World

"The Mississippi riverboat gambler ranks alongside the mountain man, frontier scout, patriot militiaman, borderlands outlaw, and cowboy as an archetypal American folk hero. Yet the scholarly literature of the riverboat gambler is sparse compared to that of his folkloric colleagues. Thomas Ruys Smith helps to correct this slight in *Blacklegs, Card Sharps, and Confidence Men*. Smith has gathered together a splendid collection of both literary and historical writings (and combinations thereof) that tell the exciting story of this nineteenth-century icon. Scholars and laymen alike will enjoy sitting back and reading these engaging tales."

—MICHAEL ALLEN, author of *Rodeo Cowboys in the*
North American Imagination

In 1836 Benjamin Drake, a midwestern writer of popular sketches for newspapers of the day, introduced his readers to a new and distinctly American rascal who rode the steamboats up and down the Mississippi and other western waterways—the riverboat gambler. These men, he recorded, "dress with taste and elegance; carry gold chronometers in their pockets; and swear with the most genteel precision. . . . Every where throughout the valley, these mistletoe gentry are called by the original, if not altogether classic, cognomen of 'Black-legs.'"

In *Blacklegs, Card Sharps, and Confidence Men,* Thomas Ruys Smith collects nineteenth-century stories, sketches, and book excerpts by a gallery of authors to create a comprehensive collection of writings about the riverboat gambler. Long an iconic figure in American myth and popular culture but, strangely, one that has never until now received a book-length treatment, the Mississippi River gambler was a favorite character throughout the nineteenth century—one often rich with moral ambiguities that remain unresolved to this day.

In the absorbing fictional and nonfictional accounts of high stakes and sudden reversals of fortune found in the pages of Smith's book, the voices of canonized writers such as William Dean Howells, Herman Melville, and, of course, Mark Twain hold prominent positions. But they mingle seamlessly with lesser-known pieces such as an excerpt from Edward Willett's sensationalistic dime novel *Flush Fred's Full Hand,* raucous sketches by anonymous Old Southwestern humorists from the *Spirit of the Times,* and colorful accounts by now nearly forgotten authors such as Daniel R. Hundley and George W. Featherstonhaugh.

Smith puts the twenty-eight selections in perspective with an Introduction that thoroughly explores the history and myth surrounding this endlessly fascinating American cultural icon. While the riverboat gambler may no longer ply his trade along the Mississippi, *Blacklegs, Card Sharps, and Confidence Men* makes clear the ways in which he still operates quite successfully in the American imagination.

Thomas Ruys Smith is a lecturer in American literature and culture at the University of East Anglia in the United Kingdom and the author of *River of Dreams: Imagining the Mississippi before Mark Twain.*

Blacklegs, Card Sharps, and Confidence Men

SOUTHERN LITERARY STUDIES

Fred Hobson, *Editor*

Blacklegs, Card Sharps, and Confidence Men

◆

Nineteenth-Century Mississippi River Gambling Stories

EDITED BY

THOMAS RUYS SMITH

LOUISIANA STATE UNIVERSITY PRESS

BATON ROUGE

Published by Louisiana State University Press
Copyright © 2010 by Louisiana State University Press
All rights reserved
Manufactured in the United States of America
First printing

Designer: Laura Roubique Gleason
Typeface: Minion Pro
Printer and binder: Thomson-Shore, Inc.

Title page illustration is from *Wild Scenes on the Frontiers; or, Heroes of the West* (1859), by Emerson Bennett.

Library of Congress Cataloging-in-Publication Data

Blacklegs, card sharps, and confidence men : nineteenth-century Mississippi River gambling stories / [edited by] Thomas Ruys Smith.
    p.   cm. — (Southern literary studies)
    Includes bibliographical references.
    ISBN 978-0-8071-3636-2 (cloth : alk. paper) 1. Gamblers—Mississippi River—Literary collections. 2. Gambling on river boats—Mississippi River—History—19th century—Literary collections. 3. River life—Mississippi River—History—19th century—Literary collections. 4. Mississippi River Valley—Social life and customs—19th century—Literary collections. 5. American literature—19th century. 6. American literature—Mississippi. I. Smith, Thomas Ruys, 1979–
    PS558.M7B63 2010
    810.9'355—dc22

                                    2009030241

The paper in this book meets the guidelines for permanence and durability of the Committee on Production Guidelines for Book Longevity of the Council on Library Resources. ⊚

For Arianna, Queen of Hearts

Contents

Contents

Epilogue

Blacklegs, Card Sharps, and Confidence Men

Introduction

The Many Lives of the Mississippi Gambler

> A numerous and peculiar race of modern gentlemen, may be found in
> the valley of the Mississippi. A naturalist would probably describe them
> as a genus of bipeds, gregarious, amphibious and migratory. They seldom
> travel "solitary and alone"; are equally at home on land or water; and like
> certain vultures, spend most of their winters in Mississippi and Louisiana;
> their summers in the higher latitudes of Kentucky and Ohio. They dress
> with taste and elegance; carry gold chronometers in their pockets; and
> swear with the most genteel precision [. . .] Every where throughout
> the valley, these mistletoe gentry are called by the original, if not
> altogether classic, cognomen of "Black-legs."
>
> —Benjamin Drake, *Tales and Sketches from the Queen City* (1838)

Almost two centuries after Benjamin Drake introduced his readers to the
"numerous and peculiar race of modern gentlemen" (27) to be found on the
steamboats of the western rivers, the iconic Mississippi River gambler still
occupies a symbolically potent role within the American imagination. As
Jackson Lears has rightly asserted, "riverboat gambling has preserved an almost mythic stature as an American cultural ritual" (116). Given the ever-
increasing prominence and acceptance of gaming, that might be truer now
than ever before. And yet, compared to other popular nineteenth-century
representatives of the national spirit—the cowboy, the backwoodsman, the
pioneer, the miner—the riverboat gambler has received relatively little critical attention. This is a shame, not least because he was a favorite character for a wide variety of nineteenth-century writers and a figure rich with
moral ambiguities that remain unresolved. This anthology, the first of its
kind, represents a step along the road of redress. Within the shifting fortunes of this important icon can be traced a wealth of societal and attitudinal
changes that continue to have importance in the present day. Furthermore,
these texts allow us to revisit seemingly familiar texts and authors and view
them in an entirely new light. Here voices from high and low culture mingle,
and these stories present a panorama of nineteenth century literature. The
mythical Mississippi gambler has lived many lives in American culture, and
the stories featured here allow us to clearly trace the transformations of his
formative decades.

However familiar the riverboat gambler might seem to us as a cultural presence, a combination of both critical neglect and the frequently illicit nature of his activities makes it difficult to establish a clear picture of his life and times. In the pages of this volume, history and fiction mingle. The wealth of texts that follow clearly attest to the fact that gambling, at least to some extent, did take place on and along the western rivers in the nineteenth century. Indeed, the Mississippi had a reputation for gambling and other forms of vice even before the first steamboat reached the river in 1811. As steamboat pilot Emerson Gould declared in 1889, the "beautiful valley of the Mississippi" had been "a veritable *elysian field,* for the successful operation of all outlaws" (268). Timothy Flint, writing about his experiences on the river frontier in the days before steam, reluctantly admitted, "It is true there are gamblers, and gougers, and outlaws" (176). The men who worked on the flatboats and keelboats that plied the rivers before the steamboat were particularly associated with gambling. Christian Schultz traveled along the western rivers in the early nineteenth century and noted that the crew of his boat were keen gamblers: "You will scarcely believe," he declared of the settlement of Smith Town, near the mouth of the Cumberland River, "that a billiard-table has been established, which is continually surrounded by common boatmen [. . .] who in one hour lost all the hard-earned wages of a two months voyage!"(1:203). As Frances Trollope put it succinctly, boatmen were "constantly gambling and wrangling" (1:22).

Catering to their needs, there developed in each river town an area renowned for gambling, prostitution, and worse. In Natchez, it was "Under-the-Hill"; in Vicksburg, "the Kangaroos"; in Memphis, "Pinch-Gut." On a much larger scale, New Orleans was famed for its casinos. Herbert Asbury has stated that by 1810 "gambling-houses were numerous, both in the French Quarter and in the new section above Canal Street, and had become the focal points of much crime and disorder" (214). In 1835, Joseph Holt Ingraham visited just such an establishment and noted: "From six to twelve well-dressed, genteel looking individuals, are always to be found in attendance, to whom salaries are regularly paid [. . .] It is this class of men who are emphatically denominated 'gamblers and black legs'" (*South-West* 1:129–30). Ten years earlier, the *New Hampshire Gazette* had given its readers a cautionary story about the dangers posed by such figures: "A young man previously of excellent character, was sent from the State of Mississippi lately to New Orleans to sell 77 bags of Cotton. After transacting the business well, and receiving pay, he was beset, intoxicated and seduced by gamblers, and lost the whole of the money.—He afterwards in despair enlisted as a soldier" (2).

Gambling, then, was well established on the river by the time the steamboat reached the Mississippi in 1811. But the advent of the steamboat on the western waters clearly marked a vital new era in the story of gambling on and along the Mississippi. The steamboat cabin created a potent setting for social interaction on the river, and inevitably this meant that it was also a fruitful environment for gamblers. It wasn't long before they made the space their own. As Frederick Marryat described the development, in unhappy terms: "the morals of the Mississippi became worse, as the mean and paltry knave, the swindler, and the forger were now mingled up with the more daring spirits, producing a more complicated and varied class of crime than before. The steam-boats were soon crowded by a description of people who were termed gamblers, as such was their ostensible profession, although they were ready for any crime which might offer an advantage to them, and the increase of commerce and constant inpouring of populations daily offer to them some new dupe for their villainy" (1:261). As John Findlay has articulated more recently, this home on the river became a necessity for gamblers when river towns became less content with their presence: "The Mississippi and its tributaries in a sense constituted a perpetual frontier, even as their shores settled down into respectability" (71). Indeed, the environment of a steamboat cabin on the Mississippi might have been tailor made for gamblers to ply their trade. As Gerda Reith's description of gambling psychology makes clear, games of chance and their area of play (like the Mississippi steamboat cabin) are "characterised essentially by their separateness, both temporally and spatially, from everyday life. They involve both a physical and a mental crossing of a threshold out of the ordinary world and into the world of play [. . .] [P]layers within it are animated by a different set of motivations from those of everyday routines in which they are free to experiment with new roles and to temporarily adopt new identities" (128).

The steamboat provided gamblers with an itinerant, ever-changing cast of potential victims removed from the moral safeguards of home with time on their hands—many of whom were carrying large sums of money. Moreover, the steamboat was an arena marked by what Karen Halttunen has described as "a system of horizontal social relations" in which outward appearance provided little indication of social status (20). In short, the normal rules of social interaction were made fluid in a way that was ripe for exploitation. For every blackleg who dressed and affected the manners of planter aristocracy, there was another gambler who adopted the appearance of a rustic and naïve cowboy returning from market. Gambler Henry Edward Hugunin remembered: "I dressed sometimes like a preacher, sometimes like a southern

3

planter, and occasionally in imitation of a regular western or south-western adventurer, with pistol in belt, but I never said in words that I was one or the other" (38). And as actor Joseph Cowell described his steamboat experience in 1844, "All moral and social restraint was placed in the shade—*there Jack was as good as his master*—and never was Republicanism more practically republicanized" (92). The gamblers' particular penchant for variations of the game of three-card monte, with its fast pace and apparently limitless potential for playacting and sleight of hand, exacerbated these tendencies.

But having established that gambling did take place in the nineteenth century on a Mississippi that could seem to be, in Jackson Lears's words, "a timeless, parallel universe of play" (116), it is still difficult to ascertain the true extent of riverboat gaming operations. The preeminent steamboat historian Louis Hunter has judged, "To separate fact from fiction in this tradition is difficult indeed, but it seems probable that the business was seldom conducted on the scale and with the thrills and excitement portrayed in the legend" (409). It is certainly of interest that tales of gambling on the river are largely absent from the writings of Mark Twain—something for which Bernard De Voto, writing about *Life on the Mississippi* (1883), upbraided him: "There is no mention [. . .] of the parasitism that was also constant in the [steamboat] trade. The skin games, the frauds, the robberies, the gambling, the cozenage, the systematic organization of the sucker trade are wholly absent" (110). As an explanation for this absence, perhaps Twain's expression of his distaste for the work of Bret Harte is revealing: "We owe Harte a deep debt of gratitude—the reverence in which gamblers, burglars & whores are held in the upper classes to-day is all due to him, & to him only—for the dime novel circulates only among the lower ranks" (*Notebooks* 312).

Regardless, in spite of Twain's gambling lacuna, other travelers left ample testimony of the prevalence of steamboat gambling. Charles Joseph Latrobe, traveling on the steamboat *Cavalier* in the early 1830s, described "a den of sharpers and blacklegs, where from morning to night the dirty pack of cards are passed from hand to hand" (1:225). Steamboat pilot John Habermehl clearly remembered, "Gambling on the western rivers in the olden time was a general custom [. . .] As late as 1855 one might have seen from four to six gambling tables stretched out in the main cabin in full blast for money" (45). Frederick Law Olmsted, traveling by steamboat through Louisiana, agreed: "Gambling was constantly going on, day and night. I don't think there was an interruption to it of fifteen minutes in three days" (2:268). As far as Aleksandr Borisovich Lakier was concerned, when he traveled down the Mississippi in 1857 the "passion" for gambling "firmly gripped the entire steam-boat": "Except for the ladies, everyone took part, some with their gestures, some with their eyes, and some by placing bets on one side or the other" (226, 222). Gambler Tom Ellison estimated that "there was 500 men who worked the boats" in the antebellum period (Lillard 50). And Henry Ward Beecher felt that the practice was sufficiently widespread to warn his readers about the men "often met on steamboats, travelling solely to gamble [. . .] He deals falsely; heats his dupe to madness by drink, drinking none himself; watches the signal of his accomplice telegraphing his opponent's hand; at a stray look, he will slip your money off and steal it" (147–48).

The degree to which these kinds of operations were tolerated is unclear. It seems that on board a steamboat, games of chance took place at the discretion of the captain. Actor Solomon Smith, for example, described a steamboat captain of his acquaintance as a man who was resolute that his passengers should "amuse themselves "'just as they d——n please' [. . .] If there were passengers on board who desired to pass away the time in playing poker, euchre, brag, or whist [. . .] poker, brag, euchre and whist be it!" (189). As in Smith's story (and numerous travel accounts), passengers who attempted to protest about such activities often found that their complaints fell on deaf ears. Other captains seem to have been more actively enthusiastic about the presence of gambling on their boats. In 1833, Thomas Hamilton encountered a steamboat captain who "was decidedly the greatest gambler on board; and was often so drunk as to be utterly incapable of taking command of the vessel" (175).

In some instances, gamblers and steamboat workers seem to have had something of a formal business arrangement in place. In *The End of the World* (1872) Edward Eggleston noted that "a percentage of gamblers' gains was one of the 'old man's' perquisites, and he was not the only steamboat captain who profited by the nice little games in the cabin upon which he closed both eyes" (198). John O'Connor also made the complicity of boat workers clear: "The marked-card player could accomplish nothing on a steamer, except by the connivance of the bar-tender, to whom he was obliged to give a certain share in his profits as the price of his assistance and silence" (J. Morris 424). Alternatively, stories abound of gamblers facing rough justice aboard steamboats or being put ashore in peremptory fashion. As Irvin Anthony noted, "Scarcely a gambler ever worked the river who did not have to both run and fight at times" (269). Henry Edward Hugunin (and others) told a story of a gambler who was "tied for an hour to the horizontal piston rod" of a steamboat: "It was absolutely essential for him to keep his eye on the rod and turn exactly with its backward movement or it would have torn his head from his shoulder" (35–6). George Devol had an equally tricky encounter with the wife of a man he and his partner had conned, who demanded: "You won my husband's money, and I will just give you one minute to hand it to me, or I will blow your brains out in this cabin" (27).

Exactly what sums of money might have been changing hands in these steamboat games is equally contested. As Tom Ellison speculated of his gambling colleagues, "there's no telling how much money they did pull off the travellers" (Lillard 50). Another old riverman remembered: "There was always a game of cards—poker usually—going on in the saloon, and the gamblers seldom got the worst of it. I have seen many a thousand dollars change hands in a single game" (Lillard 36). On the other hand, John O'Connor asserted: "As for the tales regarding the fabulous sums bet at poker-tables on our western rivers, they are all pure humbug. I have grave doubts whether a brag of two thousand dollars has ever been lost and won at a card-table on the Mississippi River, since the steamer Pennsylvania descended that stream in 1813" (J. Morris, 433–34). Not that gamblers were above playing for small stakes; Aleksandr Borisovich Lakier noted that they worked the entire social scale of a Mississippi steamboat: "Entrepreneurs with limited means and dirty cards went down to the second deck where the immigrants were, and there tried to take away from the poor whatever extra they might happen to have" (226).

The lifespan of riverboat gambling is also difficult to measure accurately. There is a common assumption that the Civil War ended the golden age of gambling on the Mississippi, just as it mortally wounded the steamboat trade, but even as early as 1851 Abraham Oakey Hall claimed that gamblers were "compelled to be cautious and diplomatic; for gambling on the western waters [. . .] has come to be understood; and there is little card-fleecing nowaday on the Mississippi first-class packets" (182). Postwar announcements of the demise of river gambling were more common. George Ward Nichols, writing an account of a journey "Down the Mississippi" for *Harper's New Monthly Magazine* in 1870, made it clear: "You can not see now, as we did ten years ago, the cabin tables surrounded by planters, merchants and politicians, calling themselves gentlemen, who would gamble from morning till night, and again till morning, staking, and often losing, their entire fortunes. We do not now encounter the elegant, gentlemanly, professional gambler, who was accomplished in every way, and not least in the use of the pistol and bowie knife [. . .] The war did splendid scavenger-work in sweeping them into the other world" (842). Similarly, Sydney Gay, writing in the *Atlantic* in April 1869, lamented the decline of the steamboat—and steamboat gambling—in the postwar years: "What is a respectable game of whist in a palace car to watching or playing, if one was so minded, a game of poker in the 'social hall' of a steamboat where a professional river gambler sat down, with a pack of marked cards in one pocket and a six-shooter in the other, and challenged the company to a game, quite ready for the chance of killing somebody or being killed before morning?" (439). On the other hand, John O'Connor was adamant that in the 1870s, "Though railways have diverted a large portion of the travel from our western waters, and consequently thinned out some what the horde of sharpers who formerly infested the river steamers, they are still numerous, and still find fools to prey upon" (J. Morris 434). And Albert D. Richardson, traveling up the Missouri in 1867, noted the presence of "a gambler with hang-dog face, wearing a white hat with broad band of black crape" enticing passengers to gamble with dice (24). Either way, by 1896 Tom Ellison was ready to declare: "There isn't any more gambling now [. . .] and no gamblers, either" (Lillard 50).

For all of these contradictions, one clear theme is discernible across the range of gambling accounts: the South was the primary location for riverboat gambling. George Byron Merrick, pilot on the upper Mississippi from 1854 to 1863, remembered that "the play was not high on the upper river [. . .] The passengers were not great planters, with sacks of money [. . .] The operators, also, were not so greedy as their real or fictitious fellows on the lower river" (138–39). Many agreed with Merrick's judgment. John Habermehl remembered, "Signs were tacked up, 'Games for money strictly forbidden,' which had some little effect in the North, but in the South, a notice of this kind was one thing, and human nature entirely a different thing" (45). Another old steamboatman, perhaps echoing the romanticism that grew up around Mississippi gambling in the late nineteenth century, exhorted: "The time to see life then was about the last of the year, when the planters were travelling home from New Orleans after selling their cotton crops. They would have, every man of them, a fortune in his pocket, and not one had the least conception of the value of money" (Lillard 35–36).

And yet the association between gambling and the South was an ambiguous one. Gambling was clearly an important part of southern culture in the years before the war. Kenneth Greenberg has noted: "Games of chance [. . .] flourished among the honorable men of the antebellum South," who "wagered with a frequency and an intensity widely noted by visitors to the region" (135). W. J. Cash concluded that the ability "to lose the whole of one's capital on the turn of a card without the quiver of a muscle" was one of the essential attributes of the southern man of honor (39). Contemporary accounts support these assertions. One antebellum writer judged that the "man of the West and South" was "a born gambler," since he had "to bet his life every day to make a great profit," and could therefore stand "at a faro-table with a stoic manner declaring *I don't give a damn*" (Klauprecht 185). In the 1850s, Emerson Bennett stressed: "Any man living on the lower Mississippi twenty years ago, who was not in favor of playing all sorts of games for all manner of sums, would have been at once pronounced no gentleman or a minister of the Gospel" (125). And as one old steamboatman clarified the issue, "every one gambled; if they had not done so the professional's occupation would have been gone" (Lillard 43).

Despite the prevalence of gambling in the South, not all gamblers were equal. A clear division was drawn between the gentleman gambler and the professional. In *The Last of the Foresters* (1856), John Esten Cooke advised that "if you have the playing mania, never play with anybody but gentlemen. You will thus have the consolation of reflecting that you have been ruined in good company, and, in addition, had your pleasure;—blacklegs ruin a man with a vulgar rapidity which is positively shocking" (241). "Falconbridge" made the social divide even clearer: "a gentleman may game with a gambler by the hour, and yet despise him and refuse to recognise him afterwards" (119). As Kenneth Greenberg has explained, "The best way to begin to appreciate the connections between gambling and honor is to examine closely the sharp contrast between a Southern gentleman's powerful love of gambling and his equally powerful hatred of professional gamblers" (136). While the North censored the professional gambler because of the way he won his money—the fact that, as Karen Halttunen has put it, gambling "undermined all desire to practice industry" (17)—the South hated him because he refused to lose it. For the professional gambler, in Greenberg's words, "the best bet was a sure bet—which was no bet at all for a Southern man of honour" (143). And to make certain of a "sure bet," as the stories and personal testimonies in this collection make clear, professional gamblers had a variety of cheating practices at their disposal. It was this, particularly, that drew the line of respectability between amateur and professional. John O'Connor lamented:

> Previous to the appearance of the card-sharper and his newly invented schemes for cheating, on the river the card-tables of a steamer were free to all persons of gentlemanly habits and manners. The gambler was not

excluded from a seat there on account of his superior skill at play; or, at least, it was an exceedingly rare thing for one person to object to another on these grounds. Pride would not permit the humiliating confession [. . .]

The votaries of chance were not yet aroused to the fact that they could be insidiously robbed at the card-table when everything seemed perfectly fair and above-board; but when that enlightening took place, the gambler was immediately classed with the sharper, because the verdant were unable to understand where the gambler left off and the thief began. (J. Morris 423)

Henry Edward Hugunin also noted that his retirement from the life of a blackleg was related to "the change in the character of gambling": "I could not have gone, if I had tried, in to the three card monte, confidence swindles or any of the 'sure thing' games. I had always, if I may be allowed to use the expression, a 'professional pride'" (50).

For some contemporary commentators, the professional gambler's prominence on the lower Mississippi was more than just a reflection of gambling's popularity in the South: it was a direct result of slavery. In his abolitionist work *Despotism in America* (1840), Richard Hildreth asserted that the "vice of gambling" was "next to universal" in the South because the "institution of slavery deprives a large portion of the people of their natural occupation." This created "a peculiar class of men [. . .] who are gamblers by profession." As far as Hildreth was concerned, professional gamblers, compelled to make a living through gambling by the peculiar social system of the South, were obliged to cheat: "If they left every thing to chance and strictly observed the laws of play, it would be impossible for them to live by their business, because, in the long run, they would be certain to lose as much as they won, and so could have nothing left whereupon to live. Hence they are compelled to play false. They must cheat, or starve." Despite the social stigma attached to professional gambling, it was still a crowded field: "Its members throng the steam-boats [. . .] of the south, and among them may be found, the most gentlemanly, agreeable, insinuating, talented, well informed men of the whole population." And because of slavery, more were drawn to the profession every day: "The planter who has ruined himself by improvidence, dissipation or losses at the gaming table, the young disappointed heir, bred up in indolence and luxury by a father who dies insolvent,—these persons find scarcely any other way of gaining their daily bread" (*Despotism*

153–55). Daniel Hundley, while ostensibly writing in defense of the South, also drew a direct connection between slavery and the professional gambler, but noted that it was only "the son of the vilest of the Southern Yankees" who ended up "a peripatetical blackleg, gambling for a livelihood. He travels on the river steamboats mostly, and lives by plucking all such poor pigeons as remind him of his former self" (246–47). The relationship between slavery and steamboat gambling seems to have been recognized across the social spectrum. In Epes Sargent's wartime emancipation novel *Peculiar* (1863), ex-overseer Quattles has his own tale of gambling to relate: "What with huntin' and fishin', thimble-riggin' an' stealin', I got along somehow, an' riz ter be a sort uv steamboat gambler on the Misippy" (242).

For the enslaved themselves, the prevalence of gambling on the lower Mississippi often augured ill. William Wells Brown, who worked on the steamboats before fleeing to the North, described the way that a slave might be used as collateral at the gambling table: "Such is the uncertainty of a slave's position. He goes to bed at night the property of the man with whom he has lived for years, and gets up in the morning the slave of some one whom he has never seen before!" In the 1890s, a river man assented: "I have seen negro women disposed of in this fashion [. . .] there was no romance to it" (Lillard 43). So popular was this kind of story that even a young William Dean Howells produced a poetic version of it for the *Atlantic Monthly* in 1860.

That said, it seems that there were moments when a curious kind of kinship emerged between the marginalized professional gambler and the enslaved. Henry Bibb had just such a story to tell. The slave of a brutal owner, Deacon Whitfield, Bibb was to be sold down the river away from his wife and children. When he was sold to "a company of [. . .] Southern sportsmen," his situation looked inauspicious. And yet, as Bibb himself marveled: "Although they were wicked black legs of the basest character, it is but due to them to say, that they used me far better than ever the Deacon did. They gave me plenty to eat and put nothing hard on me to do. They expressed much sympathy for me in my bereavement; and almost every day they gave me money more or less." Bibb's relationship with the gamblers developed to the point that they attempted to purchase his wife and children. The deacon refused, and Bibb noted a "sympathetic tear-drop, stealing its way down the cheek of the profligate and black-leg." Though they could not reunite Bibb with his family, the gamblers did help him to effect his escape (143–46). For Richard Hildreth, there was an even deeper association between gambling and slavery, since the tricks of a professional gambler could give the rich and powerful "a little experience what a nice thing it is, this being stripped and plundered!" (*White Slave* 324–25). And sometimes gambling seems to have brought its own brand of liberation. As a runaway Kentucky slave remembered in later life, "I got me a job and worked as a roustabout on a boat where I learned to gamble wid dice. I fought and gambled all up and down de Mississippi River" (Buchanan 76).

Though it may be difficult, if not impossible, to reconstruct the history of gambling on the river without being drawn into the wealth of romantic mythology that surrounds it, one thing is certain: in the nineteenth century, the morally ambiguous figure of the riverboat gambler captured the popular imagination—and did so in a way that his land-locked colleagues never did. The relationship between gambling and the Mississippi became proverbial; it is little wonder that playing cards with "a wrapper picturing a steamboat" were "popular among American makers for many years" (Hargrave 333). The creation of the fictional blackleg was something with which gambler John O'Connor was all too familiar: "Their rascalities even, bad as they were, were made the themes of marvelous romantic stories by the penny-a-liners and story-tellers of every description. Then the wonderful yarns that have been circulated from time to time by the lovers of the marvelous, relating to the outwitting of gamblers at their own games by determined heroes, who have forced them to disgorge their ill-gotten plunder and make restitution to every one whom they had duped, and many more tales, all equally improbable and without foundation, is all clap-trap" (J. Morris 432). Clap-trap it might have been, but the process of turning history into legend created archetypes that still have resonance today.

We may be used to popular culture representations of the antebellum river gambler as a figure who, if not entirely heroic, at least contains an element of what James Smith has called "gambler heroism": the "mythic archetype of a rugged individualist [. . .] involved in a specific ritual of play" who gains a "larger-than-life stature" (106, 102). But as we have already seen, in the days when the riverboat gambler actually plied his trade, in the years before the Civil War, this was not the case. As an old steamboatman remembered in the 1890s, "It's very pretty to read about, but the real thing was not so nice. The black-eyed, black-mustached hero gambler that you read about was anything but a hero. There was no chivalry in his nature, and he was ready for any dark deed that would profit him" (Lillard 42). Such was the gambler's reputation in the antebellum years.

Indeed, the changing fortunes of the Mississippi gambler in popular culture can be encapsulated in the experiences of one acting dynasty. In 1834 Irish actor William Grattan Tyrone Power traveled along the Mississippi River on his first American tour. When he arrived at the infamous Natchez-Under-the-Hill, he was shocked at what he found there: "The impunity with which these professed gamblers carry on their trade, and the course of crime contingent upon it [. . .] is one of the most crying evils existing in this society. The Legs are associated in gangs, have a system perfectly organized, and possess a large capital invested in this pursuit; they are seldom alone, always armed to the teeth, bound to sustain each other, and hold life at a pin's fee [. . .] [N]ot a steamboat stirs from any quarter, but one or more of the gang proceed on board, in some guise or other" (2:197–98). Power's profound mistrust of these characters was typical of the time. A century later, a sympathetic veil had obscured such fears. In 1953 Power's great-grandson, the matinee idol also named Tyrone Power, played the heroic Mark Fallon, the titular hero of Universal's *The Mississippi Gambler*. As the *New York Times* described the performance, "Mr. Power shows his prowess with the foils, his fists and with the cards" (A.W.).

Quickly told, then, the vicissitudes of fortune experienced by the riverboat gambler in popular culture, readily discernible within this anthology, can be condensed into a journey from villain to hero. On occasion, an antebellum description afforded the gambler some recognizable charm. *Emerson's Magazine and Putnam's Monthly,* in October 1857, asserted that riverboat gamblers "dress well, smoke well, drink well, and with a dash of swagger and a spice of blackleg, they [. . .] are not thought so ill of" (Gillespie 165). Equally, Joseph Cowell articulated a kinship between actors and gamblers that is readily apparent in a number of antebellum accounts—and is perhaps unsurprising, given that gamblers had to be accomplished actors and actors seem to have been inveterate gamblers. Cowell argued: "After the actors, there is no class of persons so misrepresented and abused behind their backs as the professional gamblers, as they are called; especially by those who sit down to bet against them every night without their wives and families knowing anything about it, and who would think it most praiseworthy *to cheat them* out of every dollar they had, *if they knew how* [. . .] [T]hey cannot be excelled by any other set of men who make making money their only mental occupation" (94–95). These were the kind of sympathetic characterizations that led Edwin Whipple to lament the growth of the "Romance of Rascality" in the late 1840s: "Rascality is now the rage," he explained, "and asserts its existence with an emphasis. It has forced the passages leading to the temple of fame, and breaks into literature as it was wont to break into houses [. . .] The thief and the cut-purse, the murderer and the incendiary, strut and swagger in the sunny land of romance" (2:106).

But these few defenses of his character only serve to highlight the degree to which the riverboat gambler was commonly cast as a villain in the antebellum years. And it was one event in particular that propelled the gambler into the national spotlight, simultaneously establishing his position in popular culture and assuring his role as an antebellum villain. The events of Independence Day 1835 in the town Vicksburg, Mississippi, lived long in the popular conception of gambling on the river. Trouble began when a brawl broke out at a Fourth of July celebration hosted by the Vicksburg militia, between some of its members and a gambler (or a known associate of gamblers), Francis Cabler. After tarring and feathering Cabler, the militia resolved upon the formation of an antigambling committee. Gamblers were given twenty-four hours to leave town. After the allotted period of time had passed, the militia and a civilian mob descended upon the "Kangaroos," the infamous waterfront district that took its name from a famous gambling house that had burned down the year before. Breaking up roulette wheels and faro tables as they went, the militia found a group of individuals ensconced in Alfred North's coffeehouse. After an exchange of shots the militia stormed the building. One of its members, Dr. Hugh Bodley, was shot dead. Five men—labeled as gamblers—were seized and promptly hanged. Other river towns followed suit, exiling, though not executing, their own gambling communities. The *Louisville Advertiser* announced that the "proceedings at Vicksburg have kindled a spirit throughout the lower country which is breaking forth at every point, and obliging the blackleg fraternity to make their escape with all haste" (*Niles' Weekly Register* 401).

The event gained national prominence. News of the lynchings even reached London late in August 1835, and the *Times* warned: "The treatment of the gamblers at Vicksburg will give some of our fashionable clubbists a crick in the neck" (6). The incident retained its notoriety for a number of years. Fifty years after the fact, Mark Twain noted in *Life on the Mississippi* that conversation still "drifted [. . .] into talk about the lynching of the gamblers in Vicksburg half a century ago" (312). The Vicksburgers erected a monument to Bodley: "Murdered by the Gamblers July 5, 1835 while defending the morals of Vicksburg" (Horwitz 201–2). While they gained some support for their actions, others were horrified at what had taken place. Reformed gambler Jonathan Green even asserted that gambling, not gamblers, was at the root of the problem: "I have no doubt that as many as three fourths of all the citizens of Vicksburg were more or less addicted to gambling [. . .] all these evils being occasioned by tolerating and encouraging Mr Hoyle's scientific amusements" (150).

The wider significance of the Vicksburg lynchings has been much debated. Ann Fabian describes the antebellum gambling fraternity as "undermining the symbolic presentation of authority that supported a threatened world run by slaveholders" (37). John Findlay concludes that middle-class mob action "heralded the closing of the frontier" and "ultimately asserted eastern culture over western ways" (69). For Christopher Morris, such actions belied "a nagging sense among Vicksburg residents that they were losing control of their city to strangers" (123). Whatever else they represented, the Vicksburg lynchings clearly inaugurated a new era in the popular iconography of the river. It was the moment at which the baton passed imaginatively from the river piracy of the frontier days to the riverboat gambling that was now felt to be expressive of its place and time. As William Faulkner expressed it, the "avatars of Harpe and Hare and Mason and Murrel" were "vanishing": "the river hero was now the steamboat gambler wading ashore in his draggled finery from the towhead where the captain had marooned him" (*Big Woods* 5–6). Or as Melville put it, "where the wolves are killed off, the foxes increase" (2). In practical terms, the actions at Vicksburg were indicative of wider movements taken by river towns to rid themselves of the gambling presence in their midst and push them, inevitably, onto the steamboats. As John Findlay argues, "Sharpers persisted by finding another ideal milieu for betting, the western steamboat, which both supplanted under-the-hill districts as a center for gaming and continued to generate additions to the culture of American betting" (71).

It is perhaps important to note, however, that this propulsion of the Mississippi gambler into the national spotlight also came at a moment when writers were eager to make use of just such a figure. Events in Vicksburg coincided with a growing fascination with literary scoundrels and sensational texts. It was a trend that began in the Old World. As Keith Hollingsworth has explained, "Between 1830 and 1847 [. . .] a series of novels having criminals as prominent characters aroused widespread attention" and "familiarized their readers with vice and crime." Frequently, and controversially, these "Newgate novels" aroused what was felt to be "an unfitting sympathy for the criminal" (14–15). Even William Makepeace Thackeray, who was no fan of the Newgate novel, featured gambler "Algernon Percy Deuceace" in his *Yel-*

lowplush Papers, noting that "for a real thorough bread genlmn, it's the esiest and most prophetable line he can take" (37). Closely associated with the Newgate novel was the rise of the romantic melodramatic villain in literature and on the stage. Juliet John has noted the way in which this significant figure was characterized by "moral ambiguity": he was "often a highwayman or pirate by trade" and yet "*genteel* despite his robberies" (56, 59). Significantly for the literary development of the blackleg, the romantic villain was also "a master at manipulating his presentation of self [. . .] and even proud of his theatrical talent" (61). Michael Booth has highlighted the degree to which, in the late 1820s and 1830s, there was a "real popularity" for "gambling melodrama," a trend that was sparked by four English adaptations of Victor Ducange's *Trente ans, ou la vie d'un joueur* in 1827 and extended through plays like Andrew Campbell's *The Gambler's Life in London* (1829) and William Moncrieff's *The Heart of London, or the Sharper's Progress* (1830) (129–30).

The publication of Edward Bulwer Lytton's *Paul Clifford* in 1830 was a crucible moment in this regard, and a demonstrable influence on some of those who turned to the Mississippi gambler for inspiration. In Lytton's novel, Paul Clifford leads a double life, alternating between respectable gentleman and highway robber. The book achieved a great deal of popularity and, in Hollingsworth's terms, was "an influence upon the decade then beginning" (65). It was also one of the most important sensational texts to cross the Atlantic. As David Reynolds has asserted, "American publishers issued many cheap reprintings of such foreign sensational writings, which found a huge market in America" (172). For example, looking for entertainment during his famous naval voyage in the early 1830s, Richard Henry Dana was handed a copy of *Paul Clifford* by a fellow sailor: "one of the men said he had a book which 'told all about a great highwayman,' at the bottom of his chest [. . .] I shall never forget the enjoyment I derived from it" (227–28). Benjamin Drake, in his early sketch of gambling on the Mississippi, made explicit the association between the rise of the riverboat gambler and the likes of Paul Clifford in the character of blackleg Major Marshall Montgomery, who, as Drake described him, was "a native of the 'Old Dominion,' belonged to the 'Paul Clifford' school; and indeed, had, for some years past, borne testimony, to the merit of Mr. Bulwer's romances, by making the hero of one of them, his great prototype" (28).

The fictional riverboat gambler was therefore, at least in part, a peculiarly American incarnation of an important Old World literary type, brought to birth by a notorious moment of violence. The fascination with the Mississippi gambler clearly helped to spearhead the American vogue for sensation writing. David Reynolds has calculated that between "1831 and 1860, when printing improvements sped the publication of cheap sensational literature (particularly yellow-covered pamphlet novels), the proportion of adventurous or darkly humorous volumes rose to almost 60 percent" of all published American fiction (183). Though he had a large role to play in this dominance, the Mississippi gambler was not limited to a place in sensation writing; he proved to be a more resilient and adaptable rascal than some of his contemporaries.

It is no surprise, then, that the first significant fictional accounts of the riverboat gambler can be dated to immediately after the events in Vicksburg; American writers eagerly seized upon this homegrown scoundrel and turned him to their own particular ends. It is also unsurprising that in the earliest stories of gambling on the river the riverboat gambler was commonly the villain, at odds with the communities and individuals on which he preys. What is perhaps unexpected is the swiftness with which the essential characteristics of the archetypal riverboat gambler were established. In 1836, the year after the Vicksburg lynchings, Philadelphia author Richard Penn Smith created the character of "Thimblerig" for his anonymous account of Davy Crockett's experiences in Texas. Thimblerig's account of his career—particularly his descent of the social ladder from frustrated suitor to failed actor to "marker to a gambling table" to finally "passing up and down the river in the steamboats" as a professional gambler himself—provided something of a template for the fictional gamblers who followed (95–96). Pointedly, Smith notes that Thimblerig had "luckily made his escape a short time before the recent clearing-out of the sleight-of-hand gentry" in Vicksburg (103). And unlike many other antebellum accounts, Smith's portrait is sympathetic. Crockett finds him a "pleasant talkative fellow" and Thimblerig follows him to a hero's death at the Alamo (96). Twentieth-century Crockett biographer Constance Rourke even gave some credence to Emerson Hough's suggestion that Thimblerig was actually based on "Jonathan Harrington Green, the great gambler of the day"—later a famous antigambling activist (269).

In 1838, William Gilmore Simms outlined another vital element of the gambler's iconography that would soon become proverbial: his clothes. In *Richard Hurdis,* the titular hero is required to disguise himself as a gambler to infiltrate a criminal gang. First, Hurdis obtains "a couple of entire suits, as utterly different from any thing [he] had previously worn as possible." Then, "having a proper regard to the usual decoration of the professed gamblers of our country, [he] entered a jeweller's establishment, and bought sundry bunches of seals, a tawdry watch, a huge chain of doubtful, but sold as virgin, gold; and some breastpins and shirt buttons of saucer size" (293). John Findlay notes the practical purposes of such items: "watch chains and diamond breastpins [. . .] constituted ready sources of cash, liquid assets in a world where currency was not always easy to come by" (74). To complement his outfit, Hurdis adds another crucial embellishment: "my beard was suffered to grow goatlike, after the most approved models of dandyism, under the chin, in curling masses, and my whiskers, in rival magnificence, were permitted to overrun my cheeks." The ensemble is topped off with "a thick cap of otter skin" and "as much of their easy impudence of demeanor as I could readily assume" (293). In the decades that followed, these models would undergo few changes.

As stories of the riverboat gambler proliferated, he appeared in a remarkable range of texts—"he," since nineteenth-century accounts of life on the Mississippi make no reference to female riverboat gamblers. And at the very least, the experience of Lottie Deno suggests that this was a significant omission. Deno is best remembered (along with other female gamblers like Kitty Le Roy and Alice Ivers) as a professional gambler in the West in the years after the Civil War, but Cynthia Rose has argued that, in conjunction with partner Johnny Golden, she was "making a living as a gambler [. . .] along the river" at the beginning of the war (22). This is a tantalizing clue to the existence of numerous lost stories. The role of women in the Mississippi underworld, particularly as gamblers and prostitutes, remains one of the most obscure aspects of antebellum river life. In this anthology, they are represented by Zilla Fitz James and her (potentially apocryphal) autobiography. Having accidentally become the "inmate of a fashionable brothel," Fitz James begins affairs with a number of riverboat gamblers—none of which end happily (19). As she laments, "it seemed to be my lot to be the paramour of such despicable men" (27).

Most commonly, antebellum stories of professional gamblers tended to fall into a number of discrete categories. Alongside the appearance of riverboat gambling in slavery narratives, it provided comic fodder for writers submitting stories to journals like the *Spirit of the Times*. Indeed, Norris Yates has noted that the *Spirit*'s gambling stories were set "especially on the riverboats" (137), something corroborated by a contemporary contributor to the journal (the "Little 'Un") in 1849: "I noticed in a Boston paper, a few days since, a remark to the effect that the 'Spirit' was abundantly fruitful in Card playing-stories, the scenes of which, however, were 'always' laid on the Mississippi river" (518). The pages of the *Spirit* might well represent the greatest single repository of Mississippi gambling tales.[1] Frequently, these sketches involved an unexpected reversal in which victim becomes victor. But the *Spirit* writers were not the only ones to play the subject for laughs. In his account of New Year's Eve on a steamboat in the 1850s, the popular humorist "Doesticks" remembered "the captain, steward, and one of the bar-keepers being occupied playing 'poker' with the passengers at one end of the boat [. . .] crew all on a 'bender' in the engine room, firemen all drunk on the boiler deck, and every body generally enjoying themselves" (169).

At other times, the intent of gambling stories was more serious. Accounts of riverboat wagers could serve as cautionary antigambling diatribes, as they often did in the works of Jonathan Green. In *Gambling Exposed,* for example, he tells of a "merchant from Philadelphia" who, though a "very intelligent man, and a shrewd business man [. . .] was far above intrigue," and unwittingly "lost over sixteen hundred dollars" to gamblers on the Mississippi (65, 68). Blackleg stories were also a favorite source of melodrama for the writers of sensational frontier tales, like Emerson Bennett and Justin Jones, whose work prefigured the dime novel fashion of the late nineteenth century. In Bennett's story of Paul Rathbun, for example, the hero outwits a group of gamblers, but is soon "found missing, with blood on the sheet of his berth" (134). The Mississippi gambler also featured in popular romances as

1. Stories in the *Spirit of the Times* featuring gambling on the Mississippi River include George W. Bradbury, "An Original Angling Sketch," 9.44 (January 4, 1840): 524; "Fun on the Mississippi," 14.9 (April 27, 1844): 106; "The Way 'Lige' Shaddock 'Scared Up A Jack!'" 15.1 (March 1, 1845): 4; Sol. Smith, "A Friendly Game of Poker," 15.13 (May 24, 1845): 144; Wisconsin, "Anecdotes of Western Travel," 15.17 (June 21, 1845): 189–90; Sol. Smith, "Breaking A Bank," 15.19 (July 5, 1845): 215; "A Game of 'Full Deck Poker,'" 15.47 (January 17, 1846): 554; "Dr. Bennet and His Game of Thimbles," 16.14 (May 30, 1846): 164–65; The Man With the Specks, "Doctor W. in a Tight Place," 16.37 (November 7, 1846): 439; Satchel, "A Game of Poker on the Mississippi," 16.38 (November 14, 1846): 445; "A New 'Dodge' in Playing 'Poker,'" 17.2 (March 6, 1847): 13; "An Old Joker in a Bad Fix," 17.4 (March 20, 1847): 37; "The Way an Old One Mistook a Green Case," 17.10 (May 1, 1847): 109; Rekrap, "A Gambling Incident," 17.27 (August 28, 1847): 314; "A Strong Hand at Poker," 17.36 (October 30, 1847): 422; "The Game of Thimbles—or Best Two in Three," 18.7 (April 8, 1848): 76; "Hez Spaulding's Account of 'Things on the River,'" 19.26 (August 18, 1849): 308; Viator, "About Steam," 19.34 (October 13, 1849): 397; Little 'Un, "Uncle Abe's 'Winnin' Hand," 19.44 (December 22, 1849): 518; "Steamboat Amusements," 19.44 (December 22, 1849): 518; M. G. Lewis, "How Dodge 'Dodged' The Sharpers," 20.32 (September 28, 1850): 375; Chips, "Them There Trays Up Again," 21.36 (November 8, 1851): 453; John of York, "Eight Aces," 22.26 (August 14, 1852): 309; "A Mysterious Gambler," 29.4 (March 5, 1859): 45.

a nefarious suitor pretending to gentlemanly status. In Laura Bibb Rogers's "The Hasty Marriage," heroine Carrie soon regrets her whirlwind courtship: "He was now a professional gambler, and was gone down the river to join a gang, and travel the Mississippi steamboats" (242). Alternatively, in Herman Melville's *The Confidence-Man* (1857), the exchange between a riverboat gambler and a potential mark could become fraught with metaphysical concerns. A multifaceted figure in antebellum American culture, the gambler would not fit neatly into any one role.

It was after the Civil War that the villainous reputation of the riverboat gambler truly began to be nuanced. Aided by postwar nostalgia, the new national climate, and the sympathetic patina of memory and distance, the gambler-hero slowly blossomed in the popular consciousness as a very different type from his antebellum predecessor. It was a two-fold process. On one hand, the gambler was rediscovered and repackaged by a variety of dime novelists. Where antebellum America had tried to banish the fearful, destabilizing presence of the gambler, the newly refurbished blackleg emerged as a charismatic figure entirely suited to the spirit of the Gilded Age. Ann Fabian has traced the riverboat gambler's newfound popularity to "northern readers" who were "increasingly confined to the small and uncertain gains of wage labor" and therefore entranced by "the Mississippi Valley's surviving myths of easy wealth" (6). Gambling "allowed the poor to challenge the rich"—and that power resonated, even if the challenge was only imaginary (38). Where once the excitement in gambling stories had come from lurid moral instruction or the fantasy of beating the gambler at his own game, now their pleasure came in identification with the gambler himself. Though previously an emasculated coward, the riverboat gambler now represented a potent masculinity. While hero gamblers like "Dan, the River Sport," "Monte Jim," "Gabe Ganderfoot," and "Sandycraw," all thrilled readers, most notable was Edward Willett's series of dime novels featuring "Flush Fred," first published by Beadle and Adams in 1884 (the year that *Huckleberry Finn* was published).[2] Willett, a newspaperman, was a longtime resident of St. Louis and was quite plausibly influenced by the reminiscences of old-time gamblers in that milieu. In the shape of Flush Fred, he created a true gambler-hero: "an

2. There were, in total, four Flush Fred adventures: *Flush Fred, the Mississippi Sport; or, Tough Times in Tennessee* (1884); *Flush Fred's Full Hand* (1884); *Flush Fred's Double* (1884); and *Flush Fred, the River Sharp; or, Hearts for Stakes: A Romance of Three Queens and Two Knaves* (1888). See Albert Johannsen, *The House of Beadle and Adams and Its Dime and Nickel Novels* (Norman: University of Oklahoma Press, 1950), 1:215, 216, 217, 224.

attractive and noticeable young man, with dark hair and eyes, a fine mustache, and a general air of good breeding and good temper." A young woman declares that Fred "is just lovely—my ideal of a man" (*Flush Fred's Double* 2–3). And a man beaten by Fred at cards happily exclaims: "I wish I had your nerve and your pluck, and I wish I had your youth and spirit; and begad sir, I wish I could play poker with your dash and spirit" (*Flush Fred's Full Hand* 3).

At the same time, real-life riverboat gamblers like John O'Connor, Mason Long, and particularly, George Devol began to publish autobiographies that immortalized their youthful escapades. They evoked a world that, though dominated by cheating, double-dealing and eventual poverty, had enough gallantry, romance, and sentiment to fire the imagination. Mark Twain famously asserted that the antebellum steamboat pilot "was the only unfettered and entirely independent human being that lived in the earth" (166). Gamblers' autobiographies suggested that they and their colleagues might have been the real claimants to that title. Devol, for example, in his account of his beginnings as a gambler, knowingly cast himself as a rebel against the oppressions of work and class:

> At last one day while we were finishing a boat that we had calked, and were working on a float aft of the wheel, I gave my tools a push with my foot, and they all went into the river. My brother called out and asked me what I was doing. I looked up, a little sheepish, and said it was the last lick of work I would ever do. He was surprised to hear me talk that way, and asked me what I intended to do. I told him I intended to live off of fools and suckers. I also said, "I will make money rain"; and I did come near doing as I said. (14)

Gamblers' memoirs also demonstrated an intrinsic sentimentality. Iconic figures like "Canada" Bill Jones emerged from their narratives as representative paragons of honest double-dealing: gamblers who only conned deserving suckers; who were kind to the poor and needy; who dressed well, spent joyfully, and repented in the morning. Canada Bill, Devol wrote, "resembled an idiot": he "walked with a shuffling, half-apologetic sort of a gait [. . .] He had a squeaking, boyish voice, and awkward, gawky manners, and a way of asking fool questions and putting on a good natured sort of a grin, that led everybody to believe that he was the rankest kind of a sucker—the greenest sort of a country jake." In truth, he was "a regular card shark" who "could turn monte with the best of them." His motto: "suckers had no business with money." And yet what Bill won from suckers with his monte routine he lost at cards to other gamblers. He died a pauper. "God bless him for it," Devol declared, "for he gave more money to the poor than a thousand professed Christians" (190, 285–87). At times, the memories of old gamblers could transform the antebellum Mississippi into a lost paradise—an Eden, but one expressly created for the serpent. In Tom Ellison's words, "The river used to be the place for gambling, but that's been dead for over twenty years, and I don't guess it'll ever come to life again. But those were the days, my boy—great days for the town, with thirty-six steamboats all at the wharf at once, the levee covered with drays, and every sport with stuff in his pockets and lots of good clothes" (Lillard 50).

From the 1880s onward, therefore, the gambler was assured of an afterlife as an icon of popular culture. In a story by George Jean Nathan published in *Harper's Weekly* in 1910, for example, a discussion of "the spectacular gambling that used to prevail on the old Mississippi River steamboats" leads to the assertion "I doubt [. . .] if gambling ever disclosed more exciting melodrama than in those days" (11). But the romanticization of the Gilded Age was soon finessed by a number of significant publications. In *Show Boat* (1926), Edna Ferber led the way with the character of riverboat gambler Gaylord Ravenal and his doomed relationship with Magnolia Hawks. While Ferber's portrait of Ravenal was clearly indebted to nineteenth-century archetypes, it was not entirely in thrall to the reveries of the Gilded Age. His first appearance is definitive: "an idle elegant figure in garments whose modish cut and fine material served, at a distance, to conceal their shabbiness." Ravenal plays "an honest and over-eager game" and finds that his finances are never quite "raised to the high level of his hopes." In short, even though he has "the habits and instincts of a gentleman," he is invariably "what the river gamblers called broke" (115–17). Like Thimblerig in reverse, Ravenal becomes an actor on the showboat, having "the gambler's love of the play" (157). While Magnolia's regard for him makes him wish "that he might leap into the Mississippi (though muddy) and wash himself clean of his sins," the effect is temporary. At least in part, he is, as Parthy Hawks describes him, a "murdering gambler" (133). The world of gambling pulls him back irresistibly. Subsequent popular stage and film versions may end happily, but the original pulled no such punches: Gaylord deserts Magnolia for the gaming table, and Ferber makes it clear that she "never saw him again" (234).

This reinvigoration of the riverboat gambler type was developed further still in the shape of two very recognizable figures. Like Ferber, it seems that both Margaret Mitchell and William Faulkner owed a debt to the antebellum blackleg in the creation of Rhett Butler and Thomas Sutpen. As Mitchell writes of Butler's past in *Gone with the Wind,* "The reports of his activities in these parts were none too savoury. Scrapes about women, several shootings, gun running to the revolutionists in Central America and, worst of all, professional gambling were included in his career, as Atlanta heard it" (221). Sutpen, on the other hand, is described in *The Unvanquished* as "underbred, a cold ruthless man [. . .] [A]ll believed he robbed steamboats, either as a card sharper or as an out-and-out highwayman" (470). In *Absalom, Absalom!* he is pictured "with a handkerchief over his face and the two pistol barrels glinting beneath the candelabra of a steamboat's saloon" (44). But perhaps even more than these telling moments, both characters—Butler with his "close-clipped black moustache," "cool recklessness" and "bold and black eyes" (97), Sutpen with his "beard" and "hard and pale and reckless eyes" (45)—share a certain style and demeanor, not to mention moral ambiguity, that marks them out as close kin of the riverboat gamblers that preceded them. From the margins, the Mississippi gambler had become a figure at the heart of southern literature and southern identity.

Throughout the twentieth century the Mississippi gambler remained a stock character in popular culture, from the various incarnations of Maverick and Elvis Presley's performance in *Frankie and Johnny* to countless other appearances on screen and in print. Of late, the gambler's stock has risen further still. In recent years, river towns like Vicksburg have been notably less antagonistic toward the idea of professional gambling than they were in the flush times of the nineteenth century. In 1990, the state of Mississippi legalized gambling. However, the Mississippi Gaming Control Act, as Matt Dowd explains, also "limited the area where gaming would be allowed to the regions where the activity had historically taken place: the Gulf Coast and along the Mississippi River" (325). With no little irony, therefore, eager gamers now board ersatz, land-locked steamboats—with employees dressed in what Frederick and Stephen Barthelme have described as "paddle-boat quaint: cheap tux shirts, black bow ties, red cartoon suspenders" (9)—where professional gamblers were once lynched. The romance attached to antebellum river gambling in the late nineteenth century, and embellished throughout the twentieth, is clearly designed to be part of their appeal. And such tactics seem to have been successful. David Cohen noted in 2001, "So unexpected was their popularity that when the casinos opened, the city had budgeted zero dollars in gaming-tax revenues for their first year of operation

[. . .] Today, the city budget has more than doubled to $30 million, mostly as a result of taxes on casino revenues" (158).

Indeed, the modern prevalence of riverboat gambling is threatening to overwrite previously dominant cultural visions of the river. Speaking to the *New York Times* in 2002, casino owner Bernie Goldstein noted that before the advent of contemporary river gambling the Quad Cities area of Iowa and Illinois "was just a river stop on I-80—a lot of people would stop and say, 'Gee, is that the Mississippi River Mark Twain wrote about?' [. . .] Now we are at the nucleus of a small recreation area" (Wilgoren). But that success has come at an inevitable price—a price that many nineteenth-century accounts of riverboat gambling were at pains to highlight. In 1996, only a few years after the inauguration of casino gambling on the Mississippi and the Gulf Coast, Rachel Volberg reported, "Both lifetime and current prevalence of problem and probable pathological gambling in Mississippi [. . .] are higher than in most other states," a state of affairs that reflected "the introduction of casino gambling" (16).

If the stories contained within this anthology speak of a time and place that disappeared sometime around the end of the Civil War, it is clear that they also have an important significance for our own times. Antebellum riverboat gamblers may no longer ply their trade along the Mississippi, but these texts make clear the ways in which they are still operating in the American imagination. The Mississippi gambler has lived many lives, and he has not yet placed his final bet.

A Note on Texts

In the selections that follow, original spelling and punctuation have been maintained in almost all instances. On a very few occasions, textual errors have been corrected for sense (indicated by square brackets).

Readers who would like to know more about the games featured in these stories are advised to do what confused nineteenth-century gamers would have done—reach for Hoyle. Edmund Hoyle published the first of his gaming reference works in England in 1742. His descriptions of the rules of card games were soon definitive, to the extent that the phrase "according to Hoyle" became proverbial. In *The Flush Times of Alabama and Mississippi*, Joseph Glover Baldwin wrote of a judge "who had read a good deal more of Hoyle than Coke" (299). But eventually, Hoyle needed updating for the New World. An American version was produced in the 1860s and reprinted well into the twentieth century. According to its editor, "Americans rarely play games which have been introduced from Europe according to European methods" (Dick iv). As a result, William Dick's *The American Hoyle* remains the most useful guide to the games played in these pieces. Even then, readers should beware. As reformed gambler and antigambling activist Jonathan Green cautioned, gamblers didn't always play by the rules: "Mr. Hoyle, I doubt not, little supposed that any one would wish to improve his games, and there is only one class of persons that would wish to do so, and that is the class of professional gamblers, who are usually quite ingenious, though their ingenuity all runs into rascality" (117–18).

Prologue

"Pretty soon he becomes a peripatetical blackleg"

From *Social Relations in Our Southern States*

DANIEL R. HUNDLEY

Daniel Hundley remains famous, in Fred Hobson's description, as "the author of a book undertaken largely to defend and justify the South but which became, despite its author's intents, a book more critical of the South than anything else written by an inhabitant of the Deep South in the years just preceding the Civil War" (64). This extract, Hundley's account of the descent of a typical "Southern Bully" to the position of "peripatetical blackleg, gambling for a living," is a good case in point. Though Hundley is careful to note that the dissipated "Southern Bully" was only one member of the blackleg family, this extract remains a unique nineteenth-century attempt to define the riverboat gambler as a particular social type. For more information see Fred Hobson, *Tell about the South: The Southern Rage to Explain* (Baton Rouge: Louisiana State University Press, 1983).

Not Plug Uglies and Rip Raps do we purpose to discourse about at this time, gentle reader, for such doughty shoulder-hitters and short-boys are not the necessary out-growth of Southern institutions, but only vegetate in the purlieus of the cities of the South, just as Dead Rabbits, *et id omne genus* of outcasts and vagabonds, grow up within the shadows of the marble palaces, gothic churches, and iron front five-storied warehouses of the cities of the North. But there is in most of the Southern States a species of Bully entirely distinct from the above—a swearing, tobacco-chewing, brandy drinking Bully, whose chief delight is to hang about the doors of village groggeries and tavern tap-rooms, to fight chicken cocks, to play Old Sledge, or pitch-and-toss, chuck-a-luck, and the like, as well as to encourage dog-fights, and occasionally to get up a little raw-head-and-bloody-bones affair on his own account. This is the Southern Bully par excellence, for in all the world else his exact counterpart is no where to be found.

[. . .]

This style of Southern Bully is found more often in the Cotton States, than elsewhere; which is owing to the fact, that fortunes are more frequently made in those States than in any others, by ignorant men—overseers, negro traders, and others of a similar class. For it is the son of the vilest of the Southern Yankees, who usually, no matter how great his wealth may be, does not even approach the comparative respectability of a Cotton Snob, but is nothing more nor less than a bully—an ignorant, purse-proud, self-conceited, guzzling, fox-hunting, blaspheming, slave-whipping, uproarious, vulgar fellow! who is at all times as willing and ready to pink a fellow-being as to wing a pheasant, or to shoot a hare. Even if sent to college, (which sometimes does happen, since his father, however ignorant, is yet anxious that his son shall know more than himself,) he seldom learns any thing from books, and cares for nothing but his daily drams, his cocktails, and brandy-straights, his pistols and his cards, his dogs and his sooty mistress, and, greatest knave of all, himself! While at college, however, he lives extravagantly, though but meanly supplied with funds by his miserly parent; and, as a matter of course, is always over head and ears in debt. But wo to the poor tradesman who menaces him with a bill! The Honorable Algernon Percy Deuceace, worthy scion of the noble house of Crabbs, knew not better how to brain a dunning tailor or starving cobbler, than does the warm-hearted noble-souled Southern Bully, of *good* family and *respectable* standing. And as for presenting one of the son's bills to his miserly father, were we an honest storekeeper, we should much prefer to bear in patience with the wrath of the hot-headed juvenile, than to run the risk of encountering the supercilious frowns of his honorable sire.

When the rich Southern Bully comes into the possession of his estates, his first care is to fill his cellars (in case he has any, otherwise his storeroom) with barrels of Old Rye, as well as brandy, gin, rum, and other kinds of strong waters, but rarely with any thing in the shape of wine. Wine may do for babes, but not for such a puissant gentleman as he fancies himself to be. Having laid in his stock of liquors, he proceeds immediately to gather about him a set of boon companions like himself—idle loafers, drunken overseers, and may be one or two other fellows of like kidney; and now he devotes his nights to gaming, drinking, and coarse libertinism, and his days to fox-hunting, horse-racing, and the like. Ah! thou blot on the fair escutcheon of the South, what a rabble is it indeed dangles ever at your heels! How they yell, and whoop, and halloo, louder than the deep-baying hounds, while they pursue the manly old English sport! One would almost fancy the whole of Bedlam had broke loose, so great is the confusion they create. And as they ride crashing and dashing through the thick underbush in the wide-reaching stretches of Southern woodlands, or through the tangled mosses which hang in festoons from the cypresses of the swamps, you will observe not infrequently two bottles of different kinds of liquors, dangling, one on either side, from the pommel of the Southern Bully's saddle—from each of which he drinks by turns, between every swallow shouting furiously, tally ho! tantivy! to his hounds, and waves to his liegemen to follow on, so that they may all be "in at the death."

Like the Cotton Snob, the rich Southern Bully is great on horse-flesh. His conversation runs chiefly on dogs and horses, horse-trappings and the like; and he himself much affects jockey caps, and other sporting articles of costume, and fills his house with wood-cuts of all the celebrated racers, as well as with whips, saddles, bridles, spurs, etc. etc. Besides, from associating so constantly with jockeys and grooms, he soon learns all the slang phrases peculiar to jockeydom, and rattles them off most volubly on all occasions; for his groveling conception of what constitutes a well-bred gentleman, never allows of his looking to any thing beyond a shrewd dealer in horse-flesh. Hence, he will tell you that he wants no scallywags about him—no *short stock,* as he delights to characterize all horses of unrecognized or uncertain pedigree. He must have the full blood or none; and in consequence his stables are filled with racers, trotters, natural pacers, and saddle and harness horses without number, all of undoubted descent from some imported stallion, and any one of which he will back against the world for almost any stake you shall name. Hence, he is all the time running his crack nags against the crack nags of the sponging worthies who dangle always at his heels; nor does he allow any of the public races near him to come off without his being in attendance, together with his horses, grooms, and motley crowd of retainers. Of course he loses money in the end; as who does not that follows the turf any length of time? But, in addition to his losses from bets, he loses also from the negligent carelessness with which his plantation and negroes are looked after; for how can these be expected to thrive, when he keeps his overseer all the time with himself, and more than half the time drunk? Moreover, to cap the whole, he is ever losing money at cards: for, if he plays in his own old tumble-down dwelling, he loses there; and if he plays in the little back-room to the village groggery, he loses there; and if he plays in the tap-room of the village tavern, with the horse-jockeys and other equally honest, hearty blades, he loses there too, since, poor ignorant simpleton! he is always fuddled with rum or brandy, and falls therefore an easy prey to every sharper who crosses his path. When, however, he has played out his last card; when he suddenly wakes up out of his sottish stupor, to find himself a thriftless beggar; when he sees the auctioneer crying off his paternal acres and the lazy blacks, (for whom he never entertained one half as much sympathy as he still cherishes for his blooded horses, that are also now snatched from him by the officers of the law,) his wits seem to return to him in a measure, and pretty soon he becomes a peripatetical blackleg, gambling for a livelihood. He travels on the river steamboats mostly, and lives by plucking all such poor pigeons as remind him of his former self; else, acts as a decoy to entice such verdants to play, so that keener sharpers may do the plucking, dividing with him the spoil. Any man who has travelled much on the Mississippi, or the Alabama, or the Red, or the Arkansas, or any other of our Southern rivers, can not fail to have noted the rich Southern Bully in this particular stage of his decline and fall. He must not be confounded, however, with the keenest and most adroit of such peripatetic *chevaliers d'industrie;* for these are nearly always foreigners, or else have served their apprenticeship to crime in some one of our large cities. The Southern Bully is not so polished or self-possessed as all such precious scamps usually are; and is besides so constantly addicted to ardent spirits, that his face is full of blotches, and has not that genteel pallor and thoughtfulness of expression so characteristic of the regularly-bred gambler.

But in a very few years we miss the Southern Bully on the river steamers, and must either search for him in an untimely grave, or else far out on the Southwestern frontier. Here he chases after buffaloes and Indians, and shoots wild cats and Comanches with equal nonchalance; and astonishes with the boastful narratives of his former exploits, the simple-minded backwoodsmen—those rude American vi-kings who wear leather breeches and buckskin shirts, and live by following the chase; but who are honest and rudely chivalrous, though unschooled in the arts of civilized life, all of which they as heartily contemn and despise, as did those ancient barbaric heroes of the Niebelungen Lied. Wearying after a while, however, of this nomadic life, the Southern Bully makes yet another change, and as a last resort turns fillibuster. Like Cortez in Mexico, or Pizarro in Peru, or the English in India, or the French in Algeria; he seeks by plundering and pillaging a helpless people, to make up for his past losses, as well as to bury in the excitement of adventure and the changeful fortunes of the tented field, all remembrances of a past life, misspent, squandered, and most wickedly wasted in riot and dissipation.

Early Days

"A numerous and peculiar race of modern gentlemen"

The Vicksburg Tragedy

On Independence Day 1835, five alleged gamblers were lynched in Vicksburg, Mississippi. This was a signal moment in the popular conception of gambling along the Mississippi River and the men engaged in the trade. The lynchings became internationally notorious and were widely debated—even a young Abraham Lincoln offered an opinion on what had taken place. The extract that follows is a justification of the actions of the citizens of Vicksburg published in the immediate aftermath of events. For more information, see Thomas Ruys Smith, "Independence Day, 1835: The John A. Murrell Conspiracy and the Lynching of the Vicksburg Gamblers in Literature," *Mississippi Quarterly* 59:1–2 (Winter-Spring 2006): 129–60.

Vicksburg, (Miss.) July 9th

The following account of some proceedings of the citizens of this town, which will excite the attention of the public, was prepared by a witness of the acts detailed, and the correctness of the account may be relied on:

Our city has for some days past been the theatre of the most novel and startling scene that we have ever witnessed. While we regret that the necessity for such scenes should have existed, we are proud of the public spirit and indignation against offenders displayed by the citizens, and congratulate them on having at length banished a class of individuals, whose shameless vices and daring outrages have long poisoned the springs of morality, and interrupted the relations of society. For years past, professional gamblers, destitute of all sense of moral obligations—unconnected with society by any of its ordinary ties, and intent only on the gratification of their avarice—have made Vicksburg their place of rendezvous—and, in the very bosom of our society, boldly plotted their vile and lawless machinations. Here, as everywhere else, the laws of the country were found wholly ineffectual for the punishment of these individuals, and, emboldened by impunity, their numbers and their crimes have daily continued to multiply. Every species of transgression followed in their train. They supported a large number of tippling houses, to which they would decoy the youthful and unsuspecting, and, after stripping them of their possessions, send them forth into the world the ready and desperate instruments of vice.

Our streets every where resounded with the echoes of their drunken and obscene mirth, and no citizen was secure from their villainy. Frequently in armed bodies, they have disturbed the good order of public assemblages, insulted our citizens, and defied our civil authorities. Thus had they continued to grow bolder in their wickedness, and more formidable in their numbers, until Saturday, the fourth of July, instant, when our citizens had assembled, together with the corps of Vicksburg volunteers, at the barbecue, to celebrate the day by the usual festivities. After dinner, and during the delivery of the toasts, one of the officers attempted to enforce order and silence at the table, when one of those gamblers, whose name is Cabler, who had impudently thrust himself into the company, insulted the officer, and struck one of our citizens. Indignation immediately rose high, and it was only by the interference of the commandant that he was saved from instantaneous punishment. He was, however, permitted to retire, and the company dispersed.

The military corps proceeded to the public square of the city, and information was received that Cabler was coming up armed, and resolved to kill one of the volunteers who had been most active in expelling him from the table. Knowing his desperate character—two of the corps instantly stepped forward and arrested him. A loaded pistol, a large knife and a dagger were found on his person, all of which he had procured since he had separated from the company. To liberate him, would have been to devote several of the most respectable members of the company to his vengeance, and to proceed against him at law would have been mere mockery, inasmuch, as, not having had the opportunity of consummating his design, no adequate punishment could have been inflicted on him. Consequently it was determined to take him into the woods and *Lynch* him—which is a mode of punishment provided for such as become obnoxious in a manner which the law cannot reach. He was immediately carried out under a guard, attended by a crowd of respectable citizens—tied to a tree, punished with stripe—tarred and feathered; and ordered to leave the city in forty eight hours. In the meantime one of his comrades, the Lucifer of the gang, had been endeavouring to rally and arm his confederates for the purpose of rescuing him; which however he failed to accomplish.

Having thus aggravated the whole band of these desperadoes, and feeling no security against their vengeance, the citizens met at night in the court house, in a large number, and there passed the following resolutions:

Resolved, That a notice be given all professional gamblers, that the citizens of Vicksburg are *resolved* to exclude them from this place and its vicinity; and that twenty four hours notice be given them to leave the place.

Resolved, That all persons permitting faro dealing in their houses, be also notified that they will be prosecuted therefor.

Resolved, That one hundred copies of the foregoing resolutions be printed and stuck up at the corners of the streets—and that this publication be deemed notice.

On Sunday morning, one of these notices was posted at the corners of each square of the city. During that day (the 5th instant) a majority of the gang, terrified by the threats of the citizens, dispersed in different directions, without making any opposition. It was sincerely hoped that the remainder would follow their example, and thus prevent a bloody termination of the strife which had commenced. On the morning of the 6th, the military corps, followed by a file of several hundred citizens, marched to each suspected house, and, sending in an examining committee, dragged out every faro table and other gambling apparatus that could be found. At length they approached a house which was occupied by one of the most profligate of the gang, whose name was North, and in which it was understood that a garrison of armed men had been stationed. All hoped that these wretches would be intimidated by the superior numbers of their assailants, and surrender themselves at discretion, rather than attempt a desperate defence. The house being surrounded, the back door was burst open, when four or five shots were fired from the interior, one of which instantly killed Dr. Hugh S. Bodley, a citizen universally beloved and respected. The interior was so dark that the villains could not be seen; but several of the citizens, guided by the flash of their guns, returned their fire. A yell from one of the party announced that one of these shots had been effectual; and by this time a crowd of citizens, their indignation overcoming all other feelings, burst open every door of the building, and dragged into the light those who had not been wounded.

North, the ringleader, who had contrived this desperate plot, could not be found in the building, but was apprehended by a citizen, while attempting, in company with another, to make his escape, at a place not far distant. Himself, with the rest of the prisoners, were then conducted in silence to the scaffold. One of them, not having been in the building before it was attacked, nor appearing to be concerned with the rest, except that he was the brother of one of them, was liberated. The remaining number of five, among whom was the individual who had been shot, but who still lived, were immediately executed in the presence of the assembled multitude. All sympathy for the wretches was completely merged in detestation and horror of their crime. The whole procession then returned to the city, collected all the faro tables into a pile and burnt them. This being done, a troop of horsemen set out for a neighbouring house to the residence of Hurd, the individual who had attempted to organize a force on the day of this disturbance, for the rescue of Cabler, and had since threatened to fire the city. He had, however, made his escape on that day, and the next morning crossed the Big Black, at Baldwin's ferry, in a state of indescribable consternation. We lament his escape, as his whole course of life, for the last three years, has exhibited the most shameless profligacy, and been a continual series of transgressions against the laws of God and man.

The names of the individuals who perished were as follows: North, Hallums, Dutch Bill, Smith and McCall.

Their bodies were cut down in the morning after execution, and buried in a ditch.

It is not expected that this act will pass without censure from those who had not an opportunity of knowing and feeling the dire necessity out of which it originated. The laws, however severe in the provision, have never been sufficient to correct a vice which must be established by positive proof, and cannot, like others, be shown from circumstantial testimony. It is practised, too, by individuals whose whole study is to violate the law in such a manner as to evade its punishment, and who never are in want of secret confederates to swear them out of their difficulties, whose oaths cannot be impeached for any specific cause. We had borne their enormities, until to have suffered them any longer would not only have proved as to be destitute of every manly sentiment, but would also have implicated us in the guilt of accessories of their crimes.

Society may be compared to the elements, which, although "order is the first law," can sometimes be purified only by a storm. Whatever, therefore, sickly sensibility or mawkish philanthropy may say against the course pursued by us, we hope that our citizens will not relax the code of punishment which they have enacted against this infamous, unprincipled and baleful class of society—and we invite Natchez, Jackson, Columbus, Warrenton and all our sister towns throughout the state, in the name of our insulted laws—of offended virtue, and of slaughtered innocence, to aid us in exterminating this deep-rooted vice from our land.

The revolution has been conducted here by the most respectable citizens, heads of families, members of all classes, professions and pursuits. None have been heard to utter a syllable of censure against either the act or the manner in which it was performed.

An anti-gambling society has been formed, the members of which have pledged their lives, fortunes and sacred honors, for the suppression of gambling, and the punishment and expulsion of gamblers.

And, so far as we know, public opinion, both in town and country, is decidedly in favour of the course pursued. We have never known the public so unanimous on any subject.

From *Col. Crockett's Exploits and Adventures in Texas*

RICHARD PENN SMITH

For many years it was believed that *Col. Crockett's Exploits and Adventures in Texas*—published in 1836, the year after Crockett's death at the Alamo—was an authentic work of autobiography. Even when it became evident that Philadelphian Richard Penn Smith was the real author, its importance was diminished little. As John Seelye has made clear, "it was so vivid an account of Crockett's last adventure that it continued to influence other writers"—down to the present day (xi). This influential extract is an important case in point. Published the year after the lynching of the Vicksburg gamblers, this portrait of "Thimblerig" represents the earliest sustained portrait of a Mississippi gambler—charming, roguish, and rich in ambiguity. For more information, see John Seelye's introduction to his modern edition of Smith's work, *On to the Alamo: Colonel Crockett's Exploits and Adventures in Texas* (New York: Penguin, 2003).

There was a considerable number of passengers on board the boat, and our assortment was somewhat like the Yankee merchant's cargo of notions, pretty particularly miscellaneous, I tell you. I moved through the crowd from stem to stern, to see if I could discover any face that was not altogether strange to me; but after a general survey, I concluded that I had never seen one of them before. There were merchants, and emigrants, and gamblers, but none who seemed to have embarked in the particular business that for the time being occupied my mind—I could find none who were going to Texas. All seemed to have their hands full enough of their own affairs, without meddling with the cause of freedom. The greater share of glory will be mine, thought I, so go ahead, Crockett.

I saw a small cluster of passengers at one end of the boat, and hearing an occasional burst of laughter, thinks I, there's some sport started in that quarter, and having nothing better to do, I'll go in for my share of it. Accordingly I drew nigh to the cluster, and seated on the chest was a tall, lank, sea-sarpent looking blackleg, who had crawled over from Natchez under the hill, and was amusing the passengers with his skill at thimblerig; at the same time he was picking up their shillings just about as expeditiously as a hungry gobbler would a pint of corn. He was doing what might be called an average business in a small way, and lost no time in gathering up the fragments.

I watched the whole process for some time, and found that he had adopted the example set by the old tempter himself, to get the weathergage of us poor weak mortals. He made it a point to let his victims win always the first stake, that they might be tempted to go ahead; and then, when they least suspected it, he would come down upon them like a hurricane in a cornfield, sweeping all before it.

I stood looking on, seeing him pick up the chicken feed from the green horns, and thought if men are such darned fools as to be cheated out of their hard earnings by a fellow who has just brains enough to pass a pea from one thimble to another, with such sleight of hand, that you could not tell under which he had deposited it, it is not astonishing that the magician of Kinderhook should play thimblerig upon the big figure, and attempt to cheat the whole nation. I thought that "the Government" was playing the same game with the deposites, and with such address, too, that before long it will be a hard matter to find them under any of the thimbles where it is supposed they have been originally placed.

The thimble conjurer saw me looking on, and eyeing me as if he thought I would be a good subject, said carelessly, "Come, stranger, won't you take a chance?" the whole time passing the pea from one thimble to the other, by way of throwing out a bait for the gudgeons to bite at. "I never gamble, stranger," says I, "principled against it; think it a slippery way of getting through the world at best." "Them are my sentiments to a notch," says he; "but this is not gambling by no means. A little innocent pastime, nothing more. Better take a hack by way of trying your luck at guessing." All this time he continued working with his thimbles; first putting the pea under one, which was plain to be seen, and then uncovering it, would show that the pea was there; he would then put it under the second thimble, and do the same, and then under the third; all of which he did to show how easy it would be to guess where the pea was deposited, if one would only keep a sharp look-out.

"Come, stranger," says he to me again, "you had better take a chance. Stake a trifle, I don't care how small, just for the fun of the thing."

"I am principled against betting money," says I, "but I don't mind going in for drinks for the present company, for I'm as dry as one of little Isaac Hill's regular set of speeches."

"I admire your principles," says he, "and to show that I play with these here thimbles just for the sake of pastime, I will take that bet, though I am a whole hog temperance man. Just say when, stranger."

He continued all the time slipping the pea from one thimble to another;

my eye was as keen as a lizard's, and when he stopped, I cried out, "Now; the pea is under the middle thimble." He was going to raise it to show that it wasn't there, when I interfered, and said, "Stop, if you please," and raised it myself, and sure enough the pea was there; but it mought have been other- wise if he had had the uncovering of it.

"Sure enough you've won the bet," says he. "You've a sharp eye, but I don't care if I give you another chance. Let us go fifty cents this bout; I'm sure you'll win."

"Then you're a darned fool to bet, stranger," says I; "and since that is the case, it would be little better than picking your pocket to bet with you; so I'll let it alone."

"I don't mind running the risk," said he.

"But I do," says I; "and since I always let well enough alone, and I have had just about glory enough for one day, let us all go to the bar and liquor."

This called forth a loud laugh at the thimble conjurer's expense; and he tried hard to induce me to take just one chance more, but he mought just as well have sung psalms to a dead horse, for my mind was made up; and I told him, that I looked upon gambling as about the dirtiest way that a man could adopt to get through this dirty world; and that I would never bet any thing beyond a quart of whisky upon a rifle shot, which I considered a legal bet, and gentlemanly and rational amusement. "But all this cackling," says I, "makes me very thirsty, so let us adjourn to the bar and liquor."

He gathered up his thimbles, and the whole company followed us to the bar, laughing heartily at the conjurer; for, as he had won some of their money, they were sort of delighted to see him beaten with his own cudgel. He tried to laugh too, but his laugh wasn't at all pleasant, and rather forced. The bar- keeper placed a big-bellied bottle before us; and after mixing our liquor, I was called on for a toast, by one of the company, a chap just about as rough hewn as if he had been cut out of a gum log with a broad-axe, and sent into the market without even being smoothed off with a jack plane; one of them chaps who, in their journey through life, are always ready for a fight or a frolic, and don't care the toss of a copper which.

"Well, gentlemen," says I, "being called upon for a toast, and being in a slave-holding state, in order to avoid giving offence and running the risk of being Lynched, it may be necessary to premise that I am neither an aboli- tionist nor a colonizationist, but simply Colonel Crockett of Tennessee, now bound for Texas." When they heard my name, they gave three cheers for Col- onel Crockett; and silence being restored, I continued, "Now, gentlemen, I will offer you a toast, hoping, after what I have stated, that it will give offence to no one present; but should I be mistaken, I must imitate the 'old Roman,' and take the responsibility. I offer, gentlemen, The abolition of slavery: let the work first begin in the two houses of Congress. There are no slaves in the country more servile than the party slaves in Congress. The wink or the nod of their masters is all-sufficient for the accomplishment of the most dirty work."

They drank the toast in a style that satisfied me that the Little Magician might as well go to a pigsty for wool, as to beat round in that part for voters: they were all either for Judge White or Old Tippecanoe. The thimble conjurer having asked the barkeeper how much there was to pay, was told that there were sixteen smallers, which amounted to one dollar. He was about to lay down the blunt, but not in Benton's metallic currency, which I find has already become as shy as honesty with an office-holder, but he planked down one of Biddle's notes, when I interfered, and told him that the barkeeper had made a mistake.

"How so?" demanded the barkeeper.

"How much do you charge," said I, "when you retail your liquor?"

"A fip a glass."

"Well, then," says I, "as Thimblerig here, who belongs to the temperance society, took it in wholesale, I reckon you can afford to let him have it at half price?"

Now, as they had all noticed that the conjurer went what is called the heavy wet, they laughed outright, and we heard no more about temperance from that quarter. When we returned to the deck, the blackleg set to work with his thimbles again, and bantered me to bet; but I told him that it was against my principle, and as I had already reaped glory enough for one day, I would just let well enough alone for the present.

[...]

After my speech, and setting my face against gambling, poor Thimblerig was obliged to break off conjuring for want of customers, and call it half a day. He came and entered into conversation with me, and I found him a good-natured, intelligent fellow, with a keen eye for the main chance. He belonged to that numerous class, that it is perfectly safe to trust as far as a tailor can sling a bull by the tail—but no farther. He told me that he had been brought up a gentleman; that is to say, he was not instructed in any useful pursuit by which he could obtain a livelihood, so that when he found he had to depend upon himself for the necessaries of life, he began to suspect, that dame nature would have conferred a particular favor if she had consigned him to the care of any one else. She had made a very injudicious choice when she selected him to sustain the dignity of a gentleman.

The first bright idea that occurred to him as a speedy means of bettering his fortune, would be to marry an heiress. Accordingly, he looked about himself pretty sharp, and after glancing from one fair object to another, finally, his hawk's eye rested upon the young and pretty daughter of a wealthy planter. Thimblerig run his brazen face with his tailor for a new suit, for he abounded more in that metallic currency than he did in either Benton's mint drops or in Biddle's notes; and having the gentility of his outward Adam thus endorsed by his tailor—an important endorsement, by-the-way, as times go—he managed to obtain an introduction to the planter's daughter.

Our worthy had the principle of going ahead strongly developed. He was possessed of considerable address, and had brass enough in his face to make a wash-kettle: and having once got access to the planter's house, it was no easy matter to dislodge him. In this he resembled those politicians who commence life as office-holders; they will hang on, tooth and nail, and even when death shakes them off, you'll find a commission of some kind crumpled up in their clenched fingers. Little Van appears to belong to this class—there's no beating his snout from the public crib. He'll feed there while there's a grain of corn left, and even then, from long habit, he'll set to work and gnaw at the manger.

Thimblerig got the blind side of the planter, and everything, to outward appearances, went on swimmingly. Our worthy boasted to his cronies that the business was settled, and that in a few weeks he should occupy the elevated station in society that nature had designed him to adorn. He swelled like the frog in the fable, or, rather, like Johnson's wife, of Kentucky, when the idea occurred to her of figuring away at Washington. But there's many a slip 'twixt the cup and the lip, says the proverb, and suddenly Thimblerig discontinued his visits at the planter's house. His friends inquired of him the meaning of this abrupt termination of his devotions.

"I have been treated with disrespect," replied the worthy, indignantly.

"Disrespect! in what way?"

"My visits, it seems, are not altogether agreeable."

"But how have you ascertained that?"

"I received a hint to that effect; and I can take a hint as soon as another."

"A hint!—and have you allowed a hint to drive you from the pursuit? For shame. Go back again."

"No, no, never! a hint is sufficient for a man of my gentlemanly feelings. I asked the old man for his daughter."

"Well, what followed? what did he say?"

"Didn't say a word."

"Silence gives consent all the world over."

"So I thought. I then told him to fix the day."

"Well, what then?"

"Why, then, he kicked me down stairs; and ordered his slaves to pump upon me. That's hint enough for me, that my visits are not properly appreciated; and blast my old shoes if I condescend to renew the acquaintance, or notice them in any way until they send for me."

As Thimblerig's new coat became rather too seedy to play the part of a gentleman much longer in real life, he determined to sustain that character upon the stage, and accordingly joined a company of players. He began, according to custom, at the top of the ladder, and was regularly hissed and pelted through every gradation until he found himself at the lowest rowel. "This," said he, "was a dreadful check to proud ambition"; but he consoled himself with the idea of peace and quietness in his present obscure walk; and though he had no prospect of being elated by the applause of admiring multitudes, he no longer trod the scene of mimic glory in constant dread of becoming a target for rotten eggs and oranges. "And there was much in that," said Thimblerig. But this calm could not continue for ever.

The manager, who, like all managers who pay salaries regularly, was as absolute behind the scenes as the "old Roman" is in the White House, had fixed upon getting up an eastern spectacle, called the Cataract of the Ganges. He intended to introduce a fine procession, in which an elephant was to be the principal feature. Here a difficulty occurred. What was to be done for an elephant? Alligators were plenty in those parts, but an elephant was not to be had for love or money. But an alligator would not answer the purpose, so he determined to make a pasteboard elephant as large as life, and twice as natural. The next difficulty was to find members of the company of suitable dimensions to perform the several members of the pasteboard star. The manager cast his eye upon the long, gaunt figure of the unfortunate Thimblerig, and cast him for the hinder legs, the rump, and part of the back of the elephant. The poor player expostulated, and the manager replied, that he would appear as a star on the occasion, and would no doubt receive more applause than he had during his whole career. "But I shall not be seen," said the player. "All the better," replied the manager, "as in that case you will have nothing to apprehend from eggs and oranges."

Thimblerig, finding that mild expostulation availed nothing, swore that he would not study the part, and accordingly threw it up in dignified disgust. He said that it was an outrage upon the feelings of the proud representative of Shakespeare's heroes, to be compelled to play pantomime in the hinder parts of the noblest animal that ever trod the stage. If it had been the fore quarters of the elephant, it might possibly have been made a speaking part; at any rate, he might have snorted through the trunk, if nothing more; but from the position he was to occupy, damned the word could he utter, or even roar with propriety. He therefore positively refused to act, as he considered it an insult to his reputation to tread the stage in such a character; and he looked upon the whole affair as a profanation of the legitimate drama. The result was, our worthy was discharged from the company, and compelled to commence hoeing another row.

He drifted to New Orleans, and hired himself as marker to a gambling table. Here he remained but a few months, for his idea of arithmetic differed widely from those of his employer, and accordingly they had some difficulty in balancing their cash account; for when his employer, in adding up the receipts, made it nought and carry two, Thimblerig insisted that it should be nought and carry one; and in order to prove that he was correct, he carried himself off, and left nothing behind him.

He now commenced professional blackleg on his own hook, and took up his quarters in Natchez under the hill. Here he remained, doing business in a small way, until Judge Lynch commenced his practice in that quarter, and made the place too hot for his comfort. He shifted his habitation, but not having sufficient capital to go the big figure, he practised the game of thimblerig until he acquired considerable skill, and then commenced passing up and down the river in the steamboats; and managed, by close attention to business, to pick up a decent livelihood in the small way, from such as had more pence in their pockets than sense in their noddles.

I found Thimblerig to be a pleasant talkative fellow. He communicated the foregoing facts with as much indifference as if there had been nothing disgraceful in his career; and at times he would chuckle with an air of triumph at the adroitness he had displayed in some of the knavish tricks he had practised. He looked upon this world as one vast stage, crowded with empirics and jugglers; and that he who could practise his deceptions with the greatest skill was entitled to the greatest applause.

I asked him to give me an account of Natchez and his adventures there, and I would put it in the book I intended to write, when he gave me the following, which betrays that his feelings were somewhat irritated at being obliged to give them leg bail when Judge Lynch made his appearance. I give it in his own words:

"Natchez is a land of fevers, alligators, niggers, and cotton bales: where the sun shines with force sufficient to melt the diamond, and the word ice is expunged from the dictionary, for its definition cannot be comprehended by the natives: where to refuse grog before breakfast would degrade you below the brute creation; and where a good dinner is looked upon as an angel's visit, and voted a miracle: where the evergreen and majestic magnolia tree, with its superb flower, unknown to the northern climes, and its fragrance unsurpassed, calls forth the admiration of every beholder; and the dark moss hangs in festoons from the forest trees, like the drapery of a funeral pall: where bears, the size of young jackasses, are fondled in lieu of pet dogs; and knives, the length of a barber's pole, usurp the place of toothpicks: where the filth of the town is carried off by buzzards, and the inhabitants are carried off by fevers: where nigger women are knocked down by the auctioneer, and knocked up by the purchaser; where the poorest slave has plenty of yellow boys, but not of Benton's mintage; and indeed the shades of colour are so varied and mixed, that a nigger is frequently seen black and blue at the same time. And such is Natchez.

"The town is divided into two parts, as distinct in character as they are in appearance. Natchez on the hill, situated upon a high bluff overlooking the Mississippi, is a pretty little town with streets regularly laid out, and ornamented with divers handsome public buildings. Natchez under the hill,— where, oh! where shall I find words suitable to describe the peculiarities of that unholy spot? 'Tis, in fact, the jumping off place. Satan looks on it with glee, and chuckles as he beholds the orgies of his votaries. The buildings are for the most part brothels, taverns, or gambling houses, and frequently the whole three may be found under the same roof. Obscene songs are sung at the top of the voice in all quarters. I have repeatedly seen the strumpets tear a man's clothes from his back, and leave his body beautified with all the colors of the rainbow.

"One of the most popular tricks is called the 'Spanish burial.' When a greenhorn makes his appearance among them, one who is in the plot announces the death of a resident, and that all strangers must subscribe to the custom of the place upon such an occasion. They forthwith arrange a procession; each person, as he passes the departed, kneels down and pretends to kiss the treacherous corpse. When the unsophisticated attempts this ceremony the dead man clinches him, and the mourners beat the fellow so entrapped until he consents to treat all hands; but should he be penniless, his life will be endangered by the severity of the castigation. And such is Natchez under the hill.

"An odd affair occurred while I was last there," continued Thimblerig. "A steamboat stopped at the landing, and one of the hands went ashore under the hill to purchase provisions, and the adroit citizens of that delectable retreat contrived to rob him of all his money. The captain of the boat, a determined fellow, went ashore in the hope of persuading them to refund, but that cock wouldn't fight. Without farther ceremony, assisted by his crew and passengers, some three or four hundred in number, he made fast an immense cable to the frame tenement where the theft had been perpetrated, and allowed fifteen minutes for the money to be forthcoming; vowed if it was not produced within that time, to put steam to his boat, and drag the house into the river. The money was instantly produced.

"I witnessed a sight during my stay there," continued the thimble conjuror, "that almost froze my blood with horror, and will serve as a specimen of the customs of the far south. A planter, of the name of Foster, connected with the best families of the state, unprovoked, in cold blood, murdered his young and beautiful wife, a few months after marriage. He beat her deliberately to death in a walk adjoining his dwelling, carried the body to the hut of one of his slaves, washed the dirt from her person, and assisted by his negroes, buried her upon his plantation. Suspicion was awakened, the body disinterred, and the villain's guilt established. He fled, was overtaken and secured in prison. His trial was, by some device of the law, delayed until the third term of the court. At length it came on, and so clear and indisputable was the evidence that not a doubt was entertained of the result; when, by an oversight on the part of the sheriff, who neglected swearing into office his deputy who summoned the jurors, the trial was abruptly discontinued, and all proceedings against Foster were suspended, or rather ended.

"There exist throughout the extreme south, bodies of men who style themselves Lynchers. When an individual escapes punishment by some technicality of the law, or perpetrates an offence not recognized in courts of justice, they seize him, and inflict such chastisement as they conceive adequate to the offence. They usually act at night and disguise their persons. This society at Natchez embraces all the lawyers, physicians, and principal merchants of the place. Foster, whom all good men loathed as a monster unfit to live, was called into court, and formally dismissed. But the Lynchers were at hand. The moment he stept from the court-house he was knocked down, his arms bound behind him, his eyes bandaged, and in this condition was marched to the rear of the town, where a deep ravine afforded a fit place for his punishment. His clothes were torn from his back, his head partially scalped, they next bound him to a tree; each Lyncher was supplied with a cow-skin, and they took turns at the flogging until the flesh hung in ribands from his body. A quantity of heated tar was then poured over his head, and made to cover every part of his person; they finally showered a sack of feathers on him, and in this horrid guise, with no other apparel than a miserable pair of breeches, with a drummer at his heels, he was paraded through the principal streets at midday. No disguise was assumed by the Lynchers; the very lawyers employed upon his trial took part in his punishment.

"Owing to long confinement his gait had become cramped, and his movements were very faltering. By the time the procession reached the most public part of the town, Foster fell down from exhaustion, and was allowed to lie there for a time, without exciting the sympathies of any one, an object of universal detestation. The blood oozing from his stripes had become mixed with the feathers and tar, and rendered his aspect still more horrible and loathsome. Finding him unable to proceed further, a common dray was brought, and with his back to the horse's tail, the drummer standing over him playing the rogue's march, he was reconducted to prison, the only place at which he would be received.

"A guard was placed outside of the jail to give notice to the body of Lynchers when Foster might attempt to escape, for they had determined on branding him on the forehead and cutting his ears off. At two o'clock in the morning of the second subsequent day, two horsemen with a led horse stopped at the prison, and Foster was with difficulty placed astride. The Lynchers wished to secure him; he put spurs to his beast, and passed them. As he rode by they fired at him; a ball struck his hat, which was thrown to the ground, and he escaped; but if ever found within the limits of the state, he will be shot down as if a price was set on his head.

"Sights of this kind," continued Thimblerig, "are by no means unfrequent. I once saw a gambler, a sort of friend of mine by-the-way, detected cheating at faro, at a time when the bets were running pretty high. They flogged him almost to death, added the tar and feathers, and placed him aboard a dug-out, a sort of canoe, at twelve at night; and with no other instrument of navigation than a bottle of whisky and a paddle, set him adrift in the Mississippi. He has never been heard of since, and the presumption is, that he either died of his wounds or was run down in the night by a steamer. And this is what we call Lynching in Natchez."

Thimblerig had also been at Vicksburg in his time, and entertained as little liking for that place as he did for Natchez. He had luckily made his escape a short time before the recent clearing-out of the sleight-of-hand gentry; and he reckoned some time would elapse before he would pay them another visit. He said they must become more civilized first. All the time he was talking to me he was seated on a chest, and playing mechanically with his pea and thimbles, as if he was afraid that he would lose the sleight unless he kept his hand in constant practice. Nothing of any consequence occurred in our passage down the river, and I arrived at Natchitoches in perfect health, and in good spirits.

[...]

I stayed two days at Natchitoches, during which time I procured a horse to carry me across Texas to the seat of war. Thimblerig remained with me, and I found his conversation very amusing; for he is possessed of humor and observation, and has seen something of the world. Between whiles he would amuse himself with his thimbles, to which he appeared greatly attached, and occasionally he would pick up a few shillings from the tavern loungers. He no longer asked me to play with him, for he felt somewhat ashamed to do so, and he knew it would be no go. I took him to task in a friendly manner, and tried to shame him out of his evil practices. I told him that it was a burlesque on human nature, that an able-bodied man, possessed of his full share of good sense, should voluntarily debase himself, and be indebted for subsistence to such pitiful artifice.

"But what's to be done, Colonel?" says he. "I'm in the slough of despond, up to the very chin. A miry and slippery path to travel."

"Then hold your head up," says I, "before the slough reaches your lips."

"But what's the use?" says he: "it's utterly impossible for me to wade through; and even if I could, I should be in such a dirty plight, that it would defy all the waters in the Mississippi to wash me clean again. No," he added, in a desponding tone, "I should be like a live eel in a frying pan, Colonel; sort of out of my element, if I attempted to live like an honest man at this time o'day."

"That I deny. It is never too late to become honest," said I. "But even admit what you say to be true—that you cannot live like an honest man, you have at least the next best thing in your power, and no one can say nay to it."

"And what is that?"

"Die like a brave one. And I know not whether, in the eyes of the world, a brilliant death is not preferred to an obscure life of rectitude. Most men are remembered as they died, and not as they lived. We gaze with admiration upon the glories of the setting sun, yet scarcely bestow a passing glance upon its noonday splendor."

"You are right; but how is this to be done?"

"Accompany me to Texas. Cut aloof from your degrading habits and associates here, and in fighting for their freedom, regain your own."

He started from the table, and hastily gathering up the thimbles with which he had been playing all the time I was talking to him, he thrust them into his pocket, and after striding two or three times across the room, suddenly stopped, his leaden eye kindled, and grasping me by the hand violently, he exclaimed with an oath, "By ———, I'll be a man again. Live honestly, or die bravely. I go with you to Texas."

Putting a Black-Leg on Shore

BENJAMIN DRAKE

Benjamin Drake was the brother of Daniel Drake, a renowned medical practitioner who was also a vital figure in the development of Cincinnati as a western cultural hub at the beginning of the nineteenth century. Among other endeavors, Daniel sponsored the Buckeye Club, one of the early West's most influential literary salons. Before his death in 1841, Benjamin himself was the author of a number of important books about life in the Queen City and its vicinity, including *Cincinnati in 1826* (1827), *The Life and Adventures of Black Hawk* (1838), and *Life of Tecumseh and His Brother the Prophet* (1841). The story that follows, taken from a collection of his sketches, is a humorous account of gambling on the river—which, judging by Drake's introduction to the story, was still a novel subject in 1838. For further information on the Drake brothers and their place and time, see Daniel Aaron, *Cincinnati: Queen City of the West, 1819–1838* (Columbus: Ohio State University Press, 1992).

A numerous and peculiar race of modern gentlemen, may be found in the valley of the Mississippi. A naturalist would probably describe them as a genus of bipeds, gregarious, amphibious and migratory. They seldom travel "solitary and alone"; are equally at home on land or water; and like certain vultures, spend most of their winters in Mississippi and Louisiana; their summers in the higher latitudes of Kentucky and Ohio. They dress with taste and elegance; carry gold chronometers in their pockets; and swear with the most genteel precision. They are supposed to entertain an especial abhorrence of the prevailing temperance fanaticism; and, as a matter of conscience, enter a daily protest against it, by sipping "mint-julaps" before breakfast, "hail-storms" at dinner, and "old Monongahela" at night. These gentlemen, moreover, are strong advocates of the race-path and the cock-pit; and, with a benevolence, which they hold to be truly commendable, patronise modest merit, by playing *chaperon* to those wealthy young men, who set out on the pilgrimage of life, before they have been fully initiated into its pleasures. Every where throughout the valley, these mistletoe gentry are called by the original, if not altogether classic, cognomen of "Black-legs." The history of this euphonious epithet, or the reason of its application to so distinguished a variety of humanity, is unknown. The subject is one of considerable interest, and worthy the early attention of the Historical Society, to which it is respectfully commended.

It was the fortune of the steam-boat Sea Serpent of Cincinnati, commanded by Captain Snake, on her return from New Orleans in the spring of 1837, to number among her cabin passengers, several highly respectable Black-Legs. One of them, Major Marshall Montgomery, a native of the "Old Dominion," belonged to the "Paul Clifford" school; and indeed, had, for some years past, borne testimony, to the merit of Mr. Bulwer's romances, by making the hero of one of them, his great prototype. In stature, the Major was over six feet, muscular, and finely proportioned. His taste in dress, was only surpassed by the courtliness of his manners, and the ready flow of his conversation. In what campaign he had won the laurels that gave him his military title, is unknown. It has been conjectured that the warlike prefix to his name, may have resulted from the luxuriant brace of black whiskers, which garnished his cheeks.

On a certain day, after dinner, the ladies having retired to their cabin for a siesta, the gentlemen, as usual, sat down to cards, chess and back-gammon. The boat had just "wooded," and was nobly breasting the current of the river at the rate of eight knots an hour. Captain Snake, having nothing else to do, was fain to join in a rubber of whist; and it so happened that he and the Major were seated at the same table. This game, at the suggestion of Major Montgomery, was soon changed to "loo"; and, played with varying success until at length, a pool of considerable magnitude had accumulated. As the contest for the increasing stake, advanced, much interest was excited among the by-standers, and still more in the players, with the exception of the Major, whose staid expression of countenance was a subject of general remark. He seemed careless about the run of the cards, and threw them, as if quite regardless of the tempting spoil that lay before him. At length the game was terminated. The fickle goddess disclosed her preference for the Major, by permitting him to win the "pool," amounting to near three hundred dollars. His success produced no outward signs of joy; he seemed, indeed, almost sorry to be compelled to take the money of his friends; and with much composure of manner, proposed to continue the play; making, at the same time, a very polite tender of his purse, to any gentleman at the table, who might need a temporary loan.

In the group of spectators, there was a tall, spindle-legged young fellow from the Western Reserve, in Ohio, who had been to the South with a lot of cheese, for the manufacture of which, that thriving New England colony, is becoming quite famous. This cheese-monger had been watching the game from the beginning, and at last, fixing his eyes upon the winning Major, said, in a low, solemn tone of voice, suited to a more lugubrious subject, "Well, now, that's right down slick, any how."

The Major, looking up, found the gaze of the company turned upon him. Knitting his brows he said, sternly, in reply,

"Let's have no more of your Yankee impertinence."

"Now, Mister," continued Jonathan in his drawling tone and with provoking coolness of manner, "you hadn't ought to let them there little speckled paste-boards, play hide and go seek in your coat sleeve."

This remark, accompanied with a knowing wink of the speaker's eye, instantly transformed the Major into a young earthquake. Springing upon his feet, as if bent on blood and carnage, he bawled out at the top of his voice,

"Do you mean to insinuate, you Yankee pedlar—you infernal wooden-nutmeg, that I have cheated?"

The young cheese merchant, leisurely rolling a huge cud of tobacco, from one cheek to the other, and looking the Major steadfastly in the eye, replied with imperturbable gravity,

"Why your the beatomest shakes, I ever seed: who insinevated that you cheated? I didn't, no how: but if you don't behave a little genteeler, I conclude I'll tell as how I seed you slip a card under your sleeve, when you won that everlasting big pond of money."

"You are a liar," thundered the Major, in a perfect whirlwind, at the same time attempting to bring his bamboo in contact with the shoulders of his antagonist; but Jonathan caught the descending cane in his left hand; and, in turn, planted his dexter fist, with considerable impulse, on the lower end of the Major's breast bone, remarking,

"I say Mister, make yourself skerse there, or you'll run right against the end of my arm."

Unfortunately for the reputation of Major Montgomery, at this moment, a card fell from his coat sleeve; and, with it, fell his courage, for he turned suddenly round to the table to secure the spoils of victory. The Captain however, had saved him the trouble, having himself taken up the money, for the purpose of returning it to those to whom it rightfully belonged. The Major finding that his winnings and his reputation were both departing, became once more, highly excited, and uttered direful anathemas against those, who might dare to question his honour.

It is, perhaps, generally known to the reader, that the captain of a steam boat on the western waters, is of necessity, almost as despotic as the Grand Turk. The safety of his boat, and the comfort of his passengers, in performing a long and perilous trip, require, indeed, that such should be the case. Between port and port, he is sometimes called to act in the triple capacity of legislator, judge and executioner. It is rumored, perhaps without any foundation, that in cases of great emergency, more than one of these commanders, have seriously threatened a resort to the salutory influence of the "second section." Be this as it may, travellers on our western boats will consult their comfort and safety, by deporting themselves according to the gentlemanly principle. We throw out this hint for the public generally; and, in the fulness of our benevolence, commend it to the especial notice of tourists from the "fast anchored Isle."

Captain Snake made no reply to the imprecations of the Major, having far too much respect for his official station, to permit himself to be drawn into a personal conflict with one of his passengers. Stepping to the cabin door, his clear shrill voice was heard above the din of the Major's volcanic burst of passion and the loud whiz of the Sea Serpent. Instantly the tinkle of the pilot's bell responded to the order of his commander, and the boat lay-to, near the lee shore. Again the Captain's voice was heard,

"Jack! man the yawl; Major Montgomery wishes to go on shore."

"Aye, aye, Sir."

The Major looked round in utter astonishment.—The Captain again called out,

"Steward! put Major Montgomery's trunk in the yawl; he wishes to go on shore!"

"Aye, aye, Sir!"

The Major turned towards the Captain with a face indicating a mingled feeling of anger and dismay. He had seen too much of life in the West, not to understand the fate that awaited him. Before he could make up his mind as to the best mode of warding off the impending catastrophe, Jack bawled out, "the yawl is ready, sir," and, the steward cried, "the trunk is on board, sir."

Captain Snake, bowed formally, and with a courteous, but singularly emphatic manner, said:

"Major Montgomery, the yawl waits."

The Major, however, retained his position near the card-table, and began to remonstrate against such very exceptionable treatment of a Virginia gentleman, whose character had never been questioned. He concluded by a broad intimation, that on their arrival at Cincinnati, he should hold the captain personally responsible under the laws of honor. In reply, the captain of the Sea Serpent, bowed again most profoundly, and turning toward the door of the cabin, said, calmly,

"Steward, call the Fireman to assist Major Montgomery into the yawl; he wishes to go on shore."

The redoubtable Major, in the vain hope that the passengers would sustain him in the contest, now threw himself on his reserved rights, ran up the flag of nullification, and ferociously brandished his Bowie knife: at this moment the Fireman made his appearance. He was a full grown Kentuckian, born on the cedar knobs of the Blue Licks, and raised on sulphur water, pone and 'possum fat.—Like many of his countrymen, he was an aspiring fellow, for he stood six-feet four in his moccasins, and exhibited corresponding developments of bone and muscle. Hatless and coatless, with naked arms, and a face blackened with smoke and ashes, he might have passed for one of old Vulcan's journeymen, who had been forging thunderbolts for Jupiter, in some *regio-infernalis*. He stalked carelessly up to the bellicose Major, and before the latter was aware of it, seized the hand that held the up-raised knife, and wrenched it from him. The next instant the Major found himself fairly within the brawny arms of his antagonist. He struggled stoutly to extricate his elegant person from such an unwelcome embrace, but in vain. The fireman, displeased with the restless disposition of his captive, gave him one of those warm fraternal hugs, which an old bear is wont to bestow upon an unmannerly dog, that may venture to annoy his retreat from a farmer's hog-pen. This loving squeeze so completely mollified the rebellious feelings of the Major, that he suffered himself to be passively led into the yawl. The Captain's shrill voice was again heard,

"Pull away, my boys, Major Montgomery wishes to go on shore."

The oars dipped into the water and the yawl glided quickly to the beach. The afternoon was cloudy and dark; a drizzling rain was falling; the cottonwood trees wore a funeral aspect; no vestige of a human habitation could be seen upon either shore, and the turbid waters of the Mississippi, were hastening onwards, as if to escape from such a gloomy place.

Many of the passengers supposed that after the Major had been disgraced by being set on shore, he would be suffered to return; but those who entertained this opinion knew very little of the character of Captain Snake. That Major Montgomery should be a black-leg, was in his estimation, no very heinous affair; for he held that in this republican country, and this democratic age, every man has a natural and inalienable right to choose his own occu-pation: But after having been permitted to play "loo" with the Captain of the fast running Sea Serpent, that the Major should slip a card, and then, lub-berly rascal, be caught at it,—this was too bad,—absolutely unpardonable: There was something so vulgar, so very unprofessional in such conduct, that it was not to be tolerated.

The yawl touched the shore and was hastily disburthened of its trunk. The Major, however, after rising on his feet, looked wistfully back upon the Sea Serpent, and manifested no disposition to take refuge in a cane-brake: Whereupon, the Capt. becoming impatient, cried out,

"Fireman, lend a hand to assist Major Montgomery on shore."

The huge Kentuckian now began to approach the Major, who, having no particular relish for another fraternal hug, sprung to the beach, and sunk to his knees in mud. Thinking forbearance no longer a virtue, he poured out on the Captain, a torrent of abuse: and, with wrathful oaths, threatened to pub-lish him and his ugly, snail creeping steamer, from Olean Point to the alliga-tor swamps of the Balize. The Captain made no reply, but the fireman, roused by hearing such opprobrious terms applied to his beloved Sea Serpent, called out in a voice, that was echoed from shore to shore,

"I say, Mr. Jack-of-knaves, it looks rather wolfy in these parts."

"Shut your black mouth, you scoundrel," retorted the Major, boiling over with rage.

"I say stranger," continued the fireman with provoking good humor, "would you swap them buffalo robes on your cheeks for a pair of 'coon-skins'?"

The Major stooped down for a stone to hurl at his annoying foe, but alas, he stood in a bed of mortar, and had no resource but that of firing another volley of curses.

"Halloo! my hearty," rejoined the fireman, "When you want to be rowed up 'salt river' again just tip me the wink; and remember Mr. King-of-Clubs, don't holler till you get out of the woods, or you'll frighten all the var-mints."

During this colloquy, the young cheese-merchant, stood on the guards of the boat, a silent spectator; but at length, as if suddenly shocked by the dread-ful profanity of the Major, he raised his voice and bawled out,

"I say Mister, if you was away down east, I guess 'squire Dagget would fine you ever so much, for swearing so wicked;—that's the how."

The pilot's bell tinkled, the wheels resumed their gyrations, and again the majestic Sea Serpent,

"Walked the waters like a thing of life."

Jonathan, with a look in which the solemn and comic were curiously blended, turned his eyes first towards the Captain, then upon the Major, and exclaimed,

"Well now the way these ere steam captains do things, is nothing to no body, no how."

And thus terminated one of those little episodes in the drama of life not uncommon on the western Waters.

From *Richard Hurdis; or, The Avenger of Blood*

WILLIAM GILMORE SIMMS

William Gilmore Simms, in Mary Ann Wimsatt's words, was the "leading exemplar of literary activity" in the antebellum South (1). The author of over eighty published books, Simms was as interested in writing about the contemporary southern scene as he was the colonial and Revolutionary past. In *Richard Hurdis,* published in 1838, he took inspiration from the recent story of outlaw John A. Murrell, believed to have been the mastermind behind an abortive slave rebellion in 1835. Here, the eponymous hero of the novel has to dress as a riverboat gambler to infiltrate a criminal gang—and in so doing, sets a fashionable template for the fictional gamblers who followed. The parson he encounters is actually gang leader (and fictionalized Murrell) Clement Foster, also in disguise. For further information, see Mary Ann Wimsatt, *The Major Fiction of William Gilmore Simms* (Baton Rouge: Louisiana State University Press, 1989). For more on Murrell, see James Lal Penick, Jr., *The Great Western Land Pirate: John A. Murrell in Legend and History* (Columbia: University of Missouri Press, 1981).

My first object was to alter my personal appearance, so as to defeat all chance of recognition by any of the villains with whom I had previously come in collision. This was a work calling for much careful consideration. To go down to Mobile, change my clothes, and adopt such fashions as would more completely disguise me, were my immediate designs; and I pushed my way to this, my first post, with all speed and without any interruption. My first care in Mobile was to sell my horse which I did for one hundred and eighty dollars. I had now nearly five hundred dollars in possession—a small part in silver, the rest in United States Bank, Alabama, and Louisiana notes, all of which were equally current. I soon procured a couple of entire suits, as utterly different from any thing I had previously worn as possible. Then, having a proper regard to the usual decoration of the professed gamblers of our country, I entered a jeweller's establishment, and bought sundry bunches of seals, a tawdry watch, a huge chain of doubtful, but sold as virgin, gold; and some breastpins and shirt buttons of saucer size. To those who had personally known me before, I was well assured that no disguise would have been more perfect than that afforded by these trinkets—but when, in addition to these and the other changes in my habit of which I have spoken, I state that my beard was suffered to grow goatlike, after the most approved models of dandyism, under the chin, in curling masses, and my whiskers, in rival magnificence, were permitted to overrun my cheeks—I trust that I shall be believed when I aver that after a few weeks space, I scarcely knew myself. I had usually been rather fastidious in keeping a smooth cheek and chin, and I doubt very much, whether my own father ever beheld a two days' beard upon me from the day that I found myself man enough to shave at all, to the present. The more I contemplated my own appearance, the more sanguine I became of success; and I lingered in Mobile a little time longer in order to give beard and whiskers a fair opportunity to overrun a territory which before had never shown its stubble. When this time was elapsed, my visage was quite Siberian; a thick cap of otter skin, which I now procured, fully completed my northern disguises, and, exchanging my pistols at a hardware establishment, for others not so good, but for which I had to give some considerable boot, I felt myself fairly ready for my perilous adventure. It called for some resolution to go forward when the time came for my departure, and when I thought of the dangers before me; but when, in the next instant, I thought of the murder of my friend, and of the sad fate of his betrothed, my resolution of vengeance was renewed. I felt that I had an oath in Heaven—sworn—registered;—and I repeated it on earth.

[. . .]

I entered a steamboat, one fair morning, and with promising auspices, so far as our voyage is considered, we went forward swimmingly enough. But our boat was an old one—a wretched hulk, which, having worked out its term of responsible service in the Mississippi, had been sent round to Mobile, at the instance of cupidity, to beguile unwitting passengers like myself, to their ruin. She was a piece of patchwork throughout, owned by a professional gambler, a little Israelite, who took the command without knowing any thing about it, and by dint of good fortune, carried us safely to our journey's end. Not that we had not some little stoppages and troubles by the way. Some portion of the machinery got out of order, and we landed at Demopolis, built a fire, erected a sort of forge, and in the space of half a day and night repaired the accident. This incident would not be worth relating, but that it exhibits the readiness with which our wildest and least scientific people, can find remedies for disasters which would seem to call for great skill and most extensive preparations. On the eleventh day we reached Columbus; but in the meantime, practising my new resolves, I made an acquaintance on board the boat. This was an old gentleman, a puritan of the bluest complexion, whom nobody would have suspected of being a rogue. Setting out to seek for, and meet with none but rogues, he yet nearly deceived me by his sanctity; and had I not maintained my watchfulness a little longer than I deemed necessary myself, I should have taken it for granted that he was a saint of the most accepted order, and, if I had not committed my secret to his keeping, I should, at least, have so far involved its importance as to make my labour unavailing. Fortunately, as I said, having put on, with the dress common to the gamblers of the great Mississippi Valley, as much of their easy impudence of demeanor as I could readily assume, I succeeded as effectually in convincing my puritan that I was a rogue, as he did in persuading me, at the beginning, that he was an honest man. It was my good fortune to find out his secret first, and to keep my own. It so happened that there were several passengers like myself, bound for Columbus on the Tombeckbe, to which place our boat was destined. As customary at that time, we had no sooner got fairly under way before cards were produced, and one fellow, whose lungs and audacity were greater than the rest, was heard throughout the cabin calling upon all persons who were disposed to "take a hand," to come forward. With my new policy in view, I was one of the first to answer this challenge. I had provided myself in Mobile with several packs, and taking a couple of them in hand, I went forward to the table which meanwhile had been drawn out in the cabin and coolly surveyed my companions. Our puritan came forward at the same moment, and in the gravest terms and tones, protested against our playing.

"My young friends," he cried, "let me beg you not to engage in this wicked amusement. Cards are, as it has been often and well said—cards are the prayer books of the devil. It is by these that he wins souls daily to his gloomy kingdom. Night and day he is busy in these arts, to entrap the unwary, whom he blinds and beguiles until, when they open their eyes at last, they open them in the dwellings of damnation. Oh, my dear children, do not venture to follow him so far. Cast the temptation from you—defy the tempter; and in place of these dangerous instruments of sin, hearken, I pray you, to the goodly outpourings of a divine spirit. If you will but suffer me to choose for you a text from this blessed volume—"

Here he took a small pocket bible from his bosom, and was about to turn the leaves, when a cry from all around me, silenced him in his homily, which promised to be sufficiently unctuous and edifying.

"No text—no text," was the general voice—"none of the parson—none of the parson."

"Nay, my beloved children—" the preacher begun, but a tall good-humoured looking fellow, a Georgian, with the full face, lively eyes and clear skin of that state, came up to him, and laid his broad hand over his mouth.

"Shut up, parson, it's no use. You can't be heard now, for you see it's only civility to let the devil have the floor, seeing he was up first. If, now, you had been quick enough with your prayer-book, and got the whip-hand of him, d——n my eyes, but you should have sung out your song to the end of the verses; but you've been slow, parson—you've been sleeping at your stand, and the deer's got round you. You'll get smoked by the old one, yourself, if you don't mind, for neglecting your duty."

"Peace, vain young man—"

He was about to begin a furious denunciation, but was allowed to proceed no farther. The clamor was unanimous around him; and one tall fellow, some-what dandyishly accoutred like myself, coming forward, made a show of seizing upon the exhorter. Here I interposed.

"No violence, gentlemen; it's enough that we have silenced the man, let him not be hurt."

"Ay, if he will keep quiet," said the fellow, still threatening.

"Oh, quiet or not," said the Georgian, "we mustn't hurt the parson. 'Dang it, he shan't be hurt. I'll stand up for him.—Parson, I'll stand up for you; but by the Hokey, old black, you must keep your oven close."

I joined in promising that he would be quiet and offer no farther interruption, and he so far seemed to warrant our assurance as, without promising himself, to take a seat, after a few half suppressed groans, on a bench near the table, on which we were about to play. I was first struck with suspicion of the fellow by this fact. If the matter was so painful to his spirit, why did he linger in our neighbourhood when there were so many parts of the boat to which he might have retreated? The suspicion grew stronger when I found him, after a little while, as watchfully attentive to the progress of the game as any of the players.

Favourably impressed with the frankness of the Georgian, I proposed that we should play against the other two persons who were prepared to sit down to the table, and my offer was closed with instantly. We bet on each hand, on the highest trump, and on the game with each of our opponents, a dollar being the amount of each bet, so that we had a good many dollars staked on the general result of the game. I know that I lost nine dollars before the cards had been thrice dealt. I now proceeded to try some of the tricks which I had seen others perform, and in particular that in which the dealer, by a peculiar mode of shuffling, divides the trumps between his partner and himself. My object was to fix the attention of one of my opponents, whom I suspected from the first to be no better than he should be, simply because he wore a habit not unlike my own, and was covered with trinkets in the same manner. But I lacked experience—there was still a trick wanting which no slight of hand of mine could remedy. Though I shuffled the cards as I had seen them shuffled, by drawing them alternately from top and bottom together, I found neither mine nor my partner's hand any better than before, and looking up with some affected chagrin in my countenance, I caught sight of what seemed to be an understanding smile between the opponent in question and the parson, who, sitting a little on one side of me, was able to look, if he desired it, into my hand. This discovery—as I thought it—gave me no little pleasure. I was resolved to test it, and ascertain how far I was correct in my suspicions. I flattered myself that I was in a fair way to fall upon the clue which might conduct me into the very midst of the gamblers, who are all supposed to be connected more or less on the western waters, and yield me possession of their secrets. Accordingly, I displayed certain of my cards ostentatiously before the eyes of the preacher, and had occasion to observe, an instant after, that the play of my opponent seemed to be regulated by a certain knowledge of my hand. He finessed constantly upon my lead; and with an adroitness which compelled the continual expression of wonder and dissatisfaction from the lips of my partner. I was satisfied, so far, with the result of my experiment, and began to think of pausing before I proceeded farther; when my Georgian dashed down his cards as the game was ended against us, and cried out to me, with a countenance which, though flushed, was yet full of most excellent feeling—

"Look you, stranger, suppose we change. We don't seem to have luck together, and there's no fun in being all the time on the losing side. The bad luck may be with me, or it may be with you, I don't say, but it can do no harm to shift it to other shoulders, whoever has it. I've been diddled out of twenty-six hard dollars, in mighty short order."

"Diddled!" exclaimed my brother dandy, with an air of ineffable heroism, turning to my partner. Without discomposure the other replied:

"I don't mean any harm when I say diddled, stranger, so don't be uneasy. I call it diddling when I lose my money, fight as hard for it as I can. That's the worst sort of diddling I know."

The other looked fierce for a moment, but he probably soon discovered that the Georgian had replied without heeding his air of valor, and there was something about his composed manner which rendered it at least a doubtful point whether any thing in the shape of an insult would not set his bulky frame into overpowering exercise. The disposition to bully, however slightly it was suffered to appear, added another item to my suspicions of the character before me. The proposition of my partner to change places with one of the other two, produced a different suggestion from one of them, which seemed to please us all. It was that we should play *vingt-un*.

"Every man fights on his own hook in that, and his bad luck, if he has any, hurts nobody but himself."

I had begun to reproach myself with a course which, however useful in forwarding my own objects, had evidently contributed to the loss by my partner of his money. If free to throw away my own, I had no right to try experiments on his purse, and I readily gave my assent to the proposition. Our bets were more moderate than before, but I soon found the game a losing one still. The preacher still sat at my elbow, and my brother dandy was the banker; and in more than one instance when I have stood on "twenty" he has drawn from the pack, though having "eighteen" and "nineteen,"—upon which good players will always be content, unless assured that better hands are in the possession of their opponents, when, by "drawing," they cannot lose. This knowledge could only be received from our devoted preacher, and when I ceased to play—which, through sheer weariness I did—I did so with the most thorough persuasion, that the two were in correspondence—they were birds of the same brood.

Moody and thoughtful, for I was now persuaded that my own more important game was beginning to open before me, I went to the stern of the boat, and seated myself upon one of the bulks, giving way to the bitter musings of which my mind was sufficiently full. While I sat thus, I was startled on a sudden to find the preacher beside me.

"Ah, my young friend, I have watched you during your sinful play, against which I warned you, with a painful sort of curiosity. Did I not counsel you against those devilish instruments—you scorned my counsel, and what has been your fortune. You have lost money, my son, money—a goodly sum, which might have blessed the poor widow, and the portionless orphan— which might have sent the blessings of the word into strange lands among the benighted heathen—which might have helped on in his labours some wayfaring teacher of the word—which might be most needful to yourself, my son; which, indeed, I see it in your looks—which you could very ill spare for such purposes, and which even now it is your bitter suffering that you have lost."

Admiring the hypocrisy of the old reprobate, I was yet, in obedience to my policy, prepared to respect it. I availed myself of his own suggestion, and thus answered him.

"You speak truly, sir; I bitterly regret having lost my money, which, as you say, I could ill spare, and which it has nearly emptied my pockets to have lost. But suppose I had been fortunate—if I was punished by my losses for having played, he who won, I suppose, is punished by his winnings for the same offence. How does your reason answer when it cuts both ways?"

"Even as a two edged sword it doth, my friend; though in the blindness of earth you may not so readily see or believe it. Truly may it be said that you are both equally punished by your fortunes. You suffer from your losses— who shall say that he will suffer less from his gains. Will it not encourage him in his career of sin—will it not promote his licentiousness—his indulgence of many vices which will bring him to disease, want, and, possibly— which heaven avert—to an untimely end. Verily, my friend, I do think him even more unfortunate than thyself; for, of a truth, it may be said, that the right use of money is the most difficult and dangerous of all; and few ever use it rightly but such as gain it through great toil, or have the divine instinct of heaven, which is wisdom, to employ it to its rightful purposes."

Excellent hypocrite! How admirably did he preach! How adroitly did he escape what had otherwise been his dilemma. He almost deceived me a second time.

"In your heart, now, my friend, you bitterly repent that you heeded not my counsel."

"Not a whit!" was my reply. "If I were sure I could win, I would stick by the card table forever."

"What! so profligate and so young. Oh! My friend, think upon your end— think of eternity."

"Rather let me think of my beginning, reverend sir, if you please. The business of time requires present attention, and to a man that is starving your talk of future provision is a mere mockery. Give me to know how I am to get the bread of life in this life before you talk to me of bread for the next."

"How should you get it, my friend, but by painstaking and labour, and worthy conduct. The world esteems not those who play at cards—"

"And I esteem not the world. What matters it to me, my good sir, what are the opinions of those to whom I am unknown, and for whom I care nothing. Give me but money though, and I will make them love me, and honor me, and force truth and honesty into all shapes, that they may not offend my principles or practice."

"But, my son, you would not surely forget the laws of honesty in the acquisition of wealth?"

This was said inquisitively, and with a prying glance of the eye, which sufficiently betokened the deep interest which the hypocrite felt in my answer. But that I was now persuaded of his hypocrisy, I should have never avowed myself so boldly.

"What are they? What are these laws of honesty of which you speak? I cannot, all at once, say that I know them."

"Not know them!"

"No!"

"Well," he continued, "to say truth, they are rather frequently revoked among mankind, and have others wholly opposite in character substituted in their place; but you cannot mistake me my young friend—you know that there are such laws."

"Ay, laws for me—for the poor—to crush the weak—made by the strong for their own protection—for the protection of the wealth of the cunning. These are not laws calculated to win the respect or regard of the destitute—of those who are desperate enough, if they did not lack the strength, to pull down society with a fearless hand, though, perhaps, they pulled it in ruin upon themselves."

"But you, my friend, you are not thus desperate—this is not your situation."

"What! you would extort a confession from me, first of my poverty—then of my desperation—you would drag me to the county court, would you, that you might have the proud satisfaction of exhorting the criminal in his last moments, in the presence of twenty thousand admiring fellow creatures, who come to see a brother launched out of life and into hell. This is your practice and creed is it?"

"No, my friend," he replied, in a lower tone of voice, which was, perhaps, intended to restrain the emphatic utterance of mine. "Know me better, my friend—I would save you—such is my heart—from so dreadful a situation— yes, I would even defeat the purposes of justice, though I felt persuaded you would sin again in the same fashion. Be not rash—be not hasty in your judgment of me, my friend. I like you, and will say something to you which you will, perhaps, be pleased to hear. But not now—one of these vicious reprobates approaches us, and what I say must be kept only for your own ears. To-night, perhaps—to-night."

He left me with an uplifted finger, and a look—such a look as Satan may be supposed to have fixed on Adam in Paradise.

Antebellum (Mis)Adventures

"gambling, drinking, smoking, and blaspheming"

From *Excursion Through the Slave States*

GEORGE W. FEATHERSTONHAUGH

George W. Featherstonhaugh was a man of many parts. In the words of biographers Edmund and Dorothy Smith Berkeley, "He was very much involved at various times in agriculture, diplomacy, geology, literature, and railroads" (xiii). Though born in England, Featherstonhaugh spent many years in America. Most famously, he played a vital role in the construction of the pioneering Albany and Schenectady Railroad and conducted important geological investigations in the territory between the Missouri and Red rivers obtained in the Louisiana Purchase. His varied career meant that he was well traveled, and his account of his American experiences, titled *Excursion Through the Slave States* (1844), achieved much popularity. The extract that follows details Featherstonhaugh's troubles with a number of riverboat gamblers—an exasperation common to many travelers. For further information, see Edmund and Dorothy Smith Berkeley, *George William Featherstonhaugh: The First U.S. Government Geologist* (Tuscaloosa: University of Alabama Press, 1988).

Upon embarking on board of this steamer I was certainly pleased with the prospect that presented itself of enjoying some repose and comfort after the privations and fatigues I had endured; but never was traveller more mistaken in his anticipations! The vexatious conduct of the drunken youth had made a serious innovation upon the slight degree of personal comfort to be obtained in such a place, but I had not the slightest conception that that incident would be entirely thrown into the shade by others a thousand times more offensive, and that, from the moment of our departure from the post of Arkansas until our arrival at New Orleans, I was destined to a series of brutal annoyances that extinguished every hope of repose, or a chance of preserving even the decencies of existence.

I had been told at the post of Arkansas that ten passengers were waiting to come on board, and that several of them were notorious swindlers and gamblers, who, whilst in Arkansas, lived by the most desperate cheating and bullying, and who skulked about alternately betwixt Little Rock, Natchez, and New Orleans, in search of any plunder that violent and base means could bring into their hands. Some of their names were familiar to me, having heard them frequently spoken of at Little Rock as scoundrels of the worst class. From the moment I heard they were coming on board as passengers I predicted to Mr. T—— that every hope of comfort was at an end. But I had also been told that two American officers, a Captain D—— and a Lieut. C——, the latter a gentleman entrusted with the construction of the military road in Arkansas, were also coming on board; and I counted upon them as persons who would be, by the force of education and a consciousness of what was due to their rank as officers, on the side of decency at least, if not of correct manners; and if those persons had passed through the national military academy at West Point, or had served under the respectable chief of the Topographical Bureau at Washington, I should not have been as grievously disappointed as it was my fate to be. It was true I had heard that these officers had been passing ten days with these scoundrels at a low tavern at this place, in the unrestrained indulgence of every vicious extravagance, night and day, and that they were the familiar intimates of these notorious swindlers. Nevertheless, believing that there must be some exaggeration in this, I continued to look forward with satisfaction to having them for fellow passengers, confident that they would be our allies against any gross encroachments of the others.

Very soon after I had retired to the steamer at sun-set, the whole clique came on board, and the effect produced on us was something like that which would be made upon passengers in a peaceful vessel forcibly boarded by pirates of the most desperate character, whose manners seemed to be what they aspired to imitate. Rushing into the cabin, all but red-hot with whiskey, they crowded round the stove and excluded all the old passengers from it as much as if they had no right whatever to be in the cabin. Putting on a determined bullying air of doing what they pleased because they were the majority, and armed with pistols and knives, expressly made for cutting and stabbing, eight inches long and an inch and a half broad; noise, confusion, spitting, smoking, cursing and swearing, drawn from the most remorseless pages of blasphemy, commenced and prevailed from the moment of this invasion. I was satisfied at once that all resistance would be vain, and that even remonstrance might lead to murder; for a sickly old man in the cabin happening to say to one of them that there was so much smoke he could hardly breathe, the fellow immediately said, "If any man tells me he don't like my smoking I'll put a knife into him."

As soon as supper was over they all went to gambling, during which, at every turn of the cards, imprecations and blasphemies of the most revolting kind were loudly vociferated. Observing them from a distance where Mr.

T—— and myself were seated, I perceived that one of them was the wretched looking fellow I had seen at Hignite's, on my way to Texas, who went by the name of Smith, and that his keeper Mr. Tunstall was with him. The most blasphemous fellows amongst them were two men of the names of Rector and Wilson. This Rector at that time held a commission under the national government as Marshal for the territory of Arkansas, was a man of mean stature, low and sottish in his manners, and as corrupt and reckless as it was possible for a human being to be. The man named Wilson was a suttler from cantonment Gibson, a military post about 250 miles up the Arkansas: he had a remarkable depression at the bottom of his forehead; and from this sinus his nose rising with a sudden spring, gave a feral expression to his face that exactly resembled the portrait of the wicked apprentice in Hogarth. The rubric on his countenance too was a faithful register of the numerous journeys the whiskey bottle had made to his proboscis.

If the Marshal, Mr. Rector, was the most constant blasphemer, the suttler was the most emphatic one. It was Mr. Rector's invariable custom, when the cards did not turn up to please him, to express a fervent wish that "his soul might be sent to ——," whilst Mr. Wilson never neglected a favourable opportunity of hoping that his own might be kept there to a thousand eternities. This was the language we were compelled to listen to morning, noon, and night, without remission, whenever we were in the cabin. In the morning, as soon as day broke, they began by drinking brandy and gin with sugar in it, without any water, and after breakfast they immediately went to gambling, smoking, spitting, blaspheming, and drinking for the rest of the day. Dinner interrupted their orgies for a while, but only for a short time, and after supper these wretches, maddened with the inflaming and impure liquors they swallowed, filled the cabin with an infernal vociferation of curses, and a perfect pestilence of smoking and spitting in every direction. Lieut. C—— occasionally exchanged a few words with me, and appeared to be restrained by my presence; he never sat down to play, but was upon the most intimate terms with the worst of these blackguards, and drank very freely with them. Capt. D——, with whom I never exchanged a word, was a gentlemanly-looking youth, and was not vulgar and coarse like the others, but I never saw a young man so infatuated with play, being always the first to go to the gambling table and the last to quit it. Such was his passion for gambling that it overcame everything like decent respect for the feelings and comfort of the other passengers; and one night, after the others had become too drunk and tired to sit up, I was kept awake by his sitting up with Rector and continuing to play at high, low, jack, and the game, until a very late hour in the morning. Perhaps, however, the most remarkable character amongst them was Smith, the New Englander, with his pale dough face, every feature of which was a proclamation of bully, sneak, and scoundrel. I never before saw in the countenance of any man such incontrovertible evidences of a fallen nature. It was this fellow that had charge of the materials for gambling, and who spread the faro table out the first evening of their coming on board, in hopes to lure some of the passengers; none of whom however approached the table except the drunken youth who had behaved so ill on a previous occasion, and they never asked him to play, probably knowing that he had no money.

Having found no birds to pluck on board, they were compelled to play against each other, always quarrelling in the most violent manner, and using the most atrocious menaces: it was always known when these quarrels were not made up, by the parties appearing the next time at the gambling-table with their Bowie-knives near them. In various travels in almost every part of the world I never saw such a collection of unblushing, low, degraded scoundrels, and I became at length so unhappy as often to think of being set on shore and taking a chance fate in the wild canebrakes, rather than have my senses continually polluted with scenes that had every appearance of lasting until the end of the voyage: but for the comfort I derived from the society of Mr. T——, who was as miserable as myself, and who relied altogether upon me to set a good countenance upon the whole matter, I certainly should have executed my intention.

Above the cabin where these scenes were enacted, was a smaller one called the Ladies' Cabin, and when I found what sort of a set we had got, I applied to the steward to give Mr. T—— and myself berths there; but he informed us this could not be done, because Capt. D's sister was there, having come on board with him at the post. She might be his sister for aught I ever learnt to the contrary, but whatever she was she kept very close, for she never appeared either below or upon deck. My remonstrances with the captain produced no effect whatever; when I talked to him about his printed rules, he plainly told me that he did not pretend to execute them; that what I complained of were the customs and manners of the country, and that if he pretended to enforce the rules, he should never get another passenger, adding, that one of the rules left it to a majority of the passengers to form their own by-laws for the government of the cabin.

On recurring to them I found it was so, the terms being that by-laws were to be so made, "provided they were in conformity with the police of the boat." As there was no police in the boat, it was evident the printed rules were nothing but a bait to catch passengers with, and I never spoke to him on the subject again. I had heard many stories of gangs of scoundrels who wandered about from New Orleans to Natchez, Vicksburg, and Little Rock, with no baggage but broad, sharp butcher knives, loaded pistols, and gambling apparatus, and I was now compelled to witness the proceedings of such ruffians. These would have been less intolerable if the two U.S. officers had kept aloof from these fellows and formed a little society with us, as I reasonably expected they would do when I first heard they were coming on board; but Capt. D—— never once offered either Mr. T—— or myself the least civility, or exchanged a word with us; and although that was not the case with Lieut. C——, yet an incident took place very early in the voyage which convinced me we had nothing to expect from him. Wilson, the man with the nose, was standing with his back to the stove before breakfast, unrestrainedly indulging in incoherent curses about some one he had quarrelled with, when Mr. C—— in the most amiable manner put his hand inside of the ruffian's waistcoat, drew forth his stabbing knife, unsheathed it, felt the edge as if with a connoisseur's finger and thumb, and was lavish in its praise. Such were the unvarying scenes which were re-enacted for the many days we were shut up in the steamer with these villains.

[. . .]

After passing a most horrible night, kept awake by the tobacco and imprecations of the drunken gamblers, we arrived early in the morning of January 1st at Vicksburg, and greatly disappointed were we not to find any steamer there bound to New Orleans. Here we remained several hours, and thought of going to a tavern to wait for a steamer, for which purpose we entered the town with the intention of looking out for lodgings.

Vicksburg is a modern settlement situated on the side of a hill very much abraded and cut up into gullies by the rains. The land rises about 200 feet above the Mississippi, but sinks again very soon to the east, forming a sort of ridge which appears at intervals as far as Baton Rouge. On returning to the steamer we were informed that eight or ten *gentlemen,* some of whom were planters of great respectability, and amongst the rest, a Mr. Vick, after whom the place was called, were coming on board with the intention of going to New Orleans. This determined us to continue on with the boat, conceiving that we should be too many for the ruffians in the cabin, and that the captain who was anxious to keep up a good understanding with the planters would now interfere to keep some order there. But supper being over, and the faro-table spread as usual, what was my horror and astonishment at seeing these Mississippi gentlemen, with the respectable Mr. Vick, sitting down to faro with these swindlers, and in the course of a very short time gambling, drinking, smoking, and blaspheming, just as desperately as the worst of them! The cabin became so full of tobacco smoke that it was impossible for me to remain in it, so wrapping myself up as warm as I could, I retreated to the deck to pass the night, Mr. T—— soon following me; there we met the captain, and told him we could not endure this any longer, and were desirous of being put on shore at the very first settlement we should reach by daylight.

He said it would be best for us to go on shore at Natchez, and that he really pitied us, but that he could not disoblige these planters, for that if he was to interfere with their amusements, they would never ship any freight with him; adding that the competition amongst the steamers was so great, that every man was obliged to look out for his own interests: as a proof that it was necessary for him to act with some policy, he told us that a captain of his acquaintance having once put a disorderly fellow belonging to Vicksburg on shore, had, when he stopped there on his return, been boarded by fifteen persons, armed with knives and pistols, who proceeded to spit in his face, kick him, and treat him in the most savage manner. Some of these fifteen persons, he said, he thought were now on board. This I could readily believe, for nothing could be more reckless or brutal than their conduct and conversation. They had escaped the restraints which society imposed in the place they inhabited—if any such existed—and seemed determined to exhaust all the extravagances that brutality and profanity are capable of. I shall never forget these specimens of *gentlemen* belonging to the State of Mississippi.

Sketches from the *Spirit of the Times*

William T. Porter's influential newspaper the *Spirit of the Times* was published in New York from 1831 to 1861. Primarily devoted to sporting pursuits, the *Spirit* also played a crucible role in the development of southwestern humor, publishing short, vernacular-filled sketches of American life. Though based in the North, it maintained a national appeal throughout the antebellum period; contributors sent in sketches from a wide variety of locations. Comic gambling stories from the Mississippi River—what one correspondent below calls "the great sporting stream"—were a favorite theme, and the *Spirit* must be considered an important factor in the development of the popular conception of riverboat gambling in the years before the war. Below are a series of characteristic sketches. Where available, author attributions are given. For more information, see Norris W. Yates, *William T. Porter and the* Spirit of the Times: *A Study of the Big Bear School of Humor* (Baton Rouge: Louisiana State University Press, 1957).

From "Anecdotes of Western Travel"

Among the passengers who came aboard at New Orleans was a "split me" young buck from New York, on a tour of pleasure through the Western States. He had never before been far from Broadway, and he regarded the time spent away from that fashionable resort as so much time thrown away; it was a blank in his existence that could never be filled up. He had been but a few weeks absent, and was already becoming disgusted with the country, and longed to return to the gaieties of the city. His peculiarities were new to the backwoodsman, and he was looked upon by them as an original, as belonging to a genus of the race biped of which they had before no conception. He had brought with him from the city all the paraphernalia of the wardrobe and toilet, and among other things, a very beautiful rose-wood dressing case, one of Tiffany's latest importations. It stood in a conspicuous place in the gent's cabin, and soon attracted the observations of the backwoodsmen.

Their curiosity was raised, and there were numerous speculations as to its use. One thought it a money-box, one a gun-case, and others, and the most knowing ones, that it was a Faro-box. The latter opinion, after a good deal of discussion, prevailed, and they arrived at the unanimous conclusion that the Broadway gent. was a travelling "Leg" in disguise.

Thereupon they resolved to give him an invitation to "open," and collecting together in the forward cabin, they appointed one of their number to intimate to the gentleman that his presence there with the necessary "tools," would be agreeable to them.

The messenger was a double-fisted Mississippian, who soon found the exquisite, and approaching him, with the right side of his face screwed up until the eye on that side closed, (intending it for a sly wink), and beckoning with his finger towards him at the same time, said in a low tone of voice—

"It's all right, my boy; get out your old 'sody box' and come along, and give us a 'turn.'"

The dandy looked in perfect amazement as he said—"Ah–ah–ah!—what you mean, fellow?"

"I say it's all OK down there"—pointing with his finger over his left shoulder—"thar's three or four of us down river boys ready to start the fires with a small pile of 'chips.' You understand, now, so come along—come along."

"Dem you, sa, what do you mean? I declare I don't comprehend you, fellar."

"Oh, come along, we'll put 'er through straight from the mark, and pile on the chips until we bust you, or get bust ourselves; so don't try to play possum on this child. I say it aint no use."

At this the dandy walked off in a furious passion, considering himself most grossly insulted, saying—"Ah, Captain, I believe—'pon me honor I do—that the savage fellar means to blow up the boat!"

The sporting gents could not understand this, and they watched his motions all day, following him from one place to another. Go where he would they were sure to keep him in sight. Having occasion to go to his dressing case before night, they all collected around him, and looked over his shoulder while he was unlocking it. On raising the lid, the first article that presented itself was a pair of boot-hooks. When they saw this, one of them, turned away with an air of disgust, saying to the others—"Why, he's one of them d——d dentistry chaps, after all."

Finding they were not likely to get up a game, they were forced to resort to other expedients to wile away the dull monotony of the voyage; and as the New Yorker was very credulous, some of them amused themselves at his expense by relating to him the most improbable tales of backwoods adventures, hair breadth escapes from savage wild beasts, the dangers of navigating Western rivers, blowing up of steamboats, running foul of snags, &c. &c.

He swallowed them all, and they had such an effect upon his imagination, that he was afraid to venture out of sight of the boat when it stopped to take in wood, for fear, as he said, of "encountewing a bear, or some other howible cweture." He was constantly on the *que vive* at night, expecting some accident to the boat, and would pace the deck for hours together, trembling at every puff of the engine, as if he expected the next to send him to the bottom. Seeing the Captain come on deck one night, he approached him, when the following dialogue ensued:—

"Ah–ah–ah, Capting, do you really have any sewious accidents upon this howible river?"

"Accidents! my dear fellow! as a matter of course we do."

"Ah! and pray, Capting, what is the nature of them?"

"Oh, sometimes we run afoul of a snag, or sawyer; then again, we occasionally collapse a boiler and blow up sky high."

"The devwal you do! you don't say so! does anybody ever get killed, Capting?"

"Nothing is more common, my good fellow; but we soon get used to such little things, and don't mind them. If we get up to St. Louis without an accident, we may consider ourselves extremely fortunate."

The dandy looked perfectly aghast, and turned blue at this announcement.

"How perfwectly howible, Capting! I wish I was back in Bwoad-way again, by quist I do."

A Game of "Full Deck Poker"

You don't know Josiah Brooks, I guess? Well, you ought to know him, and shall. Josiah is "one of the Boys" about here,—and strange to say, for the want of a phrenological chart, I suppose, he has lived to be about thirty before he found the true value of his talents, having been engaged in many trades and occupations, from an "old field school master," down to a steam Doctor; but at length, from adversity and many ups and downs, Josiah has been forced into a knowledge of the fact that he can "turn Jack" as often, and hold as many trumps, as any other man. Yet I must do Josiah the justice to say he never refuses a good place at $500 a year, when offered to oversee a business that requires a deal of looking on and not much work.

Josiah is not handsome, but can boast of a model peculiar to himself, and like all other new fashions, looks uncomely, when first introduced. Now, worse fashions of men might be got up than the pattern of Josiah. He measures just fifteen inches from the top of his crown to the point of his shoulders: fifteen inches body and three and a half feet legs, which makes him just six feet "in the clear!" Another new arrangement in Josiah's features is to dispense with the useless and unnecessary prominence of a chin, so his neck puts out just at the lower lip, making upon the whole one of the most unrivalled Julep necks extant! His eyes, too, are peculiarly adapted to the country in which he lives, being wisely placed out of harm's way—by setting very deep, and in the top of his head—for all the world like a wild cat's! His legs, too, are made for wading deep swamps, like a sand hill crow, and his chin affords no resting place for musquetoes.

Now to prove to you that Josiah knows full well the value of Aces and Kings and "full deck poker," I will give you his own words in explanation of a difficulty that occurred on board the Steam Boat "Highlander," on our way to the Memphis Races last spring.

I had left the cabin a few minutes before, where Josiah and three others were playing "full deck poker"; on my return the game appeared to be broken up and in some confusion. I immediately repaired to the scene of action, not doubting but that the odds were against Josiah. Nevertheless, I wished to see him have fair play; but to my surprise Josiah was the informer, having detected *them* in cheating, (as they were undoubtedly combined to fleece him.) I enquired of him the matter, and his story was thus:—

"Well, now, jist stop right there, and I will tell you all about it. Well you see, now, I had played along, keeping about even only, at the game, for some time, and so thinkin' I was losin' time and not getting' on as fast as I oughter, I began teu look about *thinkin' to lay aside* A FEW ACES,—but darn an Ace was to be found in that pack! Well, I sed nothin' and thought I would be satisfied with "Kings," so I kept a sharp look out for some turn of "Kings," but after playin' on a spell, I found the "Kings" all gone too! So I didn't think "Queens" very safe, and thought it time to shake, shuffle-up and begin agin, but they *didn't seem to take!* So I told 'em that it was no go! that from the best of my observations, that pack was lackin' all the Aces and Kings, and for what I knowed, the Queen's too! So that cock-eyed fellow there, jumped up and said *perhaps he had left some in his berth,* and went, and sure enough, he had, for he brought nigh about enough for a good "Three-up" pack, and he jist rammed them all up together so you couldn't see what they was,—but I guess I knowed. So then I was willing the game should go on, but they said no; it was nigh dinner and that we would rest a bit, and play after dinner. Now, I guess I've got 'em about right! They are too bad scared to try anything more, and they don't believe that *I can,* and if I get another crack at 'em, I'll fetch 'em next time, or else four Aces won't win."

And such was the fact, for Josiah *did* get another chance and *he broke the party* before we landed at Memphis.

A Strong Hand at Poker

P.U.T.

I have heard of and read a great many Poker stories, but as the following one has never been in print to my knowledge, it will probably be new to some of your readers. It happened thus wise:—

A rather elderly gentleman travelling up the great sporting stream "happened" on an acquaintance, who proposed "a friendly game of poker," which being consented to, the documents were produced, the "ardent" ordered, and the game began.

It so happened that the elderly gent had what his opponent called a bad streak, for he invariably lost when anything heavy was at stake. The game had continued some time without the suspicion of the green one having become excited, till at last he was convinced that he was being cheated. He continued on, however, and presently held four kings; and now he mentally determined to "salt" the "Leg." He made a starter by betting one hundred dollars, and "Leg" immediately "raised" him a hundred. This did not scare him, however, and he likewise raised another hundred, when, much to his surprise, "Leg" went him a thousand dollars better;—this was a puzzler;—so turning to his servant who stood near, he whispered to him that he thought he would get into trouble with his adversary, and requested him to bring him something, after which he quietly out with his money, and called a sight.

By this time the servant had returned and deposited an *axe* on the table by his master's side.

"Now," says the green one, "what have you got?"

"Four aces," says "Leg." "What have *you* got?"

"Why I have only four kings and an *axe!*" says the elderly holding up the latter instrument.

"Oh," says "Leg," "I can beat the four kings, but the *axe* knocks me; so you can rake down!"

The Way an Old One Mistook a Green Case

The South West is the place for fun; there a man meets with all kinds of people, from all parts of the universal world. I chanced to be travelling down the Mississippi River not long since, on the steam-boat "Kate Miller." At one of the numerous landings, a young fellow, from somewhere Down East, who has been in those parts for some five years, and knows pretty well the ways of the world, came on board, and took passage. It happened that no one on board knew him; he commenced looking about him with a vacant stare; and Old Sandy being on board, looking for customers, he concluded our young friend, being rather verdant, would answer. He soon learned that he answered to the name of Spike Buck, and lived away up on the Forked Deer; that his daddy had given him a heap of money to go to Orleans, and he meant to have a mighty sight of fun when he got there, though it was his first trip. Old Sandy thought he would rub some of the green spots off him, by getting his money and having the fun of a game or two; but unfortunately Spike appeared to know nothing about cards, and as there was a game of poker made up, Old Sandy told him to take a seat by his side and learn the game, and then he might play. Spike took the seat offered, and appeared very much pleased with the cards, especially those having pictures on them, which attracted the attention of most of the passengers about the table. Spike would invariably pick up Sandy's hand as it was dealt out, and take the first look at them; the third hand Spike held in such a manner that Old Sandy saw he had two pairs—deuces and fours—and an eight. The old fellow bet craftily one check, to get some one in; one other came in, and went five better. Old Sandy saw him, and went five better still; his opponent called him on a pair of aces. Old Sandy coolly raked the money down, saying that aces wouldn't win against two pair, deuces and fours. Turning his hand over, what was his surprise to find one of his fours a five. The truth flashed across his mind— Spike had thumbed the five-spot, and deceived him; he struck a terrible blow as he turned where Spike sat, which nearly dislocated his shoulder, for Spike had slipped off the chair and was skipping up the cabin, singing—

"I wonder if some one would not like to win the money daddy gave me!"

During the shouts of laughter that was going on, Old Sandy was heard to say at the top of his voice—"No, by G——! Come and licker during the trip at my expense, and I can whip the man that dare to say peas to you!"

A Gambling Incident

REKRAP

The steamer "Leviathan" was on its third day of the voyage from New Orleans to St. Louis, when she took on board from a desolate landing near M., a brown looking and apparently well seasoned chap, whose dress and appearance were such as to excite no more attention from the passengers than the usual glance of inquiry, with which the western traveller salutes every fellow passenger—nor would he in all probability have been considered a subject worthy of notice but for the singular calmness with which he bore losses at the card table, and the pertinacity which he evinced in playing against fortune.

His most frequent antagonist was a young clerk, who, as was the custom in those days of unsafe mails, was the bearer of a large quantity of bank bills, returned to St. Louis from the bank of Orleans, to be exchanged for their own paper in the north.

It was the fourth evening of the trip, and though late, the excitement of the game of Poker—then recently introduced—had kept these individuals at their table, and the passengers becoming interested in their high play had formed a circle about them, watching with eagerness the silent dropping of the cards, and admiring the fortitude with which the brown man continued to reduce the size of his pocket book.

Again the cards were dealt, and betting began—each held a strong hand, and by fifties and hundreds, the stake was raised, until the clerk, counting out the full amount of his money, and throwing it violently upon the stake, cried in an excited voice—

"There's your five hundred, and five hundred dollars better; make me or break me—'tis all I have."

Hardly was the money upon the table, when, with a cool smile from his antagonist, the money was covered and doubled.

"Your thousand dollars, and one thousand dollars better, and I give you five minutes to raise the money."

Then for the first time the truth flashed upon the young man that he was in the hands of one of the dreaded "legs" of the river, and he saw himself, by his own folly, a loser of all that he was worth, for unless he could meet the two thousand dollars of his opponent, by the rules of the game, he forfeited that already up, and as he marked the gleam of the gambler's eye as he raised it from his watch, he gave up in despair.

Each minute as it passed was noted by the brown man, but unnoticed by the clerk, until he heard that but one minute remained for him to recover his loss. Then seemingly struck with a gleam of hope, he darted through the circle of anxious spectators to his state-room, and returning, threw upon the table a sealed packet marked $100,000.

"Sir," said he, "*there is your two thousand dollars, and Ninety-eight thousand dollars better, and I give you five minutes to get the money.*"

The result can be imagined; the leg left at the next landing two thousand dollars poorer than he came on board—leaving the clerk more than that amount wiser.

The Bivouac; or, A Night at the Mouth of the Ohio, A Sketch of Western Voyaging

JOSEPH HOLT INGRAHAM

The vicissitudes of Joseph Holt Ingraham's literary career can be summed up in the following announcement, dating from 1851: "Mr J. H. Ingraham, author of 'The Southwest, by a Yankee,' 'Burton; or The Sieges,' and a large number of the vilest yellow-covered novels ever printed in this country, has been admitted to the deaconate in the Episcopal church at Natchez" (quoted in Johannsen 2:152). A prolific, popular author whose *Lafitte, the Pirate of the Gulf* (1836) was reviewed by Edgar Allan Poe, Ingraham published a large number of similarly action-packed novels before entering the church and turning his hand to theological fiction (most famously, *The Prince of the House of David*, 1855). The following account of a riverboat gambler's tragic end is a typical example of Ingraham's thrilling tales of life and death on the Mississippi frontier. For further information see Albert Johannsen, *The House of Beadle and Adams and Its Dime and Nickel Novels* (Norman: University of Oklahoma Press, 1950), 2:151–55.

A few years since I was on my way to St. Louis, and took passage at Cincinnati on board the steamer *Chief Justice Marshall,* which was bound to New Orleans, but from which I was to disembark at the mouth of the Ohio, there to wait for some New Orleans boat going up to take me to my destination. Our travelling party consisted of three ladies—a mother and two lovely daughters—deep in their teens, and a young gentleman and his bride from Louisiana, with her brother just from college. The boat was large and comfortable; a spacious state-room offered us all the retirement of a private apartment in a dwelling. It was a bright morning in October when we got under head-way from the landing, and bending our course down the river, left the queen city receding in the distance. The prospect from the decks as we swept round the noble curve which forms the peninsula of this great metropolis, was unequalled for beauty and variety. To the eye of the voyager, who gazes on the city and its opposite suburban shore, the river seems to flow through a valley peopled for centuries, rather than a region but fifty years ago a desolate wilderness. Crowded population, taste, wealth, and a high degree of agriculture on the banks, all indicate the home of a long settled people, instead of the emigrant of yesterday. Astonished at what he beholds, the traveller's mind is overpowered at the contemplation of the future destiny of the land. This feeling is not only awakened by the sight of Cincinnati and its environs, with its fleets of steamers, but it is kept alive as he proceeds down the winding and romantic river. On either bank noble farms descend with their waving fields to touch the lip of the laughing wave, and at short intervals thriving villages meet his never wearying sight. Unlike the monotony of the Mississippi, the Ohio ever presents objects of interest. The voyager of taste is ever upon deck, as he is borne through the picturesque regions, and exclamations of surprise are exhausted only to be repeated and renewed again and again.

The next morning after quitting Cincinnati we reached Louisville, its *levee* as we approached presenting a scarcely less business like air than that of her rival city. Situated just above the 'Falls,' it was then the head of large boat navigation. But a deep canal has since then been constructed around the falls nearly two miles in length, by which steamers laden in New Orleans can pass through without as heretofore, being detained and transferring their freight by drays to smaller boats above the falls, and pursue their way to Cincinnati or Pittsburg.

The river being now unusually high, the rocks of the rapids were nearly covered, and with skilful pilotage they might be ventured. After an hour's delay at the landing we shot out into the middle of the stream, and then set the boat's head to descend the rapids. As we approached them with the velocity of an arrow, there was not a word spoken on board save by the pilot, who stood forward, giving brief orders to the helmsman. Black rocks appeared on every side—the rapids reared and foamed before us, seemingly in our very path; but onward we went with irresistible power, the vast steamer rolling to and fro like drunken. But we passed them safely, the captain having risked boat and cargo, and put in jeopardy his own life and those of all on board. But human life is of little value in the West, where there is so much of it floating about, none knowing whence or whither!

Among our passengers were two, a father and daughter, that particularly attracted my attention, from the indifference to danger which both exhibited during the perilous descent of the rapids; the elder standing with folded arms looking upon the deck, gazing on vacancy,—the younger admiring with a calm but delighted look the velocity of the boat—the curling waters around her, and the wild roar and sublime confusion of the scene through which she was borne. He was about fifty-six years of age, with a noble countenance, which care and grief had deeply lined, his hair gray and his form somewhat bent, less with years than sorrow. An air of melancholy pervaded his appearance and irresistibly interested the beholder in him. His daughter had fair hair and blue eyes, and seemed destined by nature to be happy-hearted; for she spoke to him always with a sweet smile, and always smiled at seeing any scenery that pleased her. But there was a pensiveness in her look that harmonized with the sadness upon his brow. Her attentions to him, I had observed, were tender, devoted, and full of anxious solicitude to draw him away from his own thoughts. At times she would succeed, and he would look up and around at the green wooded banks and smile with momentary interest, when she would appear perfectly happy, and tears would come into her eyes—tears of joy.

During the course of the day I had an opportunity of rendering him a slight assistance as he descended from the deck, for which the daughter gratefully thanked me, adding, "My father is a little feeble, sir; I am in hopes this voyage will be of great service to him."

I warmly expressed the same desire, and as they immediately retired to their staterooms I saw no more of them that day. The ensuing morning I ascended the deck a few minutes after sun-rise and found them already promenading together, the father on the daughter's arm. The incident, and brief interchange of words the day before had conferred upon me the privilege of approaching and inquiring after his health.

"Better, sir, I thank you," he answered with a grateful look, "but," he added in a half tone which I could not help hearing, "it is not the body—it is the spirit that is sick."

"Oh, dear father!" said his daughter, glancing at me quickly, to see if I had overheard.

"Oh, my son, my son! would to God I had buried thee in thy infancy," said Mr. Townley, for such I learned was his name; and he wrung his hands and threw himself upon a seat. His child seemed much distressed, and I was turning away lest my presence should invade secrecy that she seemed solicitous to preserve, when he said, extending his hand, "Sit down. I am told you are from the South—from Natchez."

"Yes," I replied.

"I am glad to meet you. I am going there, to—"

"*Dear* father, hush!" cried the maiden with a look of distress.

"I *will* inquire of him, Charlotte. Perhaps—"

"You can hear nothing, alas, but what you already too well know. Pray, father, do not speak of Henry!—Nay, then let me inquire. Sir," she said, clasping his hand, and looking up in my face with tearful eyes, "we have a relative—a dear relative, sir, in Natchez, who, we have heard has wandered from the path of honor."

"It is my son, sir," said Mr. Townley, firmly. His daughter hung her head, and I could see the blush of shame mounting her forehead. "He is my only son. He was a clerk in New Orleans, and in an evil hour was tempted to gamble and lost all of his own money, and then embezzled that of his employer. To escape punishment he fled and joined the gamblers at Vicksburg. We have since learned that he has now become a principal leader among them, and that he remains mostly in Natchez. I am on my way to try to reclaim him. It is painful to a father to speak thus of a son! Did you ever see him, sir?"

"Townley," I repeated,—"I never heard of the name in the South except associated with men of honor."

"We have discerned that he goes by the assumed name of *Frank Carter*," said Mr. Townley. I could not confess my ignorance; for I recognized the name of the most notorious gambler or "sportsman," in the South, who from his influence with the different bands that infested the West, from Louisville to New Orleans, was called "Prince Frank." I gazed upon the father with pity, and upon the sister with feelings of the most painful sympathy. I felt that their hope of reclaiming him was destined to perish. They remarked my silence, and the daughter, now that there was no more to be told to call the tinge of shame into her cheek, lifted her head and looked into my face with anxious interest. Mr. Townley also waited earnestly to hear at least a reply from one who *might* have seen his son, and who could tell him something about him less evil than he had heard. I recollected him as a fine looking, richly dressed young man, who used to make a dashing appearance at the St. Catharine's race course, in a barouche drawn by a pair of spirited bays, with a beautiful girl, his mistress, seated by his side. He had become rich by his reckless profession, and it was said owned several dwellings in "Natchez under the Hill," the empire over which, as "Prince Frank," he ruled. But recently, since I had left the South in May, there had been a war of extermination against the gamblers, beginning at Vicksburg and sweeping the whole South-West. What had become of 'Prince Frank' in this well remembered and bloody crusade of the roused citizens of Mississippi to redeem their towns and cities from the hordes of blacklegs who infested them, I was ignorant.

"Do you know him, sir?—Pray speak freely"; asked the daughter, after watching my countenance for some time.

I frankly informed her that her information had been correct, and while

I expressed my hopes that their pious journey to effect his reformation and restoration to society, might be successful, I told her that I feared there was little prospect of it.

From this time I saw much of them, for Mr. Townley loved to sit and talk to me of his son. At length we approached the mouth of the Ohio where we were to separate, myself and my party to wait and take a boat up to St. Louis,—they to continue their sad and hopeless voyage for the recovery of a lost son and brother.

As the boat was rounding too at the beautiful point of land now the site of the infant city of Cairo, Mr. Townley came to me and asked how long I and my friends would remain in St. Louis? On learning it would be but for two days, and that we should then proceed directly down the Mississippi to Natchez, he asked if it would be agreeable to us for himself and daughter to attach themselves to our party. This accession was gladly received by all my friends to whom I had communicated the interesting object of their journey, and who were as deeply touched as myself with their peculiar affliction. Mr. Townley and his daughter, therefore, quit the boat with us; and the steamer landing our large party with our baggage upon the shore, resumed her swift course down the river, Captain Clark receiving our good wishes for his safe and speedy arrival at New Orleans.

It was late in the afternoon when we landed upon the point, and as we learned a boat was looked for momentarily from below, bound to St. Louis, we concluded not to remove our large quantity of baggage to the tavern, but remain with it, at least till night by the river side. Cairo city, as this place is now denominated, was then comprised in a two story tavern, called "Bird's Hotel," with a double gallery running around it,—in a sort of grocery store, one or two log huts and a vast forest of gigantic trees that covered nearly the whole place except 'the clearing' on the extreme point. It was a desolate looking spot, especially on the approach of night. The tavern, too, had a bad name, the point being, from its central position, a rendezvous for gamblers, and from its retired character, and the peculiar facilities it afforded for evading justice, the refuge of criminals and all kinds of desperate characters. Flat boats, also, always hauled up here on their trips for the crews to take a frolic, and here were always sure to be landed from steamers, mutinous 'hands,' or detected rogues. We had some knowledge of the character of the spot, and therefore chose to remain as long as we could on the *levee,* hoping the boat would soon appear and render further intimacy with the suspicious tavern unnecessary. We therefore placed our trunks in a hollow square, and seating

87

ourselves upon them, waited patiently for the expected boat.—When the sun at length set, and no signs of her rewarded our long and intense gazing, we began to wish we had waited at Cincinnati for a St. Louis boat, as the Broad-way House we all acknowledged, was far more comfortable than the broad side of a river bank. The landlord, now, on our application to him, roughly replied that his rooms were full.

We had observed as we went to the house, several suspicious men lurking about the tavern, one of whom I recognized as a well known Natchez gam-bler. We felt no disposition to remain in their company at the tavern, well knowing the vindictiveness which they entertained, since their expulsion, against all Mississippians, and the annoyance we might expect if we were recognized to be from the South. As the night promised to be clear, and the moon rose as the sun set, we decided on remaining on the bank all night. We arranged couches for the ladies with cloaks and buffalo skins within the space enclosed by the trunks; and suspending on four stakes a large crim-son Mexican blanket that belonged to the travelling equipment of the Loui-sianian, formed a serviceable canopy to protect them from the dew. We then opened our trunks and took out our knives and pistols, and the brother of the bride unlocked from his case a new, double-barreled fowling piece he was taking home. There were of our party seven men, including two young merchants returning home to St. Louis from the East, who were bivouacked a few paces from us, but who on invitation joined us. We had arms,—the double-barreled fowling piece just named, nine pistols and five bowie knives, and powder and ball: we therefore felt very sure of giving a good reception to any who molested us; for we knew that defenceless parties of bivouacking travelers had been attacked by armed banditti, and robbed of every article of baggage, and their jewelry stripped from their persons; we had heard also of travellers landing to the point who never embarked again. We therefore qui-etly loaded our arms, and having established a watch both for security and at look out for a steamer, and awaken the rest on its approach, we settled our-selves about our bivouac for the night. The ladies soon went to sleep, confid-ing in our guardianship as women should ever do. Mr. Townley all at once showed himself to be a man of resolute character; for the probable danger of the party roused him from the contemplation of his own sorrows to sympa-thy with the feelings of those around him.

The moon shone very bright, and the two great rivers flowed majestically past, their broad surfaces looking like torrents of molten steel, meeting a mile below the point, and blending into one dark flood which lost itself in the gloomy forests to the South. It was two in the morning. I was standing watch with Mr. Townley and the knight of the fowling piece, and one of the young merchants, when we observed a party of men suddenly issue from a path leading into the forest in the direction of two or three log huts. Hitherto the night had been still; the lights had been early extinguished in the tavern, and the groups of boatmen that were lingering about the shore had returned on board their flat boats. The party which we now saw was, when we discovered it, about three hundred yards off, moving at a quick tramp directly towards our bivouac. We instantly wakened our companions without disturbing the ladies, and having prepared our arms to give them a good reception should they prove hostile, we remained seated upon our trunks watching them. The moon now shone upon them so clearly that we could count their number—fourteen men, marching three and four abreast; it also gleamed upon weapons which some of them carried. We were now satisfied that we were the object of an open attack by some of the desperadoes who infested the point, who probably expected to find us unarmed and sleeping, and so pillage our baggage and persons, if not do murder, if resisted. We let them advance within fifty paces and then challenged. One who walked by the side of the first rank then spoke to them and they halted.

"If you approach any nearer, be your errand peaceful or hostile, we shall fire upon you," we said firmly.

"Ha! they are prepared!" said one.

"No. It is bravado. Let us on!" shouted another.

"On, then," was the general cry, and they rushed towards us in an irregular body.

We let them come within close pistol shot,—all fired a regular discharge— but over their heads. They suddenly stopped, with a cry of surprise, fired a pistol or two, and then retreated a few paces and made a stand.—One of them was evidently wounded, for we saw him fall, and with difficulty and groaning drag himself after his companions.—The challenge and firing aroused the females of our party, who at first shrieked, and were in great terror, but were prevailed upon to keep their recumbent positions sheltered from any fire of the assailants, by the trunks we had fortunately piled around their lodging place. We now reloaded our pistols, and prepared to receive them if they again attempted to molest us. Before we all got prepared for a second defence, they rushed upon us, firing pistols as they advanced, the balls of which whizzed over us, and, as we afterwards saw, pierced our trunks. Reluctant as we were to shed blood, we did not hesitate to return their fire, when they had got within five yards of us brandishing their knives and as desperate a looking set of black-legs as I should ever wish to encounter. A ball from Mr. Townley's pistol brought down their leader, and we were in the act of engaging with our knives, when a happy diversion was made in our favor by a shout close at hand, and a crew of gallant Kentucky boatmen, consisting of a father and five sons, roused by the skirmishing, came up from their boat to our rescue. They rushed upon the gamblers so unexpectedly, that, after making slight defence, they fled into the forests, leaving their chief dead not four yards from our bivouac. At the same moment, the deep "boom" of an ascending steamer reached our ears. We were congratulating each other upon our escape, and thanking the brave boatmen, when a loud wild cry from Mr. Townley chilled the blood in our veins. We looked, and saw him leaning over the body of the slain robber. His daughter flew to him, gazed at the face of the dead, shrieked and cast herself upon the body.

It was his son—her brother! He had fallen by his father's hand. Poor Mr. Townley! he never came to his reason, to realize the full extent of his misery. He grew imbecile, and perished a few months afterwards, a broken-hearted wreck. Charlotte Townley still lives, but consumption is eating the bloom from her cheek, and her fading form will soon lie in the grave beside her father's.

Taking Good Advice

MADISON TENSAS (HENRY CLAY LEWIS)

Though often affecting the demeanor of an elderly man of the world, Henry Clay Lewis was only a young man when he wrote his sketches of the life of a Louisiana "swamp doctor," which retain a significant reputation in the history of southwestern literature. As Lewis was drowned in a tributary of the Mississippi at the age of twenty-five, they represent a small but significant literary legacy. Before training as a doctor, Lewis worked as a cabin boy in the Ohio and Mississippi riverboat trade, and such firsthand experience may well have contributed to the following sketch of gambling on the western rivers. For further information, see John Q. Anderson, *Louisiana Swamp Doctor: The Writings of Henry Clay Lewis* (Baton Rouge: Louisiana State University Press, 1962).

"POOR fellow! if he had only listened to me! but he wouldn't take good advice," is the trite exclamation of the worldling when he hears that some friend has cut his throat, impelled by despair, or has become bankrupt, or employed a famous physician, or is about to get married, or has applied for a divorce, or paid his honest debts, or committed any deprecated act, or become the victim of what the world calls misfortune; "poor fellow, but he wouldn't take good advice." Take good advice! yes, if I had obeyed what is called good advice, I would be now in my grave; as it is, I am still on a tailor's books, the best evidence of a man's being alive.

When I was a boy my friends were continually chiding me for my half bent position in sitting or walking, and since I have become a man the cry is still the same, "Why don't you walk straight, Madison? hold up your head."

Had I obeyed them, a tree-top that fell upon me whilst visiting a patient lately, crushing my shoulder and bruising my back, would have fallen directly upon my head, and shown, in all probability, the emptiness of earthly things. This is one instance showing that good advice is not always best to be taken; but I have another, illustrating my position still more strongly.

Whilst a medical student, I was travelling on one of the proverbially fine and accommodating steamers that ply between Vicksburg and New Orleans. Before my departure, the anxious affection of a female friend made her exact a promise from me not to play cards; but the peculiarity of the required pledge gave me an opportunity of fulfilling it to the letter, but breaking it as to the spirit. "You've promised me, Madison, not to play cards whilst you're on earth: see that you keep it." I assured her I would do so, as it applied only to shore, and when the boat was on a sand-bar. It was more her friendly solicitude than any real necessity in my habits, that made her require the promise, as I never played except on steamboats, and then only at night, when the beautiful scenery that skirts the river cannot be seen or admired.

It was a boisterous night above in the heavens, making the air too cool for southern dress or nerves, so the cabin and social hall were densely crowded, not a small proportion engaged in the mysteries of that science which requires four knaves to play or practice it. I had not yet sat down, but showed strong premonitory symptoms of being about to do so, when my arm was gently taken by an old friend, who requested me to walk with him into our stateroom. "Madison," said the old gentleman, "I want to give you some good advice. I see you are about to play cards for money; you are a young man, and consequently have but little knowledge of its pernicious effects. I speak from experience; and apart from the criminality of gambling, I assure you, you will have but little chance of winning in the crowd you intend playing with: in fact, you are certain to lose. Now promise me you won't play, and I shall go to bed with the satisfaction that I have saved you from harm." The charm was laid too skilfully upon me; I would not promise, for what was I to do in the long nights of present and future travel? so my old friend gave me up in despair, and retired to rest, whilst I sought the card-table.

Young and inexperienced as I was, an unusual strain of good luck attended me; and when the game broke up at daylight, I was considerably ahead of the hounds.

I retired to my state-room to regain my lost sleep, and soon was oblivious of everything. How long I slept I do not know: my dreams ran upon the past game; and just as I held "four aces," and had seen my opponent's two hundred and went him four hundred dollars better, I was aroused from my slumbers by the confused cries of "Fire! Back her! Stop her! She'll blow up when she strikes!" and a thousand-and-one undistinguishable sounds, but all indicative of intense excitement and alarm.

Stopping for nothing, I made one spring from my berth into the middle of the cabin, alighting on the deserted breakfast-table, amidst the crash of broken crockery, three jumps more were taken, which landed me up on the hurricane-deck, where I found nearly all the passengers, male and female, assembled in a fearful state of alarm, preventing by their outcry the necessary orders, for the preservation of the boat, from being heard. I took in the whole scene at a glance. I forgot to mention, when I retired to rest, the wind was blowing to such a degree that every gust threatened to overset the boat. The captain, who was a prudent, sensible man, had tied his boat to the shore, waiting for the storm to subside. After the lapse of a few hours, a calm having ensued, he cast loose, intending to proceed on his way; but scarcely had he done so, when the wind, suddenly increasing, caught the boat, and, in despite of six boilers and the helm hard down, was carrying her directly across the Mississippi, towards the opposite shore, where a formidable array of old "poke-stalks" and low, bluff banks were eagerly awaiting to impale us upon the one hand, or knock us into a cocked hat upon the other. At this time I arrived upon the scene—the boat was nearly at the shore, the waters boiling beneath her bows like an infernal cauldron.

Great as was the danger, there were still some so reckless as to make remarks upon my unique appearance, and turn the minds of many from that condition of religious revery and mental casting up and balancing of accounts, which the near proximity to death so imminently required; and certainly I did look queer—no boots, no coat, no drawers—but, lady reader, don't think my bosom was false, and I had no subuculus on. "I didn't have anything else" on—more truth than poetry, I ween. Sixteen young ladies, unmindful of danger, ran shrieking away; fourteen married ones walked leisurely to the stern of the boat, where the captain had been vainly before trying to drive them; whilst two old maids stood and looked at me in unconscious astonishment, wonderful amazement, and inexpressible surprise.

"Look out!" rang the shrill voice of the captain; and, with a dull, heavy thump, the boat struck the bank, jarring the marrow of every one on board, save myself—for, just before she struck, I calculated the distance, made my jump, landed safely, and was snugly ensconced behind a large log, hallooing for some one to bring me my clothes.

No damage of consequence, contrary to expectations, was done our craft; and after digging her out of the bank, we proceeded on our way, a heavy rain having succeeded the storm.

I was lying in my state-room, ruminating sadly over the pleasureableness of being the laughing-stock of the whole boat, when my old adviser of the night previous entered the room, with too much laughter on his face to make his coming moral deduction of much force.

"You see now, Madison, the result of not having followed my advice. Had you been governed by me, the disagreeable event of the morning would never have occurred; you would have been in bed at the proper hour, slept during the proper hours, been ready dressed as a consequence at the breakfast hour, and not been the cause of such a mortal shock to the delicacy of so many delicate females, besides making a d——d unanimous fool of yourself."

I said but little in reply, but thought a great deal. I kept my room the balance of the trip, sickness being my plea.

I transacted my business in the city, and chance made my old adviser and myself fellow-passengers and roommates again, on our upward trip. Night saw me regularly at the card-table, and my old friend at nine o'clock as constantly in bed.

It was after his bed-hour when we reached Grand Gulf, where several lady-passengers intended leaving. They were congregated in the middle of the gentlemen's cabin, bringing out baggage and preparing to leave as soon as the boat landed.

At the landing a large broad-horn was lazily sleeping, squatted on the muddy waters like a Dutch beauty over a warming-pan. Her steering-oar— the broad-horn's, not the beauty's—instead of projecting, as custom and the law requires, straight out behind, had swung round, and stood capitally for raking a boat coming up along side. The engines had stopped, but the boat had not lost the impetus of the steam, but was slowly approaching the broad-horn, when a crash was hea[r]d—a state-room door was burst open, and out popped my ancient comrade, followed up closely by a sharp stick, in the shape of the greasy handle of the steering-oar. It passed directly through my berth, and would undeniably have killed me, had I been in it.

It was my turn to exult now. I pulled "Old Advice" out from under the table, and, as I congratulated him on his escape, maliciously added, "You see, now, that playing cards is not totally unattended with good effects. Had I, agreeably to your advice, been in bed, I would now be a mangled corpse, and you enjoying the satisfaction that it was your counsel that had killed me; whilst, on the other hand, had you been playing, you would have escaped your fright, and the young ladies from Nankin in all probability would never have known you slept in a red bandana." I made a convert of him to my side; we sat down to a quiet game, and before twelve that night he broke me flat.

From *Zilla Fitz James, The Female Bandit of the South-West*

ZILLA FITZ JAMES

Little is known about Zilla Fitz James beyond the pages of the biographical account apparently edited by a Rev. A. Richards in 1852. In itself, this short sketch was a companion piece to another criminal narrative, *The Arch Fiend: or, The Life, Confession, and Execution of Green H. Long,* also published by A. R. Orton in 1852. Sara Lynn Crosby has made it clear that the Rev. A. Richards was likely to have been one of the many pseudonyms used by Orton himself, a publisher, author and editor based in Philadelphia who specialized in crime pamphlets and used a variety of false names in their production. Nonetheless, even though this sensational account may have been rooted more in fiction than in fact, it still stands as one of the few accounts of a woman's experiences in the Mississippi underworld and is therefore extremely valuable. Fitz James's story provides a tantalizing glimpse into the life of a woman whose fortunes become entwined with a number of riverboat gamblers. The most complete analysis of Zilla Fitz James's narrative can be found in Crosby's unpublished doctoral dissertation, "Poisonous Mixtures: Gender, Race, Empire, and Cultural Authority in Antebellum Female Poisoner Literature," University of Notre Dame, 2005.

I was born in New Orleans, May 17th, 1827, of respectable parents. My father was a dealer in tobacco, snuff, and segars, and kept a store in Poydras street, at the time of my birth. But I was doomed not to know much of a parent's care, for when only four years of age, that scourge of the south—the yellow fever, crossed our threshold, and bereft me of both father and mother, at one fell swoop, leaving me an orphan at that tender age. Fortunately or unfortunately for me, as will be seen by the reader anon, I was taken and adopted by an aunt, my mother's sister, who was a widow. I was too young at the demise of my parents to recollect much about them, still I have a faint recollection, and that recollection is strengthened, so far as regards my mother, by a small miniature that I have of her, in a locket that I am told she hung upon my neck the day she died and to which I have ever clung as a talisman. There is a holy something about the miniature that fills me with joy and grief, awe and reverence, as I gaze upon it. It is the picture of her that gave me birth, nursed, cherished, and doted upon me in early infancy. How lovely and heavenly she seems to look upon her only child, with those coal black eyes. How placid and angelic is her countenance! Those who watched with her during her illness say, that she freely parted with the world and all else beside, with the exception of me. It was a hard struggle for her to part with me, her only child. She died with a prayer on her lips for me, commending me to the Most High. From the grave which contained the twain, I went to the house of my aunt, a splendid mansion in Canal Street, gorgeously furnished from cellar to attic. At first, I was inclined to be restive and peevish, cried for my mother, and wanted to go home. My aunt was very kind to me, and caressed me much, which soon made me forget what had passed. I soon began to look upon her as my mother, and was taught to call her so. Time wore on, and I grew in years and in stature. When I had arrived at the age of six years, my aunt engaged a young lady by the name of Lucy Wilkins, from Boston, as a governess, and I was put under her tuition. I was an uncommonly handsome child, and withal had a most excellent temper, so I won at once the heart of Miss Wilkins, who spared no pains to instruct me, and I mastered with rapidity every task that she gave me, so that at the age of ten my aunt concluded to send me to a boarding school up the river to finish my education, as Miss Wilkins had it in contemplation to return, at that time, to Boston, to spend the summer with her relatives. I liked the arrangement very much, all but parting with Miss Wilkins. I had become endeared to her by her kindness to, and patience with me for four long years, and thus regretted the separation, fearing that it would be forever. However, it was all arranged. Miss Wilkins returned to Boston, and I went up the river to Baton Rouge, to Mrs. Johnson's boarding school.

[. . .]

I was now in my fourteenth year, and was quite a woman, I had also grown tired of the place and longed to return to my aunt, in New Orleans, whom I had not seen once in all that time, for I never left Baton Rouge, from the time I first went there to attend the boarding school, until I was in my fourteenth year, and had completed my studies. I wrote to my aunt, and informed her of my desire to return to her house, etc. On the receipt of my letter, she took passage on a steamboat, and came to Baton Rouge, to see me, settle all my bills, and take me back with her to New Orleans. She was highly delighted to see me, embraced me many times, kissed my forehead, said I was a lovely girl, that she was proud of me, etc. I was quite as delighted to see her as she was to see me, I am sure, for I loved her exceedingly. The superintendent gave her flattering accounts of me and said I was the most accomplished young lady in her school, all of which tended to raise me high in the estimation of my aunt. After settling up everything, my aunt concluded to spend a few days in that delightful place, for Baton Rouge is the most lovely place in the whole South. We then took passage on one of those splendid steamers that ply on the Mississippi, for New Orleans which we reached in due time. On our arrival home, my aunt decided to give a great *fete,* on which occasion I should make my *debut* in the *beau mondes.* I shall never forget that occasion, as it is from that occasion that I date the commencement of my eventful career. Nothing was spared by my aunt that would, in any way, add *eclat* to the occasion, and conduce to my happiness. The House was arrayed gorgeously, the windows were hung with curtains of damask and crimson; sofas, lounges, ottomans, and all other furniture was nicely and tastefully arranged. Wines, fruits, and pastry were supplied, in profusion, and the best musicians in the city were engaged, for an orchestra. Cards of invitation were sent to many of the *elite, beau monde,* and *beau esprits* of the city, and to some noted strangers at the St. Charles, St. Louis, and Verandah hotels. The night came, and so did the guests. I was arrayed in the richest and costliest fabrics and the finest jewelry. At precisely nine of the clock, I was led into the parlor by my aunt, and was soon surrounded by the gaping crowd, who eagerly sought an introduction to me. I was, as Ophelia says, "The expectancy and rose of the fair state, the glass of fashion and the mould of form; the observed of all observers." I was engaged to dance the first "set" with young C. C——, the son of a celebrated statesman. He was the handsomest and most accomplished man in the room, and as I was led up by him to take my place in the first set, I felt as proud as a princess royal. He, too, seemed conscious of the loveliness of his partner, and fairly beat himself, by his gallantry. He lost no time while by my side, to pour the delicious poison of flattery into my willing ear, and which filled me with pleasure. He praised my gazelle-like eyes, and queenly form, and pressed my hands, with such ardor, that my little heart began to flutter and beat with rapture. And, when the cotillion was through, he led me to my seat, ensconced himself by my side, and began to talk of love, in accents sweet and low. Soon he led me on the floor again, to waltz. Oh! what a thrill of pleasure ran through my frame, as I whirled through the giddy waltz, in his arms, and could hear, audibly, the beating of his heart. The rules of *etiquette* demanded that I should not be monopolized by him, all the evening, so, he gave way for other gentlemen, to dance and waltz with me, with the best grace he could command. But the moment he saw me disengaged, he was by my side, talking most bewitchingly. From the moment I saw him first, I was drawn irresistibly towards him, preferring him before all others. This will not appear strange, when it is remembered that I was hardly fourteen years of age, just ripening into womanhood, and, as such, having a soft, warm heart to dispose of, free to hold a thousand tender pleasures, and, unsophisticated, withal, and he being of pleasing exterior, and insinuating address, gave great force to his honied words, to which I listened without suspicion. I can not say that I fell in love with him, at that time, for I hardly knew my own feelings. I looked upon him with no small degree of pleasure, and felt highly honored by his attentions to me. I also felt no small degree of pride, when I saw that I eclipsed all the other ladies in the room.

The *fete* was at last over, the company dispersed, all passing off as such *fetes* generally do, and I retired to my room, with the proud consciousness that I was the belle of the season. I had just made my *debut* in a new sphere; I was no longer looked upon as a child, but was recognized as a woman, and one of the loveliest of my sex. And I felt quite certain, from C. C——'s advances, throughout the evening, that I had captivated one of America's noblest sons.

[. . .]

I asked him, why not elope at once, and, that without delay. He said that certain things had got to transpire, before he could be able to do so, and begged me to wait a little while longer, and not be rash, and ruin all his hopes in life. By such deceit I was kept on for nearly four months, when I saw that it was necessary to do something, as I was, in fact, becoming a mother, and my condition could not long be concealed. Charles soon saw that it was necessary that something should be done speedily, and, at last, informed me that he was now ready to fulfill his promise with me. So it was arranged, that, at our next meeting, I should have everything prepared to elope with him. I packed all my jewelry into a nice casket, a present from him, and a few of my best clothes into a small valise, both of which old Martha conveyed to the arbor, in the garden, just after nightfall, and, at the hour of ten, I went there too, when I found Charles C—— there, ready to receive me. He had a carriage near by, to which my things were carried, and we soon followed, bidding old Martha good-bye. I supposed that we were going to drive to the house of a clergyman, and be indissolubly united that very hour, but such was not his intent. Whilst driving, he informed me that he dare not publicly make me his wife, just then, as his father would disinherit him if he married against his will, but, that he was now going to take me to the house of his cousin, with whom he had made arrangements for me to stay a few weeks, till he could soften the heart of his father, and thus be allowed to take me home as his wife. He said, also, that he had informed his cousin that we had been privately married. He told such a plausible story, that I could not but believe him, so I said nothing, but went cheerfully with him. When we drove up to the door of what I supposed was his cousin's house, we were met at the door by a very handsome woman, of some twenty-five summers, to whom he introduced me, as his cousin. She seemed to be a very kind and good woman, as she kissed me affectionately, shook my hand cordially, and welcomed me to her house with great warmth. A very nice suit of rooms were already prepared for us, and, to which we repaired, I feeling quite happy. Charles then sat down by my side, and talked lovely and sweetly of domestic felicity, and of our future happiness, when he could take me home to his father's house.

A few days after this, I noticed some half a dozen beautiful young ladies passing to and fro, in dishabille, which much surprised me. I also noticed that a great number of young and middle aged men came and went. I asked Charles what this all meant. When I put the question to him, he started, changed color, and answered me vaguely, and in a confused manner. This aroused my suspicion that all was not right, and I determined to know what it all meant. I said no more to him about it, but kept a strict watch on all in the house, when, at last, oh! horror of horrors, I became sensible of the awful truth, that I was an inmate of a fashionable brothel! The mystery was now unveiled. I was the victim of a designing villain, who had, under the guise of love, and a promise of marriage, robbed me of all that was dear to a woman,—her chastity,—and consigned me to that loathsome cess-pool, a house of ill-fame. When I became fully conscious of the awful state of degradation to which I had been brought, all my love for the villain that had brought me to such a state, was turned from love to hate; hate such as only a despised and ruined woman can possess, for the author of her shame. I was now transported with the very quintessence of such dark hate against Charles C——, and felt as did Othello,

> "Oh! that the slave had forty thousand lives,
> One is too poor, too weak for my revenge.
> All my fond love thus do I blow to heaven—'tis gone.
> Arise, black vengeance, from thy hollow cell,

Yield up, oh! love, thy crown and hearted throne, to tyrannous hate!
Swell, bosom, with thy fraught, for 'tis of aspic's tongues."

I resolved to murder the villain, but how to accomplish his death, without
detection, was the next thing to be taken into consideration. The most effectual way to do this, and escape detection, was to murder him in the street,
as he was in the habit, lately, of staying out very late, sometimes not coming
home before two or three o'clock in the morning. I possessed myself of a very
nice poniard, that he had laid away; I then questioned him, at different times,
in a careless way, which way he went, and where he went, etc., so that I soon
became informed of the different streets he was most apt to walk through.
Shortly after questioning him thus, he informed me, one Sunday night, that
he was going to the theatre, in Charles Street, and asked me to accompany
him. I made an excuse, as I determined to meet and murder him on his return home. He went, and I staid in my room till about eleven o'clock, when
I stole softly out the back way, and proceeded down to the corner of Charles
and Poydras streets, where I laid in wait for him. I had not been there more
than half an hour, before I saw a great many people coming along Charles
street, from the direction of the theatre, and I knew the theatre was let out, so
I stationed myself close to the building on the corner of Charles and Poydras
streets, in readiness for action, as I knew that he would come that way. I had
not long to wait, as he soon came along with three of his companions. When
he and his companions had got opposite to me, I stepped quickly out in front
of them and cried, "Stand!" Then, quick as thought, I plunged the poniard up
to the hilt in his black heart, and then ran for dear life down Poydras street to
Old Levee street, then down Old Levee street to Canal street, then up Canal
street to Charles street, and then went directly home, got in the back way,
and retired to bed, and soon fell asleep.

The next morning I awoke at the usual hour, and felt quite cheerful. I
knew not whether I had been recognized by Charles C——'s companions,
when I stabbed him the night before, or not, neither did I care; I had now had
my revenge. Soon the morning newspaper was thrown into my room, and I
caught it up with eagerness, and soon found a paragraph which stated, in
substance, that one of the first young men in the city, by the name of Charles
C——, was stabbed to the heart with an old-fashioned poniard, by what appeared to be a crazy woman, at the corner of Charles and Poydras streets,
the previous night, as he, with three young gentlemen, was going home from
the theatre, and that the stab caused instant death. The sudden appearance

of the woman, and the shrill cry of "stand!" that she uttered, her stabbing Charles C—— so quickly, and her sudden flight, so paralyzed all three that they could not move, nor utter a word, till she was out of sight. They then raised the cry of murder, and soon had the police in pursuit of the murderess; but all search had, as yet, proved futile. Then followed a long eulogy on his many virtues, and what a bereavement his loss was to society, etc. When I had read all this, I threw the paper away with disgust, as I thought of the hypocrisy of men—men that would canonize as a saint, a heartless libertine.

[. . .]

I was now vitiated and depraved, and cared not what I did. As many of the *beau monde* were visitors at the house, I was not long in becoming acquainted with them, and soon chose one John Smith as Charles C——'s successor. It may not be amiss to give a short sketch of John's life, prior to my acquaintance with him. I will give it in his own words, as he told it to me, on my becoming acquainted with him:

"I am," said he, "the only son of a wealthy planter, whose plantation is within an hour's drive of Natchez, Mississippi. My father, who doted upon me from early infancy, had me educated for the bar, and at the age of twenty, I gave every promise of being a most excellent jurist, which delighted my fond parents beyond measure.

"At this time, I took it into my head to take a trip to New Orleans and remain there through the winter. My father saw no impropriety in that, so he furnished me with the means, and I started without delay. While going down the river, from Natchez, I was induced to play eucher and poker, at first, only for a pastime, but soon I got to playing in dead earnest, being led on by those gamblers that are to be found on board of all the steamboats on the Mississippi and Ohio rivers. Becoming excited, as the games progressed, I took to drinking liquor quite freely, which soon intoxicated me, and I played recklessly, until my last dime was gone, and I arrived in New Orleans without a picayune. By this time, I was quite sober and sensible, and felt in very low spirits. I put up at the St. Charles, and immediately wrote to my father, and gave him 'a plain, unvarnished tale,' of all that had transpired with me, from my first setting out from home, to the very moment I wrote him. I expressed contrition for my folly, and swore to do better if he would send me a thousand dollars. My letter moved the old gentleman, and he sent me the thousand dollars that I requested, forthwith. When I had received the money, the thought flashed through my brain, that I could now play with this thousand and win back the thousand I had lost. So I went to playing again, but met with no better success than at first; for, soon the excitement of the game made me drink deep of the intoxicating bowl, which crazed me, and left me to the tender mercies of the gamblers with whom I was playing. At the end of the last game, when I saw the last dollar of the thousand gone, I arose from the table, drew a pistol, and was about to blow my brains out, when the gamblers at the table sprang upon me, wrested the pistol from me, and then confined me for a few hours in a dark room. When I had become sobered and sane, they took me out, gave me some drink, and then set me down among them, and made overtures to me to join them. They told, me it would be impossible for me to get any more money from my father, as he would be informed of my second mishap before I could write to him, and that he would discard me forever; and, that if I would join them, they would initiate me into the hidden mysteries of gaming, and supply me with abundant means, etc. I could see no other alternative, so I at once gave my consent to be initiated, which ceremony was immediately gone through with, and I became one of the fraternity. I entered, at once, into the spirit of the thing, and soon became very expert at cards, dice, etc. Gaming led me to commit many other crimes, of which I shall not speak at this time," said he, and our conversation dropped, for that time.

Thus, it will be seen by the reader, that two congenial spirits were now together. Both of us depraved, and lost to all that was virtuous and good, and ready to commit the darkest crimes. I told him how I had murdered Charles C——, which pleased him not a little. I staid at the same place with him, till about a month after my child was born. Then I went up the river, to St. Louis, with him, as he had a speculation in view, at that city. When we arrived there, we took board at a private boarding house. He there left me, for a short time, and went into southern Illinois, to get a large quantity of counterfeit notes from a gang of counterfeiters that had their rendezvous there.

While Smith was gone into Illinois, I amused myself by reading, walking, etc. One day, as I was walking along in front of the Planter's hotel, I noticed that I attracted the notice of a very fine-looking man of about forty years of age, as near as I could judge, who followed me, at a distance, till I arrived at the house where I boarded. I did not think much about it, at that time, but, when I noticed, that every day, as I walked past the hotel, the same individual watched and followed me, I thought there must be something in it. So the next time that I passed that way, I determined to let him follow me, as he had done before, and, when near home, to turn upon him and inquire his meaning. So, agreeably to the resolution I had come to, the next day I took my every day walk, and was noticed and followed by him, as on previous occasions. When I had arrived nearly home, I turned suddenly, and walked towards him, and, when about to pass him, I spoke, and asked him why he watched me so narrowly, and dogged my steps. My speaking so suddenly, caused him to stammer, and blush with confusion, at first, but, soon becoming assured, he told me that my beauty had captivated and charmed him, and he longed to learn my name, as he supposed he had already learned my place of residence. Something whispered to me to tell him my name was Smith, and to ask him to call upon me, in the evening, which I did. After giving me William Cobb, from Boston, as his name, we separated, and I returned home. The same evening, at eight o'clock, Mr. Cobb called upon me, and I received him in a very cold and formal manner. He seemed to be well acquainted with such receptions, as he sat down, and soon made himself quite familiar with me; told me that he had fallen desperately in love with me, and, that if I would leave Smith he would spend two thousand dollars a year upon me, take me to all the fashionable watering places in the states, and then take me to Europe, etc. He said that he was worth two million dollars, and that I should be mistress of his heart and his purse too, if I would only accept of both. This was a very tempting offer, and I finally concluded to accept of it. However, I told him that I would let him know at the expiration of three days, what I would do. He then gave me a purse containing five hundred dollars in gold, kissed me, bade me to think kindly of him, and then he took his leave. The five hundred completely won me over to him, and I resolved, if I could get rid of my child, I would go with him. But how to get rid of the child was a serious question. It was a beautiful male child, the very image of Charles C——, its father. I resolved to murder it. When I had come to this resolution, I gave out to the people that I boarded with, that I was going on a journey with my uncle, and that I was going to put my child out to nurse, so that there should be no suspicions aroused. The same evening of the day in which I had given out my intentions of putting the child out to nurse, I took and wrapped the child up nicely, left the house, and wended my way to the river.

When I had arrived there, I took the child up, looked at him, and said to him, You are a child of shame, and it is better that you die now, than live to be a man, and become such a villain as your father. You are too young to speak yet, therefore you have never deceived any person, nor took the name of God in vain. It is in justice and mercy to you that I, your unnatural mother, put an end to your existence. After speaking thus to my child, I took the poniard with which I stabbed his father, and plunged it several times into his little bosom, from which the warm blood flowed copiously. He writhed, struggled, and gave a few sobs, and expired. I then tied a clock weight, which I had brought with me for the purpose, to his neck, and tossed him into the river. I then stooped down to the water and washed all the blood off my hands, and off from the poniard, which I stuck into its scabbard, and replaced it in my bosom. Then I retraced my steps, and loitered on the way till nearly ten o'clock, when I arrived home. After I had got in and seated, I told the folks that I had found an excellent nurse, who had taken my child, which it pleased them to hear.

It will probably be thought by many, that I would feel a remorse of conscience for the terrible deed that I had just committed, and that life must forever after be a burden to me. Let no one suppose such a thing of me for a moment. I was on the contrary elated with joy, to think that both the father and the son were dead and out of my sight. Both the sower and the fruit were distasteful to me, and I murdered them.

At the expiration of the three days, Mr. Cobb came to see me again, and desired to know the result of my meditations. I told him that if he would take me and leave the city at once, I would go with him. This filled him with a transport of joy, and he caught me in his arms and buried me with kisses. We then sat down and talked the matter over rationally for a couple of hours, at the expiration of which time, it was agreed that we should start for Louisville, Kentucky, the next day. After he took his leave, I packed my trunks, and then retired to rest.

I awoke at an early hour the next morning, breakfasted, and paid my bill, and told the folks that I was going to start that morning for Nauvoo, Illinois; and I also desired them to tell my husband, Mr. Smith, that I had gone there to spend a few weeks with my relatives, in company with my uncle, and if he got tired waiting for me, to come up to Nauvoo and see me. I had hardly finished telling the folks this, before a carriage with Mr. Cobb inside drove up to the door. I was soon helped in, my trunks packed on behind, and away we went to the boat that was just ready to start. As soon as we were on board, she started, and soon St. Louis was left far astern. I was right glad we were off, for I was not without my fears that Smith would return and stop me in my flight.

Mr. Cobb was very attentive to me at first, but he left me after all was nicely arranged, and joined a party that were playing poker in the social hall, near the bar, where I could hear him laugh and bet money, as the play progressed in interest. This surprised me, as I had supposed that he was free from that vice of vices—gaming. But it seemed to be my lot to be the paramour of such despicable men, for ere we had arrived at Louisville, I learned that my gentleman, Mr. Cobb, was a professional gambler, thief, assassin, highway robber, utterer of counterfeit money, and a cool-blooded murderer, as he was pleased to inform me confidentially. He also informed me that he was captain of a gang of counterfeiters, highway robbers, etc., that had their headquarters in a cave near Silver Creek, Stephenson county, Illinois, where he intended taking me, after he had arranged certain things in Louisville.

[. . .]

When he had been gone two days, I began to think that I had had enough of him, so I concluded to leave him. As soon as I had come to this resolution, I packed my trunks, called a carriage, and went on board of a boat that was just leaving for New Orleans, which place I arrived at in seven days from Cincinnati. I went back to my old place there, where I used to live with Charles C——. I had not been there but about ten days, when I took a fancy to visit a masquerade ball that was soon to come off, with great *eclat*. I went, and there I first saw Green H. Long. He being a great observer of character, knew that I was a charming female, although I was masked, and, he having any quantity of impudence, began to flirt with me, which aroused the jealousy of a gambler who had been to see me, and had learned the costume that I intended to appear at the masquerade ball in. This gambler, seeing us thus coquetting and flirting, came up to Long and bade him desist, and then drew a knife, and made a demonstration towards Long, which, on Long's perceiving, he drew a knife, and stabbed the gambler and then sprang out of the window. The gambler was costumed as a wolf, and Long as a lion. A man by the name of Birchead, who was a friend and pal of Long's, stood by and saw the fight, and when I had said that I was glad that the gambler was killed, and could love the man that killed him, Birchead took me aside and told me who the man that did the deed was, which, upon learning, I requested him to bring Long, to see me. We fell in love with each other, at first sight, and I at once commenced to travel with him, and share an equal part with him in all his good and evil deeds, for years, up to the time he deserted me, and left me in the city of Mexico. Since that time, there has been a great change wrought in me. I have seen the error of my ways; have become converted to a better life; have changed my name, and become a novice in the nunnery, and, as soon as my novitiate expires, I shall take the black veil, and forever seclude myself from the world, and do penance the rest of my days, for the many dark and black crimes that I have committed.

Turning the Tables

"I HAVE BROKEN THAT BANK!"

Breaking a Bank

SOLOMON SMITH

Solomon Smith, along with his business partner Noah Ludlow, was one of the most important figures in the development of theatrical entertainment in the South and West in the years before the Civil War. Among other notable achievements, Ludlow and Smith opened the New St. Charles Theatre in New Orleans in 1843—becoming, in Charles Watson's words, "the dominant theatrical force" in the Mississippi valley (49). But beyond the stage, where he specialized in comic roles, "Old Sol" was also a popular figure in the pages of newspapers like the *Spirit of the Times*—as both an author of comic sketches and as a character for others to employ. Smith's longer works, like *Theatrical Management in the West and South* (1868), from which this sketch is taken, have been described by John Hanners as "minor classics in Americana," providing the "modern reader with rich and varied insights into the lives of itinerant entertainers who practiced their trade while battling bad weather, poor traveling conditions, fickle audiences, and a hostile clergy and press" (9). In this sketch, Old Sol breaks up a game of faro on board a riverboat. For more information see John Hanners, *"It Was Play or Starve": Acting in the Nineteenth-Century American Popular Theatre* (Bowling Green, Ohio: Bowling Green University Press, 1993); and Charles S. Watson, *The History of Southern Drama* (Lexington: University Press of Kentucky, 1997).

Captain Summons was a very clever fellow and the "Dr. Franklin" was a very superb boat, albeit inclined to rock about a good deal, and nearly turn over on her side when visited by a breath of air in the least resembling a gale. Captain Summons was a clever fellow. All steamboat captains are clever fellows, or *nearly* all; but what I mean to say is, Captain Summons was a *particularly* clever fellow; a clever fellow in the widest sense of the term; a fellow that is clever in every way—anxious that his passengers shall be comfortably bestowed, well fed and well attended to, and *determined* that they shall amuse themselves "just as they d——n please," as the saying is. If he happened to have preachers on board, he put on a serious countenance of a Sunday morning, consented that there should be preaching, ordered the chairs to be set out, and provided Bibles and hymn-books for the occasion, himself and officers, whose watch was below, taking front seats and listening attentively to the discourse. Likely as not, at the close of the service, he would ask the reverend gentleman who has been officiating, with his back in close proximity to a hot fire in a Franklin furnace, to accompany him to the bar and join him in some refreshments! If there were passengers on board who desired to pass away the time in playing poker, euchre, brag, or whist, tables and chairs are ready for *them*, too—poker, brag, euchre, and whist be it! All sorts of passengers were accommodated on the Dr. Franklin; the rights of none were suffered to be infringed; all were free to follow such employments as should please themselves. A *dance* in the evening was a very common occurrence on this boat, and when cotillions were *on the carpet,* the captain was sure to be *thar.*

It sometimes happened that, at the commencement of a voyage, it was found somewhat difficult to reconcile *all* the passengers to the system of Captain Summons, which was founded on the broad principle of equal rights to all.

On the occasion of my voyage in the "Doctor," in December, 1844, I found myself surrounded by a crowd of passengers who were *entire strangers* to me—a very rare occurrence to one who travels so often on the western rivers as I do. I wished my absence from New Orleans to be as brief as possible, and the "Doctor" was the fastest boat in port at the time of my leaving the Crescent City; so I resolved to secure a berth in her, and trust in luck to find a St. Louis boat at the Mouth.

I don't know how it is, or *why* it is, but by strangers I am almost always taken for a PREACHER. It was so on this voyage. There were three Methodist *circuit* riders on board, and it happened that we got acquainted and were a good deal together, from which circumstance I was supposed to be *one of them,* which supposition was the means of bringing me into an acquaintance with the female passengers, who, for the most part, were very pious, religiously inclined souls. We had preaching every day, and sometimes at night; and I must say, in justice to brothers Twitchell and Switchell, that their sermons were highly edifying and instructive.

In the mean time, a portion of the passengers "at the other end of the hall" continued to play sundry games with cards, notwithstanding the remonstrances of the worthy followers of Wesley, who frequently requested the captain to interfere and break up such unholy doings. The captain had but one answer—it was something like this: "Gentlemen, amuse yourselves as you like; preach and pray to your hearts' content—none shall interfere with your pious purposes; some like that sort of thing—*I* have no objection to it. These men prefer to amuse themselves with cards; let them; they pay their

passage as well as you, gentlemen, and have as much right to *their* amusements as you have to *yours,* and they shall not be disturbed. Preach, play
cards, dance cotill[i]ons, do what you like, *I* am agreeable; only understand
that *all games* (preaching among the rest) *must cease at 10 o'clock.*" So *we*
preachers got very little comfort from Captain Summons.

Up, up, up, up we went. Christmas day arrived. All the *other* preachers
had holden forth on divers occasions, and it being ascertained that it was my
intention to leave the boat on her arrival at Cairo, a formal request was preferred that *I should preach the Christmas sermon!* The women (God bless them
all!) were *very* urgent in their applications to me. "Oh *do,* Brother Smith! we
want to hear *you* preach. All the others have contributed their share to our
spiritual comfort—you *must* oblige us—indeed you must." I endeavoured to
excuse myself the best way I could, alleging the necessity of my leaving the
boat in less than an hour—my baggage was not ready—I had a terrible cold,
and many other good and substantial reasons were given, but all in vain;
preach I must. "Well," thinks I, "if I must, I must." At this crisis, casting my
eyes down towards the Social Hall, and seeing an unusual crowd assembled
around a table, I asked one of the brethren what might be going on down
there. The fattest of the preaching gentlemen replied—"The poor miserable
sinners have filled the measure of their iniquity by opening a FARO BANK!"
"Horrible!" exclaimed I, holding up my hands and "horrible!" echoed the
women and missionaries in full chorus. "Can not such doings be put a stop
to?" asked an elderly female, addressing the pious travelers. "I fear not,"
groaned my Methodist colleague (the fat one). "We have been trying to con-
vince the captain that some dreadful accident will inevitably befall the boat
if such proceedings are permitted, and what do you think he answered?"
"What?" we all asked, of course. "Why, he just said that, inasmuch as he permitted *us* to preach and pray, he should let other passengers dance and play,
if they chose to do so; and that if I didn't like the 'proceedings' complained
of, *I might leave the boat!* Yes, he did; and, moreover, he mentioned that it was
11 o'clock, and asked me if I wouldn't 'liquor!'" This announcement of the
captain's stubbornness and impiety was met with a general groan of pity and
sorrow, and we resumed the conversation respecting the unhallowed faro
bank. "It is much to be regretted," remarked the gentlewoman who had spoken before, "that *something* can't be done. Brother Smith," she continued, ap-
pealing directly to me, and laying her forefinger impressively upon my arm,
"can not *you* break up that bank?" "Dear Madam," I answered, "you know
not the difficulty of the task you impose upon me; FARO BANKS ARE NOT

SO EASILY BROKEN UP as you may imagine; however, as you all appear so anxious about it, if you'll excuse me from preaching the sermon I'll see what can be done." "Ah! that's a dear soul!" "I knew he would try!" "He'll be sure to succeed!" "Our prayers shall not be wanting!" Such were the exclamations that greeted me as I moved off toward the faro bank. Elbowing my way into the crowd, I got near the table in front of the dealer, and was for a time completely concealed from the view of my pious friends near the door of the ladies' cabin. I found the bank was a small affair. The betters were risking trifling sums, ranging from six to twenty-five cents.

"Mr. Dealer," I remarked, "I have come to break up this bank." "The deuce you have!" replied the banker; "let's see you do it." "What amount have you in bank?" I inquired. "Eleven dollars," was his answer. "What is your limit?" asked I. "A dollar," he replied. "Very well," said I, placing a ragged Indiana dollar behind the queen—"turn on." He turned, and the king won for me. I took the two dollars up and let him make another turn, when I replaced the bet, and the queen came up in my favor. I had now four dollars, which I placed in the square, taking in the 5, 6, 7, and 8, and it won again! Here were seven dollars of the banker's money. I pocketed three of them, and bet four dollars behind the queen again; the jack won, and the BANK WAS BROKEN! The crowd dispersed in all directions, laughing at the breaking up of the petty bank, and I made my way toward the ladies' cabin, where my new friends were anxiously awaiting the result of my bold attempt. "Well, well, well," they all exclaimed, "what success? Have you done it? Do let us hear all about it!" I wiped the perspiration from my brow, and, putting on a very serious face, I said solemnly, "I HAVE BROKEN THAT BANK!" "You have?" they all exclaimed. "Yes, I'll be d——d if he hasn't!" muttered the disappointed gamester, the keeper of the late bank, who was just going into his state-room. In the midst of the congratulations which were showered upon me, I received a *summons* from the captain to come forward with my baggage—we were at Cairo.

Dialogue Between a Gambler and a Travelling Agent

JONATHAN GREEN

Jonathan Green, the self-styled "Reformed Gambler," spent the 1830s gambling throughout the Mississippi valley; he spent the 1840s trying to prevent others doing the same. Even though his antigambling campaign ultimately failed to gain the kind of widespread support enjoyed by other popular movements of the time (abolition and temperance in particular), Green's career as a reformer produced some of the most prominent antebellum images of gambling on the Mississippi. As well as staging public performances wherein he demonstrated the tricks of the gambling trade, Green also published a variety of antigambling books, which went through numerous editions. Frequently, it was on and around the riverboats that he set his cautionary tales. As Ann Fabian has noted, "Green worked within a very old literary tradition of foolish young men who lost inherited wealth, but he gave the stories a particularly American turn by setting them in the Mississippi Valley [. . .] and by playing representations of a gambling South off against representations of an industrious North" (92). In *The Secret Band of Brothers* (1847) Green went even further, resurrecting the specter of a widespread and highly organized conspiracy of gamblers and criminals along the Mississippi. In this extract, however, Green applies a comic touch, imagining a steamboat conversation between a hapless gambler and a newspaper agent. For further information, see Ann Fabian, *Card Sharps and Bucket Shops: Gambling in Nineteenth-Century America* (1990; New York: Routledge, 1999).

The following dialogue is a true one, and was taken from a conversation between a gambler and an eastern gentleman, who was acting as agent for different houses and newspapers in the south.

Gambler. Halloo! old fellow, how are you?

Agent. How do you do yourself?

Gambler. Not altogether as well as I could wish; the times have been pretty hard on me.

Agent. Ah! how so? and how did you get here, if that is the case?

Gambler. Well, now, let me tell you. I have been on board eight different steamboats from Memphis to New Orleans, besides on one flat-boat;—now, what do you think of that?

Agent. Well, that was hard, sure enough!—But how did that happen?

Gambler. Well, I will tell you. I got on one boat, and travelled about one hundred miles before they asked me for my passage money, and when they found out that I had none, they set me ashore. It was not long before the second one came along, and I got on her, and such was her speed that we caught up to the first one in about an hour, when I, forgetting myself in my great desire to assume important airs, (in which we sporting gentlemen are not deficient,) stepped upon the hurricane deck, pulled off my hat, and gave them three cheers. This, of course, would make the passengers on the other boat notice me, as well as those on the boat where I was. No sooner had I given my cheers, than the captain of the other boat said, "Hallo, captain! I set that fellow ashore, about an hour ago, as I found out he was trying to pass himself off for a gentleman, though he had no money to pay his passage." I tell you what it is, I then would have given a round hundred dollars, had it been convenient, to have not given the cheers, and five hundred if they had not returned them in the way they did. Well, sir, in a few minutes up comes the clerk, in a very polite way. Said he, "Excuse me, but it is our rule for gentlemen, when they have no baggage, to pay their passage upon the entering of their names." At this I affected to be highly offended, and told him to set me ashore instantly, as I was grossly insulted. "Certainly," replied he, "that is just what we will do." So in a few minutes I was on shore again. I, however, got on the next boat, and, after travelling all night and the next morning, I was asked to pay my passage, and then, as usual, I had to "walk the plank." And this was the way with all the boats, until I got on the eighth, and they put themselves to a great deal of trouble to reach the shore in order to accommodate me; and when I got on board, they asked me for my passage money, (being then about thirty miles from the city.) I replied that I would pay when we arrived at the city, and that I was a merchant there. This had scarcely been out of my mouth, when up stepped a fellow, who had seen me set on shore a few days before; then my cake was dough once more. "Well," said the captain, (for he was up to snuff, being an old codger,) "have you any objections to working your passage?" "Indeed," says I, "captain, I cannot work—see how tender my hands are!" "O," said he, "the work I require you to do will not affect your hands; come with me." I followed him down into the engine room; he then made a rope fast round my two wrists, and attached it to the engine, and told me I had to keep with the motion of the engine; and, as there was no other alternative, I had to travel backwards and forwards as the piston went! and thus he kept me running until the boat landed about ten miles above the city, when I begged him to let me go on shore, as I certainly would prefer walking. This request he granted, telling me never to try such projects again. I got leave to ride down from there on a flat-boat.

Agent. Indeed, you have had a hard time of it; and you are the last man I should have expected to see in this city.

Gambler. Why so? Is it any more singular that I should get here than the rest of the boys? since, when I saw you last in Louisville, you had not much yourself. But as there are several listening, we had better stop talking until some more convenient time.

Agent. O, no; that makes no difference to me. I do not think you know me; the only places I ever saw you, are in Nashville, Tennessee, and other places in that state—but never in Louisville.

Gambler. (*Aside.*) Confound the fellow! I have been talking to a man that knows me, and I know nothing about him, but took him to be one of the boys. (*Aloud.*) O, I say, old fellow, this confab of mine was a mere romance; no such thing ever happened to me; I am a different man altogether. But pray, sir, why were you so astonished at seeing me here?

Agent. You do not know me, do you? I say I saw you at the races in Tennessee last week.

Gambler. O, yes, I was all through Tennessee at the different races, and won many of the purses through the state.

Agent. Ah! in what way?

Gambler. (*Aside.*) Confound the fellow! he appears to know me; but I will make out every minute as if he never saw me.—(*Aloud.*) Why, sir, in what way does any gentleman sportsman win purses?

Agent. Well, sir, that is a class of men that, fortunately, I never had much acquaintance with, and never intend to have.

Gambler. I won the purses by entering horses, as other gentlemen did. How did you expect me to have won them?—Sir, I demand an explanation! This is a pretty way for you to throw out insinuations before these strangers. Explain yourself!—(*Aside.*) I would a little rather he would not.

Agent. Well, now, Mr. Importance, since you are so anxious that I should explain myself, I will do so. I must let you know who I am, and the capacity I am in. I am an agent and collector from the east, having bills to collect from men that call themselves sportsmen, in that part of the country. I called on them, and presented my accounts. Many of them told me that I must go to the race-course; that they were playing different games, and there they would pay me, if they got any game; and this was the way I found it throughout all of the states among this gentry. And as the race-course was the only place where I could make any collections, of course I had to attend them.

Gambler. My good sir, you are entirely off the subject. You see, gentlemen, the young man does not know what he wishes to say himself. He is a good sort of a fellow, I have no doubt, and wished to say something, but did not know what it should be; but it is all right, since it shall make no difference with you and me; but hereafter, mind and know what you are talking about.

Agent. If you are through, sir, I will proceed, and finish what I have to say in relation to yourself and some of your acquaintances.

Gambler. Certainly, sir, proceed.—(*Aside.*) But I would much rather he would stop where he is.

Agent. On my first visit to the race-course at Nashville, I saw you, braced back, dealing faro, with a large regalia cigar and a ruffled shirt, and that ruffle so large you could scarce see over it. I believe you have the same shirt on now, but the ruffle is turned in; is it not? The next place on the track I saw you, you were playing at roulette. On the same track, the next day, you had on an old slouched hat, and were playing chucker-luck; and the next time I saw you, it was at the entrance of the track on the outside, with your foot up on a stump, playing the thimbles: and these are the different attitudes I saw you in, on the Nashville track.

Gambler. Ah! I just know now whom you have reference to: it is a brother of mine. Poor, unfortunate fellow! He was misled by some of the class you speak of; and I have heard of his smart tricks many times, and I tell you, colonel, he is hard to beat!—From what I have heard myself, if he gets broke dealing faro, he flies to roulette; if he cannot make money sufficient at that, he, like all the sporting gentry, plays the three little thimbles, or the grandmother's trick of the three cards, or most any thing else, until he gets sufficient money to promote him. But for my part, I never have been addicted to card-playing. I, as I said before, run fine horses, and win a purse; and that is the amount of my gambling.

Agent. Look here! you need not put on any airs with me. You are the man I have reference to, and no brother about it.

Gambler. Me, sir!

Agent. Yes, no other but you, sir!

Gambler. Do you pretend to say that I never run for a purse?

Agent. O no, certainly not; I had no reference to your running yourself for a purse. But I had reference to your never entering of horses to run for any.

Gambler. Look here, young man; you will get my dander up, the first thing you know. You see, gentlemen, he is trying to quiz me. Now, sir, come out and explain yourself.

Agent. Well, now, sir, that is quite easy. You know, gentlemen, there are various kinds of purses that are run for; and there is one kind entirely different from all the rest. This purse is generally run for by a class of men that call themselves *sportsmen,* but are nothing more nor less than gamblers or blacklegs. This purse that I speak of is what is generally called the landlord's purse, or bill; and that is the kind that this gentleman ran for, I believe. At the end of every race week, he ran off without paying his bill; whether he had money or not, I cannot say. And the way they do this is, one of the clan, or perhaps two, will claim all the baggage when they go to leave, and, paying their own bills, take the baggage that they bring, or at least they have in their own room; and the landlord has no right to take their trunks for the other man's bill. True, when they come to the tavern, you will think they are all brothers; but when they leave, they are all strangers to one another, with the exception of one or two who carry the rest! This number they select for baggage carriers at the beginning of the races, and the caravan travels from one part to another in this way; but the baggage men always are bound to pay their own bills. And thus they have their baggage carried from one place to another, swindling honest people of their honest dues. Then, you see, the purse or bill I speak of is very interesting for this class to run for on the last day!

Gambler. Look here, my good sir; do you say that I run off every time that I attend the races?

Agent. Yes; to my knowledge you ran off without paying your bills five different times at different tracks, and attempted it at the sixth; but, the landlord having heard what a villain you were, the last night of the races at Memphis, he locked your door, and put a watch at your room, to prevent your leaving without your paying your bill; and that night, about eleven o'clock, you were found trying to get out, which you effected, and the landlord caught you, and made you tell where you carried your baggage—and that was in your hat! You had, as your wardrobe, one shirt, one pair of socks, one chuckerluck box, two or three sorts of dice, one deck of cards, and about half a dozen thimbles! The landlord, with an officer, led you off to jail; and when I left, the next day, they told me about thirteen out of twenty of your apparently most intimate friends had left between two days, without paying their bills, or even bidding the landlord farewell. And when I left, you were still in jail, and that was the reason of my surprise when I saw you here!

Gambler. Well, I give it up. You can tell any thing the smoothest, and get over it slicker, and make the fattest joke out of it, and tell it with a better face than any other man I ever saw.—But look ye here; I will not stand such talk about me. I will let you know that I will not be trifled with by such a man as you.

Agent. Mind! I will tell something more, if you don't hush; and you know it is the truth.

Gambler. Well, sir, I have one request to make of you—that is, for you to leave me, and never speak to me again!

Agent. Now you are talking sensibly!—That I will certainly do, as I feel ashamed of myself for having been caught talking so long to you in public; and had it been in private, sir, I would not have been seen by an honest man for any consideration whatever. But now, after this, take my advice, and never put on airs without knowing whom it is with.—So I leave you.

How Dodge "Dodged" the Sharpers

M. G. LEWIS

The star of this story is the euphoniously named Ossian Euclid Dodge. Dodge achieved a significant measure of fame in the early 1850s as the so-called Boston Voice. Though primarily known as a singer, often performing songs with a comic theme, Dodge was also a journalist and newspaper publisher. Arguably, he achieved his greatest moment of notoriety when he bid $625 in a public auction to hear Jenny Lind sing when she gave her first concert in Boston in 1850. Shifts in musical taste meant that Dodge eventually returned to obscurity, but this sketch of his experiences with three riverboat captains playing at being gamblers (later reprinted in *Southern and South-Western Sketches,* "edited by a Gentleman of Richmond" [Richmond: J. W. Randolph]) was published at the height of his fame. Readers may also be interested to note that the "Peter Funk" referred to by the boat captains was a popular term for a confidence man (technically, one used by auction houses to bid-up lots). For more information, see Philip D. Jordan, "Ossian Euclid Dodge: Eccentric Troubadour," *Historian* 31.2 (February 1969): 194–210.

Where's the man residing in any part of the United States, that has not heard of OSSIAN E. DODGE, the joker, vocalist, and delineator of character? Echo answers, *whar?*—we will therefore give a *dodge* of Dodge's.

Some few years since, when the demoralizing habit of gambling was still greater than at the present day, the inveterate punster and Yankee vocalist found it for his professional and pecuniary interest to remain for some time in the flourishing villages to be found along the banks of the muddy, though world-renowned Mississippi—on whose waters men are done, overdone, and undone—water only taken by the deck passengers and divers into eternity, and where the "papers," "documents," "pocket companions," "hymn books"—in vulgar parlance called *cards,* and all games pertaining thereunto, are as plenty as brass buttons and bogus pennies in a contribution box.

It being a fine field for studying human nature, and enjoying an occasional bit of private fun, the vocalist travelled *incog.,* that he might, like the wise man in the parable, double his talents and pick up all the percentages that an overruling Providence might please to fore-ordain for his especial benefit.

His travelling apparel has once undoubtedly belonged to the *ton,* but alas!

it now looked more like the last remaining stock of an old woman's curiosity shop; his bell-crowned tile, judging from its size, must have been the measure alluded to when our forefathers were so affectionately spoken to, concerning their valuable light being hid under a bushel.

His flaxen hair (or rather that of his wig,) fell in rich profusion over a huge stock—enclosing a dickey double starched, and standing erect, like the sail of a sloop in a fog, and apparently conscious of its power in operating on the ears like the teeth of an old wood-saw, so that in front, the comical looking face had the appearance of being enclosed in a pen, or of peaking at the beholder through the interstices of a worn-out cotton carpet. The short-waisted, long-skirted, swallow-tailed blue coat, with large brass buttons and high greasy collar, sat on the square-shouldered and sinewy frame of the wearer like a door mat on a pitchfork; while a dingy cotton skirt, covered in front with a ruffled frill, gave a finishing touch to a pair of bottle-green pants, with a narrow flap, and still narrower bottoms, ornamented with a large golden watch-seal hanging pendant on a leather string from the watch-pocket, in a manner that would have made graver men than travellers on the Mississippi roar with laughter. In fact, it was too *big* a man for so *little* cloth, and what little there was seemed to have a strong tendency to meet midway, and discuss whether it would be better to stand the strain, or stretch a feet or a feet and half further, and reach the "insect killers," now visible below the pants in a pair of boots that would have answered very well for lumber and coal river boats for a wholesale dealer.

Our hero came on board of the fine (and at the time, very popular,) steamer G—— W——, bound down to New Orleans, (as she was wooding up at one of the many wood-yards ever to be found on the banks of the Mississippi,) and coming up to the Captain's office with his valise and guitar-box in hand, he exclaimed—

"Heow de dew, Cap'n—heow de dew? Wall, I've cum aboard."

"Yes, sir."

"Thought as heow I might let you know I'd arrived, so yer could make calkerlations about fodderin' on me."

"Fare, sir!"

"O! I shan't be pertikerlar abeout *that,* even if 'taint fust chop—coze I 'spose you didn't know I wus comin'; but I kin eat what anybody kin, and ef ye only have a nuff on't, I shall be as happy as a clam at high tide,—but I say *yeou*! if the vittles gits a little short, I'll whisper in your ear."

"Passage, sir!" said the Captain, looking up for the first time, and holding out his hand for the fare.

"Heow dew yer dew?" (grasping and shaking the Captain's hand)—"you needn't put yourself tew enny trouble, for I feel to hum a'ready, and I'll do all I kin to make myself comfortable; but I say, Cap'n! I guess there's sunthin' on your mind" (nodding, winking, and smiling,) "I noticed yeou was an allfired spell a gettin' ready to be perlite; but here! I'll tell you what 'tis" (passing the guitar-box through the window, and placing it on the Captain's secretary), "I want yeou to take 'special keer of that 'ere trunk, for I love my old fiddle better'n all the purty gals in Punkintown."

"O yes, certainly!" snickered the Captain, hurrying off to give the item to Brown, Strong, and Walker—three up-river captains who were laid up by low water, and were now taking a trip down as "dead hands," to have a "*time*" unbeknown to their employers.

"I say, boys," says Brown, "that's rich, ain't it?"

"The richest thing we have heard for a long time," echoed the party. "Only to think of his grasping the Captain's hand!—*ha! ha! ha!* Sticking his old fiddle-box into the office window!—*he! he! he!* A Mississippi captain foddering a real live Yankee!—*ho! ho! ho!*" And thus roared the whole party till the old boat echoed again.

"What do you say, boys—let's turn 'artists' and take a contribution of a '*ten spot*' from the Yankee, to pass over to our credit at the bar," said Brown, a fat rubicund-visaged lump of mortality, weighing some two hundred and seventy, and who was the greatest practical joker and story teller on the river.

"What game shall we stick him on?" asked Walker, a long, lank, and lean specimen of bones and sinews, loosely made up, with a hatchet-looking phiz, as dry as a chip.

"I'm in for anything that's rich," replied Strong, whose name contradicted itself—he being a little, dried up, diminutive, weasel-faced man, who would, in New England, have been termed "trundle-bed trash." "Yes, boys, I go it blind for anything that's rich—but hold! perhaps our worthy host, the Captain of the boat, can suggest something for us."

"O no, I can't have anything to do with it," replied the Captain. "In the first place, it's my own boat—and in the second, I don't think it's exactly fair for such old heads to bleed a poor fellow that's so decidedly good-hearted, and verdant withal. No! you must manage it among yourselves, I'll have nothing to do with it—but don't be *too* hard on the boy; you may be fathers yourselves some day."

"Well, let's see," says Strong, addressing his jovial companions. "'Swinging Jack'—too old. 'Calling Jack'—too complicated. 'Raising Jack'—that's better. 'Changing Jack'—that's *new,* and just the thing to take with the Yankee. '*Changing Jack*' it is, and *I'll* handle the books—who'll be Peter Funk?"

"Well, I think I'll make a very respectable looking Peter," chuckled Brown, glancing over his well-stuffed corporation.

"Strong, my dear fellow, you're rather *small* to play the principal character in the drama," exclaimed the long and cadaverous looking Walker, "but I rather think you're shrewd enough to make it up; so let's see! what shall I do for *my* share of the profits? Ah! I have it, no one can do the 'roping in' better than myself. I'll pretend to belong to the ministry—get the fellow's confidence—talk about camp-meetings—the blessed heathen, and all that sort o'thing, and if we don't make game out of a young flax-head in less than two hours from his arrival, then we're a set of dough-heads every one of us."

During this colloquy among the *sharps,* Dodge was walking around the spacious and richly furnished cabin, with his hands affectionately clasped behind, under the extremity of his swallow-tailed blue, and with all the verdancy imaginable—peering into the state-rooms, and talking to himself about "the allfiredest skiff to carry folks in, that was ever made since Sampson swallowed the whale."

The majority of the passengers, including the professionals, were seated at the farthest end of the cabin, deeply engaged in the exciting and intoxicating game of *eucre, whist, poker,* and *forty-fives,* at which games hundreds of dollars were almost constantly changing owners.

As Dodge gradually came nearer and nearer to the trio of wild and frollicksome captains, Walker put on an expression of deep solemnity and ministerial gravity, and, after a few slight coughs, ahems, and adjusting the borrowed pair of blue specs, he slowly advanced, offered his hand, and exclaimed—

"Ah! my dear young friend, how do you do? I am very happy, indeed, to meet you, although perhaps you may not fully recollect me, but I really hope you are well!"

"Wal, yes, putty well as common, I thank-ee, considerin'."

"How long is it since you left our blessed New England?"

"I jest cum *eout;* but I say, yeou! ain't you a few pints the start on me? I don't remember yeou, darned ef I do!"

"I am from the same section myself, my young friend, and it affords me great joy to meet you now at this time, for if a young man is ever in need of a friend, it is when he is travelling on the Western waters, amidst the bright and dazzling temptations that are here thrown out to trap the unsuspecting and virtuous."

"Wal, now, I feel ra-al *obliged* to yeou, and no mistake, and ef I could dew anything to show yeou how glad I is, I'd dew it in a minute, I *would* ra-ally; but I say, yeou! what dew yeou work at for a trade?"

"I am emerged in the Missionary business, young man, and now I come to think of it, you *can* be of great service to me, if you have a heart that feels for the poor unfortunate and bleeding heathen. Do you see that small red-faced man, with cards in his hand?" (pointing to Strong.)

"What! that air little feller, what looks like a drinking man?"

"The same, my good friend—the very same. Well, he won three thousand dollars with a lottery ticket, and it has completely turned his brain, for he is now foolish enough to think that he can win money at *every*thing; but he is only proving the old adage that 'a fool and his money are soon parted,' for he is losing ten and twenty dollars every few minutes, at a simple trick of cards, with that large and reckless fellow"—(pointing to Brown)—"who is one of the most noted gamblers and cut-throats on the river."

"Let's see how it's did—I don't know nothing about *keerds,* only its an orful sin to play 'em for munny."

"You are right, my friend, never gamble. I am a very humble worker in the Missionary cause, and it pains my philanthropic heart to see all this bright and beautiful gold, that would do the poor unfortunate suffering heathen *so* much good, all going to so bad a use. No doubt but that some of it will even go for rum—intoxicating and ruinous rum. If the poor deluded man is de-termined—regardless of threats or pleadings—to lose his money with *some* one, I must say, that I think it would be serving the Lord to secure a part of it for the benefit of suffering humanity. It isn't betting, nor gambling, for the game is not a *chance* one, but the man who holds the cards is sure to win; and I *must* say," continued Walker, in a drawling, sanctimonious tone, "that if the devil *brought* the money to us, the Lord undoubtedly *sent* it!"

"Wal, that's a fact!—ef a feller's sure to win, and 'taint no bettin'; of course we orter dew somethin' for them air charitable heathen niggers. But now dew you ra-ally think that 'twouldn't be wicked for us to take his money?"

"As I hope for future salvation, my dear friend, I think it wouldn't!" an-swered Walker, as they arrived at the table.

Strong was standing with a half pack of cards in the palm of his hand—his thumb across the middle of the Jack of Spades.

"You see that is the Jack of Spades," said he to Brown, holding up the leg of the Jack.

"Of course," says Brown, "do you think I'm such a fool as not to know the Jack of Spades?"

"Take hold and hold tight, then," says Strong.

"All right!—go on with your fun," says Brown.

"Pull now," says Strong, turning the face down.

"Here it is!" says Brown, pulling it out from the pack, and laying it face down on the table.

"Hocus, pokus, presto, change!" says Strong. "Now I'll bet you fifty dollars that it's the *Jack of Clubs* under your hand!"

"I'll take that bet!" says Brown, "and here's the money."

The stakes were piled, and of course Brown won, as they were preparing the hook with bait to catch the Yankee.

"Fix 'em again—I'll double on you till I win your pile; it's as easy as rolling off a greased log!" laughed Brown, flourishing his money about like so much waste paper.

"O! I'm in the ring yet, my boy, with a plenty of cash where the rest came from," says Strong, hauling from his pocket-book a large roll of bills, and throwing them upon the table.

Whilst this conversation was going on between the sharpers, Dodge was unobservedly fingering a pack with similar backs, (that happened to lay on an adjoining table,) for a card which he slipped into the top of his bell-crowned hat, under his bandanna, and once more commenced whistling in a low and verdant manner, "The girl I left behind me."

The second game at "Changing Jack" ended the same as the first, neither of the operators noticing Dodge or Walker. The latter, who had been leaning his head on a centre-table near, as if in prayer for the benefit of the poor heathen, and the success of this flaxen-headed Yankee, now approached his "dying friend," and whispered, with tears in his eyes—

"Couldn't you possibly save some of it? It is a great pity to see it all going so!—it would do the poor benighted heathen *so* much good!"

"I say, *yeou!* look yere," says Dodge, moving slowly and sideways up to the little Strong man, and winking at Walker at the same time, as much as to say the heathen should not be neglected—"I say yeou, I don't know nothing about keerds, but I'm willing to risk a heap of money on that 'ere game just for a benevolent purpose, for (turning to Walker,) 'taint gambling is it?"

"Oh no! certainly not," replied the *pseudo* Dominie, who could now hardly keep from roaring with laughter, on witnessing how easily the game was bagged.

"Very well—I'm with you, stranger," exclaimed Strong, snapping his fingers in a devil-may-care sort of manner; "there's plenty more money where this came from, and I'm willing to risk all I've got in the world, that I can, by repeating a few short sentences in swine Latin, change the Jack of Spades while under your hand, into the Jack of Clubs, and that you can't tell, by the sense of feeling, when the Spade takes its departure!"

"Look a' here, old flax head," exclaimed Brown, swelling out his large form to its fullest dimensions, and bristling up to Dodge as if for a fight. "Look a' here, Mr. Philgarlic, you are interfering in other people's business! I have set to that man's pile myself, and I don't want no man to interfere."

"I ax your pardon, if I intrude," says Dodge, "for I only want to save a little on it for a benevolent purpose!"

"Very well; you may jest bet *once!*" says Brown, looking at Dodge very closely, "for I see you are not a sporting man. You may bet once, if you wish; mind, only *once!* as it's my game; but hereafter, as a general thing you had better not interfere with stranger's games, for you might get into a muss!"

While Dodge's attention was thus drawn off by the perspective fight, Strong cut the Jack of Spades directly through the centre, with his jack-knife—hid the legs, and placed the head part evenly over the head of the Jack of Clubs, crossing his thumb over the cut edge, so, to all appearances, the legs of the Jack of Clubs belonged to the head of the Jack of Spades.

"You see that is the Jack of Spades," said he, turning to Dodge.

"Is that air spot genewine?" says Dodge, wetting his finger and touching the spade at the head of the Jack.

"You find it so, don't you?" pressing it close with his thumb to prevent its moving.

"Wal, yeas, it 'pears to be—so now go on with the *show,* for I want tew make some money allfired bad!" says Dodge, taking hold, with both hands, of what appeared to be the leg of the Jack of Spades.

"Very well, then," says Strong, turning the pack over—"now pull the card, and keep it bottom side upward."

Dodge pulled the apparent Jack of Spades out on the table, holding his left hand over it, while with the right he took off his bell-crowned hat, and sweeping the card off between the palm of both hands, had the appearance of placing the drawn card into the top of the old beaver, but, in fact, only into the folds of the old bandana, upon which he placed his doubled fist, remarking at the time—

"By ginger! ef yeou kin git that air Jack o' Spades eout of that air hat by way of yeour Latin, I hope I may be stuffed to death with biled unyuns!"

While the party were in the highest state of frolic and excitement over the verdancy of the victim, Dodge took from his pocket a large jack-knife, and, opening it with his teeth, held it over his hat, and taking out the bandana, which held the card he had drawn from the pack, he jabbed the blade of the knife clear through the other card, hat, and into the table, exclaiming—

"Dang my buttons, ef I keer for the hat—I'll jab her anyhow! cause, if I make a hull lot of money, even if 'tis for a beneverlunts, I kin buy a new hat, can't I" (winking to Walker.)

"O certainly!" says Walker, "however small the sum that you may be inclined to place at my disposal, it shall be registered as lent to the Lord!"

While Dodge was holding on to the knife, and looking as if he expected every minute that the hat would take wings, the trio could hardly keep in, but it was too good to spoil, so they only winked to one another, as much as to say—

"A sure thing of it! Got him on the dead!! What an excellent thing to tell!!!"

The crowd, *smoking* something extraordinary rich, gathered around the party, and revealed by their anxious faces, that every one aboard had now become deeply interested in the result of the professional skinning.

"Now, then," says Strong, looking the victim sharply in the eyes, and holding up his right arm, while he repeated in slow and measured tones, as solemn as a High Sheriff at a public execution—"now then, my friend, prepare for the miracle:

"Now look out for tricks that's strange—
Hocus—pocus—presto, change!"

"I'll be ker-walloped to death with cabbages, old feller! if that air keerd *is* changed anyhow!"

"I'll go a thousand dollars that it *did*!" says Strong—"and that the card that your knife is now sticking through, is the Jack of Clubs!"

"Wal, I comed eout West here for to buy a considerable of a farm, and ef

I kin make a thousand dollars in one pile, I s'pose I might as well dew it; but mind, neow, I don't call it bettin', for that would be wicked, and I only take this 'ere thousand dollars for a beneverlent purpose, but as fa-ather used to say—'in for a pence, in for a pound'—so here goes."

Suiting the action to his words, Dodge deliberately drew from an inside vest pocket an old greasy wallet, and taking therefrom ten one hundred dollar bills, on a Philadelphia bank, held them in his hand, and exclaimed—

"Well, neow, yeou feller! ef yeou're determined to throw away yeour money where yeou don't stand no chance a winnin', why jest pull oeut yeour dough!"

During this time, the *pseudo* missionary had worked his way along through the crowd, and getting behind Strong, though (as he supposed) un-observed by Dodge, remarked in a low tone—

"O! Strong, this is *too* good! If you don't hurry through and take the ninny's money soon, I shall explode with laughter. I can't hold in much longer; but I say, Strong, equal shares, you know!—honor bright! us three!"

"Of course!" chimed in Brown, with a wink of the eye and a twist of the mouth—"*partners!*"

"Only for a benevolent purpose!" whispered Strong—"this is the richest '*sell*' of the season—but if you say so, why partners it is."

"O! the dear heathen!" observed Walker, opening his mouth as if imbibing a julep—"I'm as dry a powder horn!"

Dodge had meanwhile been gazing intently in the hat, and a person not acquainted with the peculiar twinkle of his large eyes, would have sworn that he had seen nothing else for the last five minutes.

"Captain, I want you to hold these 'ere thousand dollars, and as a man of honor, in the presence of these 'ere passengers, see that fair play is did tew a stranger."

"I would rather have nothing to do with the affair," replied the Captain—"but, if you wish for me to hold the stakes I will do so, and call upon my passengers to see that everything is honorable."

"Well, Captain," exclaimed Strong, in a voice loud enough to be heard by all present, "there's a thousand dollars in current bills and gold to cover the Yankee's pile."

"See that it's genewine, Captain, and no geouging."

"All right," replied the Captain, "and now, gentlemen, please inform me, loud enough for all present to hear, the precise character of the bet."

"Well, that air chap there, what's got red whiskers and big watch chain, and my own self, what don't want to hev it called bettin', puts up in yeour hand, one thousand dollars each, and ef that air keerd in that air hat with that air knife jabbed through it, is the Jack of Spades, the hull tew thousand dollars *is* mine, but if that air keerd, in that air hat, with that air knife jabbed through it, is the Jack of Clubs, then the tew thousand dollars *is* his'n—ain't that right, yeou feller?"

"That is perfectly right, gentlemen," replied Strong, drawing his hand across his mouth to hide a laugh, and edging around sideways, for he could hardly keep in. "Yes, Captain, the Yankee's statement is correct."

The idea of a verdant nutmeg Yankee putting up a thousand dollars on the cut throat game of "Changing Jack," was so extremely ludicrous, that the crowd could only by the greatest exertion, refrain from yelling. Walker, who, of course, expressed a firm belief that the Yankee must, beyond a doubt, get the entire two thousand dollars, here winked to the clerk of the bar, and smacked his lips with hilarity, as much as to say—"Juleps for the crowd at my expense, in a few minutes, my boy."

Strong and Brown very slyly performed a few mysterious gyrations with the fingers, such as imitating the cutting of the throat, a rope around the neck, and a dive into the river, three very common ways of committing suicide, and too often adopted by young adventurers from the North and East, who blindly stake their all after falling into the hands of these Western river chaps.

Smiling at the earnestness and unbounded confidence of the heartless cut-throats, whose slightest movements had not escaped his eagle eye, Dodge merely remarked—"Let them laff that wins; there's tew sides to all jokes, tew sides to this keerd, and tew sides tew to all of yeour mouths tew laff eout of, so here she comes."

Drawing out the knife and turning over the card, to the astonishment of the entire crowd, it was the Jack of Spades!

As the Captain passed the money over to Dodge the lower jaws of the disappointed sharpers fell about a feet, and almost simultaneously exclaimed—

"Jewed by—!"

"Yankee'd by—!"

"Bit by—!"

The crowd, who were bound to have a good time any way; and more especially now that the joke was so much richer than was expected, were in a collapsed state—they yelled, cheered, and shouted until the cabin fairly shook again.

The boat soon after landing again for wood, at a small yard on the banks of the river, the trio of sharp Captains took their departure for up-river settlements, thinking, undoubtedly, that there would be a sudden rise on the river soon; and as the boat slowly moved away from her moorings, they cast a glance on her hurricane deck, where stood the comical Dodge, giving imitations of a cut across the throat, a rope around the neck, and a dive into the river.

Should any Yankee ever ask either of the trio to relate that thrilling "*story that'll do to tell,*" he will be chalked free of charge the whole length of the river.

The Gamblers Outwitted

EMERSON BENNETT

In the antebellum years, Emerson Bennett was a highly popular and prolific writer of adventure stories set on the frontier. Today, however, he is probably best known as the butt of one of Mark Twain's jokes in *Roughing It* (1872)—his reference to literary backwoodsmen who are "one part critically grammatical, refined and choice of language, and the other part just such an attempt to talk like a hunter or a mountaineer, as a Broadway clerk might make after eating an edition of Emerson Bennett's works" (149). Nonetheless, in the years before the Civil War, Bennett produced some of the most influential accounts of frontier life, most famously *The Prairie Flower* (1849). Unsurprisingly, the theme of gambling on the Mississippi was grist to his mill, and the following story was not the only time that he wrote about riverboat gambling. As he warned in *Viola, or, Adventures in the Far South-West* (1852), "Whoever has travelled much on the Western waters, needs not to be told that gambling on the boats is a very prominent feature; and that, as a consequence, scenes sometimes occur of a nature to make one's blood run chill with horror" (16). In its denouement, this story is no exception.

The following story was narrated by a gentleman who desires his name withheld from [. . .] the public:

"Any man living on the lower Mississippi twenty years ago, who was not in favor of playing all sorts of games for all manner of sums, would have been at once pronounced no gentleman or a minister of the Gospel. I was myself not a little scandalized, on my first going South, at being asked by a gentleman to play cards for money; but universal custom is every thing in settling a man's mind upon the matter of right or wrong; and I regret to say I soon found myself as much disposed for the exciting sport as the most ardent of my companions, though never at any time so much attached to it as to play with a professional gamester.

"In this latter respect I materially differed from a friend of mine—a young planter by the name of Paul Rathbun—who, having become a great adept in the handling of cards, rather prided himself on the belief that he could outwit the most adroit gambler to be found; and he never went aboard a passing steamer without trying his hand with one or more of the chance-operating fraternity.

"Now Paul Rathbun and myself had agreed to take a trip to New Orleans, to enjoy a few week's pleasure and recreation in that great city of the South; and as he was going to take down a large sum of money, to meet some notes of country merchants falling due, his father, knowing his penchant for cards and adventure, called me aside, and requested me as a friend to have an eye to him and restrain him from carrying his proclivities to the extent of ruin.

"It was a cold, dark, stormy night that we embarked on board a downward steamer, from the then pleasant little town of Grand Gulf; and though we were in fine sprits, exhilarated to a highly talkative degree by a few parting glasses with the jovial friends who had seen us off, yet I felt nothing like intoxication, and was very much astonished and mortified to discover that my friend did, and within fifteen minutes after our appearance in the splendid saloon of the boat.

"What could it mean? Was it the effect of the liquor he had drank on shore? or had he been imbibing since? I had left him but a few minutes only; and now, on my return to the saloon from the guards, I found him almost reeling, and surrounded by a group of four or five dark-visaged, villanous-looking fellows, whom I believed to be pick-pockets, or gamblers of the lowest order, and with whom he was conversing with a familiarity that both astonished and vexed me. Whether sober or otherwise, I felt in duty bound to withdraw him from such company, and immediately approached him for that purpose.

"'Come, Paul, my dear fellow,' said I, quietly running my arm through his, "let us retire to our state-room; I have something important to communicate to you."

"'You have?' he replied with a strong emphasis on the pronoun, and partially turning his face to me, with a drunken man's quizzical leer. 'You've got something to communicate, have you, old boy?'

"'Yes, Paul, I have something very important to tell you.'

"'That's a (hic) lie!' returned he, straightening himself up with drunken dignity, and winking at his delectable companions, who laughed approvingly, at my expense. 'You've got nothing to tell me—you only think I'm drunk, and want to be a father to me. But I'm not drunk yet, and you're not a going to be a father to me. Ain't I right, (hic) gentlemen, eh?'

"'Of course you are,' chorused the villanous group, with a general laugh. 'You want no father at your age.'

"'Ha! ha! ha!' laughed my friend, in drunken glee; 'it's funny enough, and I know you'll (hic) laugh; but this old fellow is my paternal progeni-(hic)-tor.'

And griping my arm in a manner to cause pain, he began to push me around from one to the other, remarking to each: 'I want you to know the old chap that's a father to me.'

"'Paul,' said I sternly, attempting to force him away, 'come with me.'

"He threw me from him with force, and made use of an insulting expression that I need not repeat.

"'Paul Rathbun,' I angrily rejoined, 'if you were sober, that remark should cost your life or mine.'

"'Oh, don't be afraid!' he rejoined, with a hiccough; 'I'm not so drunk as I look. I know exactly what I'm saying, and hold myself responsi-(hic)-ble for it.'

"Grieved, angered, and mortified, I left him abruptly, and went out upon the guards. A furious northeaster was blowing, bringing wintry airs to a summer clime, but they felt delicious to my heated brow and burning temples.

"For half an hour I stood there, looking off upon the blackness, listening to the howling wind, driving sleet, coughing steam, and gurgling waters, but thinking that the whole pleasure of my trip, if not of my life, would be marred by the misfortune that had turned the brain of my friend. Suddenly it occurred to me that it was my duty to stand by and protect him till sober, let him be never so insulting, and forthwith I returned to the saloon.

"I found him, as I did not wish to find him, seated at a table, with a large pile of money before him, engaged in playing cards with the five villanous fellows in whose company I had left him. What could result from such a condition of affairs but his entire ruin, and the ruin perhaps of others?—for, as I have mentioned, he was taking down to New Orleans large sums for his friends, which would probably be as freely staked as his own money. And should I not, to a certain degree, be held accountable for this loss, since I had been empowered by his father to restrain him from the excess of ruin? It was certainly my duty to act, and my resolution was soon taken. Advancing to the table, I laid my hand upon his shoulder, and said, calmly but firmly:

"'Paul Rathbun, if you are intoxicated, this is no place for you, and I shall take you away by force; and if you are sober enough to comprehend the words of a friend, permit me to inform you, that you are in the hands of the lowest order of Mississippi gamblers.'

"The five strangers simultaneously started to their feet; and the one nearest to me said, in a low, threatening tone, fixing his eyes sullenly upon mine, as he thrust his hand into his bosom for a weapon:

"'Take that back, sir, and acknowledge us to be gentlemen, or I will have your heart's blood!'

"'Wait a moment,' said I, returning his gaze with an unquailing eye; 'wait a moment, and I will show you how I recant. Now you dare not touch me, let me say what I will, and for two reasons: first, you would lose your victim, and a few thousands; and secondly, what is of less consequence, you would all lose your unworthy lives; therefore, I boldly defy you to do your worst, and deliberately repeat here that you are gamblers and no gentlemen.'

"These remarks were made impulsively, under the excitement of anger, and with my hand upon a pistol, which I intended to use should I perceive the least attempt upon my life. What the consequences might have been, had not Paul Rathbun interfered, I cannot say; but he started suddenly to his feet, and, reeling forward a step, thus effectually covered my person with his.

"'Gentlemen,' he said to the gamblers, 'sit down, and don't mind this (hic) boy! If there's to be any quarrel with him, I'm the man for that. Don't let us spoil our night's sport to please him. There, that's (hic) right, gentlemen—sit down. And now, boy,' turning to me, 'go to bed, and don't bother (hic) yourself about matters too old for your compre-(hic)-hension. Here,' he added, producing a large pocket-book, as I stood looking sorrowfully into his face, considering what course was best to pursue: 'take this, Frank, and don't bother (hic) me. In there you'll find all the money that don't belong to me; and the rest's my own, and I'll do as I (hic) like with it. Take that, now, and go to bed—that's a (hic) good fellow!'

"I seized the pocket-book with avidity, thankful that I could get possession of what would save my friend from utter ruin and disgrace; and finding I could do nothing with him in his present condition, without resorting to force, I left him, as it were to his fate.

"But I did not retire to bed; it was impossible, under the circumstances, for me to sleep; and I spent hour after hour in alternately clambering over the cotton-piled deck, exposed to a cold, furious storm—in standing on the guards, dripping with rain—and in walking up and down the saloon, pitying the weakness of my friend, who still drank and played with men who had the same regard for him that so many wolves would have for a lamb.

"One round after another of liquor was brought and drank, pack after pack of cards disappeared under the table, large sums of money changed hands continually, and still my poor, demented friend, as I considered him, sat among five human fiends, the victim of all.

"Almost wearied out with long-continued excitement and loss of rest, I had at last taken a seat some distance from the players, and, with my head upon my hand, was just giving way to an overpowering somnolency, when I was suddenly aroused, and much astonished, at hearing my friend exclaim, in that sharp, clear, cold, determined tone peculiar to him when carrying his point at the point of a Bowie-knife or the muzzle of a pistol:

"'Hold! The first man that lays his hand on a dollar, I will kill as I would a dog!'

"I started up, and beheld an unlooked-for tableau. The gamblers were all upon their feet, standing around the table, three with hands extended, as if to grasp a large pile of money, which one hand of my friend carelessly covered, while his other held death for the most daring in the shape of a loaded pistol. He was still seated in his chair, his cold, penetrating gray eye looking up unflinchingly from under his massive brow, and turning deliberately with his pistol from one to the other of those dark men, whose swarthy features expressed astonishment, rage and fear.

"'It's a swindle!' said the boldest, suddenly, with his hand still extended as if to grasp the money. 'You never got them cards honest; that money's ours, and we'll have it!'

"'Take it!' said Paul Rathbun, quietly, without the change of a muscle; and with the words there came a sharp click, as his thumb drew back the hammer of his pistol.

"By this time I was standing at his back, with a Bowie-knife in my teeth, and a cocked and levelled pistol in either hand.

"'Be modest, fellows, and only claim what is your own,' said I.

"'Ah, Frank, are you there?' cried Paul, with animation, partly turning his head to me, though without removing his eyes from his antagonists. 'A thousand pardons, my dear fellow, for the way I abused and insulted you! So you thought I was in liquor, eh? Ha! ha! you may be pardoned for that, considering that these shrewd sharpers thought the same. But it was necessary to deceive you, my boy, in order to deceive them—and so forgive me! Drunk, eh? I tell you, old gamblers, you are caught for once, and by a mere boy—for I am only a boy; and so if you were to play with men, where would you be? It is a swindle, is it? and no honest hand? Look there, Frank!—four aces against four kings! Is not that honest, eh? And see, my dear fellow, what those four aces won—seventeen hundred dollars—all the money these rascals have, and enough to pay our trip to New Orleans and back. Go to, for shame! five against one, and that one a youth! Do me the favor to play next with a mere

child, and never pride yourselves on being the equal of any Southern gentleman of any age.'

"While Paul Rathbun continued to rattle on in this manner, sometimes
addressing me and sometimes the gamblers, several gentlemen came out of
their state-rooms and gathered around us. On learning the true state of affairs, they greeted with a laugh the discomfited villains, who, in attempting
to fleece my friend, had themselves been fleeced by him.

"Though at first evidently determined to fight for their money, the gamblers soon became cowed by the appearance of numbers, gradually slunk
away, with crestfallen looks, and finally left the boat at the next landing,
swearing vengeance.

"Paul Rathbun hugely enjoyed what he termed his practical joke, but
promised me he would never attempt the like again.

"Poor fellow! I believe he never did. At New Orleans he spent most of his
downward winnings in charity, and was suddenly recalled home by a letter
from his father, announcing the illness of a beloved sister. He left the city a
couple of days before me, but I arrived first at his father's mansion. In fact he
never arrived; and what became of him is not certainly known to this day.
He had a state-room to himself on his upward trip, and one morning he was
found missing, with blood on the sheet of his berth. It is supposed he was
stabbed in his sleep, and his body thrown into the river. The murderer or
murderers rifled his baggage, and probably robbed him of a large amount in
money and jewels.

"But whether or not his death indirectly arose through revenge of any
of the parties who figured in the scenes I have described, is a matter I have
never been able to decide. All is mystery, and will probably ever remain so.
Peace to his ashes!"

From *The Confidence-Man: His Masquerade*

HERMAN MELVILLE

As Jonathan Cook has argued, *The Confidence-Man* (1857), Melville's last published novel, is still a question in search of an answer: "There has been little consensus on the novel's meaning and it continues to be the author's most problematic and forbidding text" (ix). In brief, the novel follows events on board the steamboat *Fidèle* as it journeys from St. Louis to New Orleans on April Fool's Day. Melville uses the social panorama of a Mississippi steamboat (a "ship of fools") to effect a rigorous and far-reaching satire of the contemporary American scene. In the following extract, the eponymous confidence man, in the guise of cosmopolitan Frank Goodman, has an encounter with Charlie Noble, a riverboat gambler who attempts to get Goodman drunk—but gets a lot more than he bargained for in the process. Melville's portrait of Noble and his methods might have been based on personal experience, since he traveled to Galena, Illinois, in 1840 and is likely to have spent some time on board a steamboat. This conversation is given added interest by the suggestion that Noble was modeled on none other than Melville's sometime friend Nathaniel Hawthorne. For more information see Jonathan A. Cook, *Satirical Apocalypse: An Anatomy of Melville's* The Confidence-Man (Westport, Conn.: Greenwood, 1996).

"And now," said the stranger, cordially retaining his hand, "you know our fashion here at the West. It may be a little low, but it is kind. Briefly, we being newly-made friends must drink together. What say you?"

"Thank you; but indeed, you must excuse me."

"Why?"

"Because, to tell the truth, I have to-day met so many old friends, all free-hearted, convivial gentlemen, that really, really, though for the present I succeed in mastering it, I am at bottom almost in the condition of a sailor who, stepping ashore after a long voyage, ere night reels with loving welcomes, his head of less capacity than his heart."

At the allusion to old friends, the stranger's countenance a little fell, as a jealous lover's might at hearing from his sweetheart of former ones. But rallying, he said: "No doubt they treated you to something strong; but wine—surely, that gentle creature, wine; come, let us have a little gentle wine at one of these little tables here. Come, come." Then essaying to roll about like a full pipe in the sea, sang in a voice which had had more of good-fellowship, had there been less of a latent squeak to it:

> "Let us drink of the wine of the vine benign,
> That sparkles warm in Zausovine."

The cosmopolitan, with longing eye upon him, stood as sorely tempted and wavering a moment; then, abruptly stepping towards him, with a look of dissolved surrender, said: "When mermaid songs move figure-heads, then may glory, gold, and women try their blandishments on me. But a good fellow, singing a good song, he woos forth my every spike, so that my whole hull, like a ship's, sailing by a magnetic rock, caves in with acquiescence. Enough: when one has a heart of a certain sort, it is in vain trying to be resolute."

The wine, port, being called for, and the two seated at the little table, a natural pause of convivial expectancy ensued; the stranger's eye turned towards the bar near by, watching the red-cheeked, white-aproned man there, blithely dusting the bottle, and invitingly arranging the salver and glasses; when, with a sudden impulse turning round his head towards his companion, he said, "Ours is friendship at first sight, ain't it?"

"It is," was the placidly pleased reply: "and the same may be said of friendship at first sight as of love at first sight: it is the only true one, the only noble one. It bespeaks confidence. Who would go sounding his way into love or friendship, like a strange ship by night, into an enemy's harbor?"

"Right. Boldly in before the wind. Agreeable, how we always agree. By-the-way, though but a formality, friends should know each other's names. What is yours, pray?"

"Francis Goodman. But those who love me, call me Frank. And yours?"

"Charles Arnold Noble. But do you call me Charlie."

"I will, Charlie; nothing like preserving in manhood the fraternal familiarities of youth. It proves the heart a rosy boy to the last."

"My sentiments again. Ah!"

It was a smiling waiter, with the smiling bottle, the cork drawn; a common quart bottle, but for the occasion fitted at bottom into a little bark basket, braided with porcupine quills, gayly tinted in the Indian fashion.

[...]

"Oh, oh," taking a moderate sip, "but you, why don't you drink?"

"You have forgotten, my dear Charlie, what I told you of my previous con-vivialities to-day."

"Oh," cried the other, now in manner quite abandoned to the lyric mood, not without contrast to the easy sociability of his companion. "Oh, one can't drink too much of good old wine—the genuine, mellow old port. Pooh, pooh! drink away."

"Then keep me company."

"Of course," with a flourish, taking another sip,—"suppose we have cigars. Never mind your pipe there; a pipe is best when alone. I say, waiter, bring some cigars—your best."

They were brought in a pretty little bit of western pottery, representing some kind of Indian utensil, mummy-colored, set down in a mass of tobacco leaves, whose long, green fans, fancifully grouped, formed with peeps of red the sides of the receptacle. Accompanying it were two accessories, also bits of pottery, but smaller, both globes; one in guise of an apple flushed with red and gold to the life, and, through a cleft at top, you saw it was hollow. This was for the ashes. The other, gray, with wrinkled surface, in the likeness of a wasp's nest, was the match-box.

"There," said the stranger, pushing over the cigar-stand, "help yourself, and I will touch you off," taking a match. "Nothing like tobacco," he added, when the fumes of the cigar began to wreathe, glancing from the smoker to the pottery, "I will have a Virginia tobacco-plant set over my grave beside the Catawba vine."

"Improvement upon your first idea, which by itself was good—but you don't smoke."

"Presently, presently—let me fill your glass again. You don't drink."

"Thank you; but no more just now. Fill your glass."

"Presently, presently; do you drink on. Never mind me. Now that it strikes me, let me say, that he who, out of superfine gentility or fanatic morality, de-nies himself tobacco, suffers a more serious abatement in the cheap pleasures of life than the dandy in his iron boot, or the celibate on his iron cot. While for him who would fain revel in tobacco, but cannot, it is a thing at which philanthropists must weep, to see such an one, again and again, madly re-turning to the cigar, which, for his incompetent stomach, he cannot enjoy, while still, after each shameful repulse, the sweet dream of the impossible good goads him on to his fierce misery once more—poor eunuch!"

"I agree with you," said the cosmopolitan, still gravely social, "But you don't smoke."

"Presently, presently, do you smoke on. As I was saying about—"

"But why don't you smoke—come. You don't think that tobacco, when in league with wine, too much entrances the latter's vinous quality—in short, with certain constitutions tends to impair self-possession, do you?"

"To think that, were treason to good fellowship," was the warm disclaimer. "No, no. But the fact is, there is an unpropitious flavor in my mouth just now. Ate of a diabolical ragout at dinner, so I shan't smoke till I have washed away the lingering memento of it with wine. But smoke away, you, and pray, don't forget to drink."

[...]

"Well, this all along seems a division of labor," smiled the cosmopolitan. "I do about all the drinking, and you do about all—the genial. But yours is a nature competent to do that to a large population. And now, my friend," with a peculiarly grave air, evidently fore-shadowing something not unimportant, and very likely of close personal interest; "wine, you know, opens the heart, and—"

"Opens it!" with exultation, "it thaws it right out. Every heart is ice-bound till wine melt it, and reveal the tender grass and sweet herbage budding below, with every dear secret, hidden before like a dropped jewel in a snowbank, lying there unsuspected through winter till spring."

"And just in that way, my dear Charlie, is one of my little secrets now to be shown forth."

"Ah!" eagerly moving round his chair, "what is it?"

"Be not so impetuous, my dear Charlie. Let me explain. You see, naturally, I am a man not overgifted with assurance; in general, I am, if anything, diffidently reserved; so, if I shall presently seem otherwise, the reason is, that you, by the geniality you have evinced in all your talk, and especially the noble way in which, while affirming your good opinion of men, you intimated that you never could prove false to any man, but most by your indignation at a particularly illiberal passage in Polonius' advice—in short, in short," with extreme embarrassment, "how shall I express what I mean, unless I add that by your whole character you impel me to throw myself upon your nobleness; in one word, put confidence in you, a generous confidence?"

"I see, I see," with heightened interest, "something of moment you wish to confide. Now, what is it, Frank? Love affair?"

"No, not that."

"What, then, my dear Frank? Speak—depend upon me to the last. Out with it."

"Out it shall come, then," said the cosmopolitan "I am in want, urgent want, of money."

"In want of money!" pushing back his chair as from a suddenly-disclosed man-trap or crater.

"Yes," naïvely assented the cosmopolitan, "and you are going to loan me fifty dollars. I could almost wish I was in need of more, only for your sake. Yes, my dear Charlie, for your sake; that you might the better prove your noble kindliness, my dear Charlie."

"None of your dear Charlies," cried the other, springing to his feet, and buttoning up his coat, as if hastily to depart upon a long journey.

"Why, why, why?" painfully looking up.

"None of your why, why, whys!" tossing out a foot, "go to the devil, sir! Beggar, impostor!—never so deceived in a man in my life."

While speaking or rather hissing those words, the boon companion underwent much such a change as one reads of in fairy-books. Out of old materials sprang a new creature. Cadmus glided into the snake.

The cosmopolitan rose, the traces of previous feeling vanished; looked steadfastly at his transformed friend a moment, then, taking ten half-eagles from his pocket, stooped down, and laid them, one by one, in a circle round him; and, retiring a pace, waved his long tasselled pipe with the air of a necromancer, an air heightened by his costume, accompanying each wave with a solemn murmur of cabalistical words.

Meantime, he within the magic-ring stood suddenly rapt, exhibiting every symptom of a successful charm—a turned cheek, a fixed attitude, a frozen eye; spell-bound, not more by the waving wand than by the ten invincible talismans on the floor.

"Reappear, reappear, reappear, oh, my former friend! Replace this hideous apparition with thy blest shape, and be the token of thy return the words, 'My dear Frank.'"

"My dear Frank," now cried the restored friend, cordially stepping out of the ring, with regained self-possession regaining lost identity, "My dear Frank, what a funny man you are; full of fun as an egg of meat. How could you tell me that absurd story of your being in need? But I relish a good joke too well to spoil it by letting on. Of course, I humored the thing; and, on my side, put on all the cruel airs you would have me. Come, this little episode of fictitious estrangement will but enhance the delightful reality. Let us sit down again, and finish our bottle."

"With all my heart," said the cosmopolitan, dropping the necromancer with the same facility with which he had assumed it. "Yes," he added, soberly picking up the gold pieces, and returning them with a chink to his pocket, "yes, I am something of a funny man now and then; while for you, Charlie," eying him in tenderness, "what you say about your humoring the thing is true enough; never did man second a joke better than you did just now. You played your part better than I did mine; you played it, Charlie, to the life."

Gamblers and Slaves

"And you promised to give me my freedom!"

From *Clotel; or, The President's Daughter*

WILLIAM WELLS BROWN

As well as being one of the more prominent figures in the antislavery movement, William Wells Brown was also one of the most prolific. He published a wide range of volumes both before and after the Civil War, ranging from autobiography to history, travel writing, and drama. Perhaps most significant, and certainly most notorious, was one of his forays into fiction: *Clotel; or, The President's Daughter*, published in London in 1853. Now considered to be the first novel published by an African American, *Clotel* remains an extraordinary book. Its central conceit is an audacious one: it takes as its heroine the enslaved daughter of Thomas Jefferson and one of his slaves and then imagines her experiences of slavery. Ultimately, Clotel commits suicide to avoid being taken back into bondage. In the extract that follows, Brown gives a definitive telling of an oft-repeated theme of riverboat gambling stories: the slave put up as gambling collateral. Brown's account is given an extra sense of authenticity by his own experiences of slavery: before his escape, he worked as a steward on the steamboats of the western rivers. For further information, see Ann duCille, "Where in the World Is William Wells Brown? Thomas Jefferson, Sally Hemings, and the DNA of African-American Literary History," *American Literary History* 12.3 (Autumn 2000): 443–62. See also Robert S. Levine, ed., *Clotel; or, The President's Daughter* (Boston: Bedford/St Martin's, 2000).

At eight o'clock on the evening of the third day, the lights of another steamer were seen in the distance, and apparently coming up very fast. This was a signal for a general commotion on the *Patriot,* and everything indicated that a steamboat race was at hand. Nothing can exceed the excitement attendant upon a steamboat on the Mississippi river. By the time the boats had reached Memphis, they were side by side, and each exerting itself to keep the ascendancy in point of speed. The night was clear, the moon shining brightly, and the boats so near to each other that the passengers were calling out from one boat to the other. On board the *Patriot,* the firemen were using oil, lard, butter, and even bacon, with the wood, for the purpose of raising the steam to its highest pitch. The blaze, mingled with the black smoke, showed plainly that the other boat was burning more than wood. The two boats soon locked, so that the hands of the boats were passing from vessel to vessel, and the wildest excitement prevailed throughout amongst both passengers and crew. At this moment the engineer of the *Patriot* was seen to fasten down the safety-valve, so that no steam should escape. This was, indeed, a dangerous resort. A few of the boat hands who saw what had taken place, left that end of the boat for more secure quarters.

The *Patriot* stopped to take in passengers, and still no steam was permitted to escape. At the starting of the boat cold water was forced into the boilers by the machinery, and, as might have been expected, one of the boilers immediately exploded. One dense fog of steam filled every part of the vessel, while shrieks, groans, and cries were heard on every hand. The saloons and cabins soon had the appearance of a hospital. By this time the boat had landed, and the *Columbia*, the other boat, had come alongside to render assistance to the disabled steamer. The killed and scalded (nineteen in number) were put on shore, and the *Patriot*, taken in tow by the *Columbia*, was soon again on its way.

It was now twelve o'clock at night, and instead of the passengers being asleep the majority were gambling in the saloons. Thousands of dollars change hand during a passage from Louisville or St. Louis to New Orleans on a Mississippi steamer, and many men, and even ladies, are completely ruined. "Go call my boy, steward," said Mr. Smith, as he took his cards one by one from the table. In a few moments a fine looking, brighteyed mulatto boy, apparently about fifteen years of age, was standing by his master's side at the table. "I will see you, and five hundred dollars better," said Smith, as his servant Jerry approached the table. "What price do you set on that boy?" asked Johnson, as he took a roll of bills from his pocket. "He will bring a thousand dollars, any day, in the New Orleans market," replied Smith. "Then you bet the whole of the boy, do you?" "Yes." "I call you, then," said Johnson, at the same time spreading his cards out upon the table. "You have beat me," said Smith, as soon as he saw the cards. Jerry, who was standing on top of the table, with the bank notes and silver dollars round his feet, was now ordered to descend from the table. "You will not forget that you belong to me," said Johnson, as the young slave was stepping from the table to a chair. "No, sir," replied the chattel. "Now go back to your bed, and be up in time to-morrow morning to brush my clothes and clean my boots, do you hear?" "Yes, sir," responded Jerry, as he wiped the tears from his eyes.

Smith took from his pocket the bill of sale and handed it to Johnson; at the same time saying, "I claim the right of redeeming that boy, Mr. Johnson. My father gave him to me when I came of age, and I promised not to part with him." "Most certainly, sir, the boy shall be yours, whenever you hand me over a cool thousand," replied Johnson. The next morning, as the passengers were assembling in the breakfast saloons and upon the guards of the vessel, and the servants were seen running about waiting upon or looking for their masters, poor Jerry was entering his new master's state-room with his boots. "Who do you belong to?" said a gentleman to an old black man, who came along leading a fine dog that he had been feeding. "When I went to sleep last night, I belonged to Governor Lucas; but I understand dat he is bin gambling all night, so I don't know who owns me dis morning." Such is the uncertainty of a slave's position. He goes to bed at night the property of the man with whom he has lived for years, and gets up in the morning the slave of some one whom he has never seen before! To behold five or six tables in a steamboat's cabin, with half-a-dozen men playing at cards, and money, pistols, bowie-knives, &c. all in confusion on the tables, is what may be seen at almost any time on the Mississippi river.

[. . .]

On the arrival of the boat at Baton Rouge, an additional number of passengers were taken on board; and, amongst them, several persons who had been attending the races. Gambling and drinking were now the order of the day. Just as the ladies and gentlemen were assembling at the supper-table, the report of a pistol was heard in the direction of the Social Hall, which caused great uneasiness to the ladies, and took the gentlemen to that part of the cabin. However, nothing serious had occurred. A man at one of the tables where they were gambling had been seen attempting to conceal a card in his sleeve, and one of the party seized his pistol and fired; but fortunately the barrel of the pistol was knocked up, just as it was about to be discharged, and the ball passed through the upper deck, instead of the man's head, as intended. Order was soon restored; all went on well the remainder of the night, and the next day, at ten o'clock, the boat arrived at New Orleans, and the passengers went to the hotels and the slaves to the market!

From *Narrative of the Life and Adventures of Henry Bibb*

HENRY BIBB

Henry Bibb was a notable figure in the antislavery movement. Even before he published the story of his escape from slavery, he was well known as an abolitionist orator. His *Narrative* remains one of the most remarkable slave autobiographies, not least because of the centrality of Bibb's wife and child to his account. He experiences a variety of hardships in his numerous (and ultimately unsuccessful) attempts to free them from slavery, including the incidents found in the following account of his time with a group of gamblers who become sympathetic to his plight. Bibb's portrait of these "Southern sportsmen" is unlike anything else to be found in nineteenth-century literature. In 1850, Bibb left America for Canada. There, he founded an antislavery newspaper, *The Voice of the Fugitive,* in which he advocated emigration to Canada for all black Americans. The most thorough analysis of Bibb's narrative can be found in Charles H. Heglar, *Rethinking the Slave Narrative: Slave Marriage and the Narratives of Henry Bibb and William and Ellen Craft* (Westport, Conn.: Greenwood, 2001). See also Roger W. Hite, "Voice of a Fugitive: Henry Bibb and Ante-bellum Black Separatism," *Journal of Black Studies* 4.3 (March 1974): 269–84.

The reader will remember that this brings me back to the time the Deacon had ordered me to be kept in confinement until he got a chance to sell me, and that no negro should ever get away from him and live. Some days after this we were all out at the gin house ginning cotton, which was situated on the road side, and there came along a company of men, fifteen or twenty in number, who were Southern sportsmen. Their attention was attracted by the load of iron which was fastened about my neck with a bell attached. They stopped and asked the Deacon what that bell was put on my neck for? and he said it was to keep me from running away, &c.

They remarked that I looked as if I might be a smart negro, and asked if he wanted to sell me. The reply was, yes. They then got off their horses and struck a bargain with him for me. They bought me at a reduced price for speculation.

After they had purchased me, I asked the privilege of going to the house to take leave of my family before I left, which was granted by the sportsmen.

But the Deacon said I should never again step my foot inside of his yard; and advised the sportsmen not to take the irons from my neck until they had sold me; that if they gave me the least chance I would run away from them, as I did from him. So I was compelled to mount a horse and go off with them as I supposed, never again to meet my family in this life.

We had not proceeded far before they informed me that they had bought me to sell again, and if they kept the irons on me it would be detrimental to the sale, and that they would therefore take off the irons and dress me up like a man, and throw away the old rubbish which I then had on; and they would sell me to some one who would treat me better than Deacon Whitfield. After they had cut off the irons and dressed me up, they crossed over Red River into Texas, where they spent some time horse racing and gambling; and although they were wicked black legs of the basest character, it is but due to them to say, that they used me far better than ever the Deacon did. They gave me plenty to eat and put nothing hard on me to do. They expressed much sympathy for me in my bereavement; and almost every day they gave me money more or less, and by my activity in waiting on them, and upright conduct, I got into the good graces of them all, but they could not get any person to buy me on account of the amount of intelligence which they supposed me to have; for many of them thought that I could read and write. When they left Texas, they intended to go to the Indian Territory west of the Mississippi, to attend a great horse race which was to take place. Not being much out of their way to go past Deacon Whitfield's again, I prevailed on them to call on him for the purpose of trying to purchase my wife and child; and I promised them that if they would buy my wife and child, I would get some person to purchase us from them. So they tried to grant my request by calling on the Deacon, and trying to make the purchase. As we approached the Deacon's plantation, my heart was filled with a thousand painful and fearful apprehensions. I had the fullest confidence in the blacklegs with whom I travelled, believing that they would do according to promise, and go to the fullest extent of their ability to restore peace and consolation to a bereaved family—to re-unite husband and wife, parent and child, who had long been severed by slavery through the agency of Deacon Whitfield. But I knew his determination in relation to myself, and I feared his wicked opposition to a restoration of myself and little family, which he had divided, and soon found that my fears were not without foundation.

When we rode up and walked into his yard, the Deacon came out and spoke to all but myself; and not finding me in tattered rags as a substitute for clothes, nor having an iron collar bell about my neck, as was the case when he sold me, he appeared to be much displeased.

"What did you bring that negro back here for?" said he.

"We have come to try to buy his wife and child; for we can find no one who is willing to buy him alone; and we will either buy or sell so that the family may be together," said they.

While this conversation was going on, my poor bereaved wife, who never expected to see me again in this life, spied me and came rushing to me through the crowd, throwing her arms about my neck exclaiming in the most sympathetic tones, "Oh! my dear husband! I never expected to see you again!" The poor woman was bathed with tears of sorrow and grief. But no sooner had she reached me, than the Deacon peremptorily commanded her to go to her work. This she did not obey, but prayed that her master would not separate us again, as she was there alone, far from friends and relations whom she should never meet again. And now to take away her husband, her last and only true friend, would be like taking her life!

But such appeals made no impression on the unfeeling Deacon's heart. While he was storming with abusive language, and even using the gory lash with hellish vengeance to separate husband and wife, I could see the sympathetic tear-drop, stealing its way down the cheek of the profligate and blackleg, whose object it now was to bind up the broken heart of a wife and restore to the arms of a bereaved husband, his companion.

They were disgusted at the conduct of Whitfield and cried out shame, even in his presence. They told him that they would give a thousand dollars for my wife and child, or any thing in reason. But no! he would sooner see me to the devil than indulge or gratify me after my having run away from him; and if they did not remove me from his presence very soon, he said he should make them suffer for it.

But all this, and even the gory lash had yet failed to break the grasp of poor Malinda, whose prospect of connubial, social, and future happiness was all at stake. When the dear woman saw there was no help for us, and that we should soon be separated forever, in the name of Deacon Whitfield, and American slavery to meet no more as husband and wife, parent and child—the last and loudest appeal was made on our knees. We appealed to the God of justice and to the sacred ties of humanity; but this was all in vain. The louder we prayed the harder he whipped, amid the most heart-rending shrieks from the poor slave mother and child, as little Frances stood by, sobbing at the abuse inflicted on her mother.

"Oh! how shall I give my husband the parting hand never to meet again? This will surely break my heart," were her parting words.

I can never describe to the reader the awful reality of that separation—for it was enough to chill the blood and stir up the deepest feeling of revenge in the hearts of slaveholding black-legs, who as they stood by, were threatening, some weeping, some swearing and others declaring vengeance against such treatment being inflicted on a human being. As we left the plantation, as far as we could see and hear, the Deacon was still laying on the gory lash, trying to prevent poor Malinda from weeping over the loss of her departed husband, who was then, by the hellish laws of slavery, to her, theoretically and practically dead. One of the black-legs exclaimed that hell was full of just such Deacons as Whitfield. This occurred in December, 1840. I have never seen Malinda, since that period. I never expect to see her again.

The sportsmen to whom I was sold, showed their sympathy for me not only by word but by deeds. They said that they had made the most liberal offer to Whitfield, to buy or sell for the sole purpose of reuniting husband and wife. But he stood out against it—they felt sorry for me. They said they had bought me to speculate on, and were not able to lose what they had paid for me. But they would make a bargain with me, if I was willing, and would lay a plan, by which I might yet get free. If I would use my influence so as to get some person to buy me while traveling about with them, they would give me a portion of the money for which they sold me, and they would also give me directions by which I might yet run away and go to Canada.

This offer I accepted, and the plot was made. They advised me to act very stupid in language and thought, but in business I must be spry; and that I must persuade men to buy me, and promise them that I would be smart.

We passed through the State of Arkansas and stopped at many places, horse-racing and gambling. My business was to drive a wagon in which they carried their gambling apparatus, clothing, &c. I had also to black boots and attend to horses. We stopped at Fayettville, where they almost lost me, betting on a horse race.

They went from thence to the Indian Territory, among the Cherokee Indians, to attend the great races which were to take place there. During the races there was a very wealthy half Indian of that tribe, who became much attached to me, and had some notion of buying me, after hearing that I was for sale, being a slaveholder. The idea struck me rather favorable, for several reasons. First, I thought I should stand a better chance to get away from an Indian than from a white man. Second, he wanted me only for a kind of a body servant to wait on him—and in this case I knew that I should fare better than I should in the field. And my owners also told me that it would be an easy place to get away from. I took their advice for fear I might not get another chance so good as that, and prevailed on the man to buy me. He paid them nine hundred dollars, in gold and silver, for me. I saw the money counted out.

After the purchase was made, the sportsmen got me off to one side, and according to promise they gave me a part of the money, and directions how to get from there to Canada. They also advised me how to act until I got a good chance to run away. I was to embrace the earliest opportunity of getting away, before they should become acquainted with me. I was never to let it be known where I was from, nor where I was born. I was to act quite stupid and ignorant. And when I started I was to go up the boundary line, between the Indian Territory and the States of Arkansas and Missouri, and this would fetch me out on the Missouri river, near Jefferson city, the capital of Missouri. I was to travel at first by night, and to lay by in daylight, until I got out of danger.

From *The White Slave; or, Memoirs of a Fugitive*

RICHARD HILDRETH

Though best known in his day for his many volumes of American history, Richard Hildreth was also the author of what is held to be the first anti-slavery novel published in America. *The Slave; or, Memoirs of Archy Moore* was first published in 1836, long before the flood of abolitionist novels that would follow the publication of *Uncle Tom's Cabin* (1852). In later life, William Dean Howells remembered that the novel "left an indelible impression [. . .] still so deep that after a lapse of nearly forty years since I saw the book, I have no misgivings in speaking of it as a powerful piece of realism" (*Literary Friends and Acquaintance,* 85). In the wake of Stowe's novel, Hildreth released a new, extended version of his pioneering story as *The White Slave; or, Memoirs of a Fugitive* in 1852. The 1836 edition closes with Archy Moore, having escaped to England, resolving to return to the South to liberate his wife and child from slavery; the 1852 edition describes that successful rescue mission. The following extract is taken from the 1852 edition. During his adventures in the South, Archy strikes up a friendship with gambler John Colter and experiences the aftermath of the Vicksburg lynchings. For more on Hildreth, see Donald E. Emerson, *Richard Hildreth* (Baltimore: Johns Hopkins Press, 1946). For more on his novel and its influence, see Evan Brandstadter, "Uncle Tom and Archy Moore: The Antislavery Novel as Ideological Symbol," *American Quarterly* 26.2 (May 1974): 160–75.

The stage coach stopped for dinner at a dirty, uncomfortable tavern, the management of which seemed to be altogether in the hands of the slaves, of whom there was a great superabundance, the landlord being a sort of gentleman guest in his own house. The head servant of the establishment, a large, portly, soft-spoken mulatto, but very shabbily and dirtily dressed, seemed, for some reason or other,—perhaps from my politeness to him,—to take quite a fancy to me. After dinner he called me aside, and inquired if I was acquainted with the gentleman who had sat opposite to me at the table. This was the supposed planter, my stage companion, in his younger days, as he had informed us, clerk and bookkeeper, and afterwards partner of Gouge and McGrab.

"No," I answered, "I did not know him except as my fellow-traveller from Charleston; I should like very well to know his name."

"As to his name," said my mulatto friend, "it would not be so easy to tell that. He goes by a good many names. Most every time he comes this way he has a new one. Have a care of him, master; he's a gambler. I thought I'd tell you, lest you might get cheated by him."

As this information seemed to come from pure good will on the part of my informant, I had no reason to distrust its correctness. I knew very well that gambling was not only practised in these southern slave states, as it is in the overgrown capitals of Europe, as a means of relieving the ennui of idleness, but that here, as there, a regular class of professional gamblers had sprung into existence, who lived by fleecing the unskilful and unwary. It was by no means unusual for members of that fraternity to have all the external marks of gentlemen; nor was there any improbability in the suggestion that my new acquaintance belonged to it.

Though he had inclined to differ, in the course of the morning, from our two northern companions on some questions of politics and morality, I could not but admire the grace and art with which he contrived, in the course of the afternoon, to worm himself into their confidence. When the stage coach stopped, for the night, at another tavern still more dirty, un-comfortable, and every way untidy,—if that could well be,—than the one at which we had dined, he proposed, after supper, a game of cards by way of whiling away the time. The other two were ready enough for it, and the three were soon busy at the game, in which they were joined by one or two plant-ers of the vicinity, who happened to be lounging about the house. For myself, I positively declined to join them, declaring that I never touched a card, and never played at any game for money; and perceiving from my manner that I was quite inflexible on that point, the alleged gambler remarked, with some significance, that I had taken a very wise and safe resolution for a stranger travelling through the southern states.

After watching the game for some time, I retired to bed; and rising pretty early the next morning, since the journey was to be renewed at five o'clock, I found them still at it: the two northern dupes haggard with want of sleep, and their very lengthened faces, distorted with ill-suppressed anxiety and suffering, seeming to have grown ten years older in that single night. They bore, in fact, but a distant resemblance to the two spruce, sleek gentlemen with whom I had ridden the day before. The other seemed as fresh and self-possessed as at the moment he had sat down; and as I entered the room, he took up and pocketed, with a graceful nonchalance that was quite admirable, the last stakes, and as it proved, too, the last money of his two companions.

Having sat down, as I afterwards learned, with only ten dollars in his pocket, as his whole means and stock in trade, he had made a good night of it. In the morning he had not less than two thousand, besides a fine mulatto boy of fifteen or sixteen, whom one of the planters had made over to him by way of squaring accounts.

Finding our two companions quite drained, he insisted upon paying their tavern bills himself, and upon lending each of them fifty dollars, as a fund to go upon till they could obtain further remittances; and this he did with as unconscious an air of sympathy and commiseration as if they had lost their money by some accident, instead of his having himself been the agent of their loss, by means not merely of his superior coolness and skill, but probably, also, by some other tricks of his profession. Not the master, who tosses a dollar to his slave by way of Christmas present, could do it with a greater air of generosity.

It was curious to remark the crestfallen air of the Boston cotton broker and the New York editor, after the loss of their money. The day before, they had held up their heads; they had had their opinions, and pretty positive ones too; nor had they been at all slow or modest in asserting them. To-day they seemed quite sunk into nobodies, the stiffening all taken out of them, moody and silent, with nothing to say about any thing, eyeing the person to whom their money had been transferred, and to whom, the day before, they had paid such court as a rich planter, with a singular mixture of dislike and terror, much like that with which I had often seen an unfortunate slave eye a master whom he feared and hated, but from whom he felt it impossible to escape.

Indeed, I could not but think, that strip those two northern gentlemen of their fine clothes, and set them up in their present crestfallen and disconsolate condition on the auction block of Messrs Gouge and McGrab, or some other slave dealers, especially with the cool, keen eye of their late depredator upon them, and they might very easily have passed muster, as two "white niggers," born and bred in servitude, and stupid fellows at that, easily to be kept in order, and from whom very little mischief or trouble need be apprehended.

Finding these two disconsolate individuals sad, solemn, and as dry as a squeezed lemon, and quite insensible to all his efforts to amuse them, the gambler, whose victims they had become, directed his conversation to me. I cannot say but that I decidedly enjoyed their predicament. "O, my fine fellows," said I to myself, "you now have a little experience what a nice thing it is, this being stripped and plundered! You think it mighty hard to part with a few hundred dollars, the earnings, by means I don't know how particularly honest, of perhaps only a few weeks—money lost, too, not less by your own consenting folly, than by the skill and tricks of a man more knowing and adroit than yourselves. Now learn to sympathize a little with multitudes of poor fellows in natural gifts and endowments not so very much, if at all, your inferiors—some of them, indeed, vastly your superiors,—regularly stripped and plundered, minute by minute, hour by hour, day by day, week by week, month by month, year by year, through a whole lifetime; and that, too, by pure fraud and force, without any consenting folly on their part; plundered, too, not only of the earnings of their hands, but, it may be, of the very wives of their affections, and children of their love, sent off to a slave auction, to suit the convenience, or to meet the necessities, of the men that call themselves their owners; and with just about as much right and title of ownership as this gambler has in you—the right of the weak over the strong, and of the crafty over the simple!"

As the late clerk, bookkeeper, and partner of Gouge and McGrab, now, as it seemed, professional blackleg and gambler, might be able, from his former connection with that respectable slave trading firm, to afford me information essential to the search in which I was engaged, I received his advances very graciously. In fact the manliness of sentiment which he had evinced the day before in the defence of his favorite candidate for the vice-presidency had inclined me in his favor; and as to his present pursuits, I was disposed to think them quite as honest and respectable as the slave trading business in which he had formerly been engaged, or as the slave breeding business by which so many southern gentlemen of unquestioned respectability gained at least a part of their livelihood.

I found him, indeed, a very agreeable companion, free, in a great measure, from those local provincialisms and narrownesses almost universal among even the best educated and most liberal-minded Americans—keen in his observations, acute in his judgments, (a vein of sly satire running through his conversation,) but good natured rather than bitter.

Such was the beginning of a companionship which gradually ripened into something of a confidential intimacy. I did not conceal from Mr John Colter (for that was the name by which he chose to be known to me) my knowledge of his rather dubious profession; at the same time, I was willing to accept, at their full value, his graces, talents, agreeable parts, and the frequent indications which he gave, at least in words, of a naturally generous and kindly disposition. Why not make allowance for his position and circumstances? Why not regard him with as much charity as is asked generally for slaveholders?

As if to confirm me in this toleration, by which he was evidently not a little flattered, and to which he did not seem much accustomed, in the course of a second night's stoppage, in a ramble by moonlight, Mr Colter having at hand no more pigeons to pluck, let me pretty fully into his history.

It appeared that he was the son of a wealthy planter, or of one who had once been wealthy, and who, while he lived, had maintained the reputation of being so. He had, of course, been brought up in habits of great profusion and extravagance. His literary instruction had not been neglected, and he had been sent to travel a year or two in Europe, where he spent a great deal of money, and fell into very dissipated habits, and whence he was recalled by the death of his father, whose estate, when it came to be settled, proved insolvent, the plantations and slaves being covered by mortgages, and a large family of children left wholly unprovided for.

Thus thrown entirely on his own resources, he had great difficulty in finding means to live. The general resource of decayed families was to emigrate to the new lands of the west; but this was hardly possible, unless one could take a few slaves with him, and he had none, nor the means of procuring any, his character for profusion and extravagance being too well established for any of his father's old friends to be willing to trust him. Indeed, since the estate had turned out insolvent, it was curious to remark, notwithstanding his father's numerous acquaintance, and the ostentatious hospitality with which for so many years he had kept open doors, how very few friends the family had.

Being a good scholar, he might have found occupation as tutor in some family; but this was looked upon as a servile position, incompatible with the dignity of a southerner, and only fit to be filled by fellows from the north. "The Romans, you know,"—so he remarked to me,—"intrusted the education of their children to slave pedagogues; we generally get ours from New England." As to going into mercantile business, that would require capital; and that business, too, was mostly engrossed by adventurers from the north, who generally procured their clerks and assistants from the same quarter.

At length, unable to do any better, he had obtained employment from the rich slave trading firm of Gouge and McGrab, rising presently to be their first clerk and bookkeeper, and being finally admitted as a partner.

But this kind of business he had found objectionable on several accounts. In the first place, it was not considered respectable, though on what grounds he was puzzled to tell. He could well understand how I, an Englishman, and even how one of these Yankee fellows—if it were possible to find one, which might be doubted, with courage enough to say that his soul was his own—might find something objectionable in this business of trading in human muscles and sinews, buying and selling men, women, and children, at auction or otherwise. For himself, he did not pretend to any great piety or morality, he left that to the other members of the firm. McGrab was not actually a Methodist, but his wife and children were devoutly so, and as the old man himself frequently attended their meetings, the Methodists expected to get him, too, at last. Gouge was a very devout Baptist, who had been regularly converted and dipped, and had built a church at Augusta, almost entirely at his own expense; but with all his piety he had never been able to see any harm in the business, buying and selling fellow church members with as little scruple as the mere unconverted heathen. Indeed, Gouge thought slavery and slave-trading a very good thing every way, not only in the concrete, but in the abstract also. Didn't St. Paul say, "Slaves, obey your masters?" And didn't that settle the question that some were to be slaves, and some were to be masters, and that the slaves had nothing to do but to obey? Such was the way that Gouge reasoned, putting the matter with wonderful force and unction ; so much so, that once—when on a visit to New York in search of three or four prime house-servants, who had been purchased in Baltimore, but had broken prison the night after, and whom Gouge had traced to that city—falling into an argument on the subject at the hotel where he was stopping, and having a very grave address and clerical aspect, he had been mistaken by a clergyman, who happened to be present, for a D.D., and had been invited to preach on the divine origin of slavery, in one of the most fashionable churches of that city.

"Still," said Colter, "in spite of the reasoning and the texts of my pious partner, I never have been able to approve either of slavery or the slave trade in the abstract. What, indeed, could be more contemptible, than for a parcel of intelligent and able-bodied white folks to employ their whole time, pains, and ingenuity, in partly forcing, partly teasing, and partly coaxing a set of reluctant, unwilling negroes into half-doing, in the most slovenly, slouchy, deceptive, and unprofitable manner, what those same white people might do fifty times better, and with fifty times less care and trouble, for themselves ? Viewed thus in the abstract, the whole system, I must say, seems to me a very pitiful affair. [. . .]

"Thus ousted from the slave trading business, it became necessary for me to find some other occupation; but that was not so easy. The occupations that a southern gentleman can adopt without degradation, are very few indeed. My manners, address, the good songs I could sing, and good stories I could tell, had made me rather a favorite in society; and as I never drank, and understood a thing or two about cards and dice, billiards and faro tables, I was able to replenish my pockets in that way; and finally, for want of a better, that became my regular profession."

"And," said I, wishing to pay him off a little for his late tantalizings, "is this one of those few occupations which a southern gentleman can adopt without degradation?"

"The gentility of gambling can't be denied," he said, "since it is very freely practised by the larger part of southern gentlemen. Once in a while the legislatures are seized with a fit of penitence or virtue, and pass laws to break it up; but nobody ever thinks of paying any attention to those laws, or attempting to enforce them, except, now and then, some poor plucked pigeon, who undertakes to revenge himself in that way. But though gambling is just as genteel as slaveholding, some how or other, by an inconsistency like that in the case of the slave traders, we who make a profession of it, though we associate constantly with gentlemen, are not, I must confess, reckoned to belong precisely to that class, except, indeed, we get money enough to buy a plantation and retire."

"It is charged," said I, "upon those of your profession, that, not content with the fair chances of the game, you contrive to take undue advantages."

"Yes; and so do half of the gentlemen players, as far as they know how, and have the opportunity. There is always a tendency, in games of chance, to run a little into games of skill. Suppose we do plunder the planters—don't they live by plundering the negroes? What right have they to complain? Isn't sauce for the goose sauce for the gander? I tell you our whole system here is a system of plunder from beginning to end. 'Tis only the slaves, and some of the poor whites who own no slaves, who can be said to earn an honest living. The planters live on the plunder of the slaves, whom they force to labor for them. The slaves steal all they can from the planters, and a good many of the poor whites connive at and help them in it. A parcel of bloodsucking Yankee pedlers and New York agents overrun our country, and carry off their share of the spoils; and we who have cool heads and dexterous hands enough to overreach the whole set, planters, Yankees, and New Yorkers—we stand, for aught I see, upon just as sound a moral basis as the rest of them. Every thing belongs to the strong, the wise, and the cunning; that is the foundation stone of our southern system of society. The living upon the plunder of others is one of the organic sins of this community; and the doctrine, I believe, has been advanced by a celebrated northern divine, that for the organic sins of a community, nobody is individually responsible. Now, if this good-natured sort of doctrine, which, for my part, I don't find any fault with, is going to save the souls and the characters of Gouge and McGrab, or of the planters who patronize and support them, shan't we professional gentlemen also have the benefit of it?"

It was not very difficult to discover under the volubility and vivacity, a little forced, of this philosophical blackleg, into whose intimacy I had been so suddenly introduced, a deep-seated and bitter chagrin, and even shame, at living as he did; however he might urge, by way of apology, that it was only one of the applications of the fundamental principle of every slaveholding community. This, indeed, was an idea upon which he seemed to pride himself, and upon which he dwelt with a good deal of pertinacious ingenuity. To gain a living by the plunder of the weak and simple, was, he admitted, in the abstract, not to be defended. Yet, if he did not do it, somebody else would. His abstinence would not save them. The weak and simple were destined to be plundered; and plundered they would be by somebody. Bred up as he had been to extravagant habits, could he be expected to renounce an employment—liable indeed to some fluctuations and uncertainties, as well as to some moral objections, but, on the whole, one that paid—and to run the risk of starving, just to gratify his conscientious scruples? He trusted, he said, that, though a professional gambler, he had a conscience. His quarrel with Gouge and McGrab, and his abandonment of the slave trading business, at which he might have made a fortune, was, he thought, evidence enough of that. But there was a limit to all things. A man must live, and live by such means, too, as his position and gifts allow him to adopt; and, all things considered, he did not see that he could be expected to give up his profession any more than the slaveholders their slaves. Nor can I say that I did, either.

On the whole, besides the necessity I was under of using him, and the additional information he might give me, in the search in which I was engaged, there was something in his straightforward, downright way of looking at things, as well as in his lively conversation and agreeable manners, which rather pleased me.

I therefore proceeded to make a return of his confidence, at which he seemed to be a good deal flattered. Complimenting his sagacity, I admitted my intimacy with a female slave, many years ago, whom, from his description of her, and the circumstances he had mentioned, I believed to be the very one whom McGrab had purchased in North Carolina, and whom he had sold to the Mississippi planter; and I added, that I believed her boy to be my child. What was the name of the planter, and could he aid me any further in finding them out?

"And suppose you find them," he asked, "what do you intend to do?"

"Buy them," I answered, "if I can, and set them free."

"Better think twice," he replied, "before you set out on any such adventure. Time, you know, makes changes. You can't expect to get back the young girl you left in North Carolina. O, the deceitful baggage! Didn't she tell me, with tears streaming down those great black eyes of hers, and such an air of truth that I couldn't help believing her, that she had a husband, the only man she had ever known any thing about, who was the father of her child, and who had been carried off by the slave traders a year or two before, and whom she expected yet to meet, by some good providence, some where in the south! Don't flatter yourself with the idea of any constancy to you. Even had she wished it, it could hardly have been in her power. Like as not you will find her, if at all, grown as plump as a beer barrel, housekeeper, and something else besides, to her master; or may be, by this time, cook or washerwoman, and the mother, as Gouge said she might be, of a dozen additional children, and perhaps with an agreeable variety of complexions; though, for that matter, slave women of her color are in general mighty squeamish and particular—quite as much so as the white women—as to any connection with men of a darker hue than themselves."

Painful to me as these suggestions were, I could not but admit their high degree of probability. To what might not twenty years of servitude have reduced the wife of my heart! To what humiliations, dishonors, miserable degradations, corrupting connections might she not have been subjected, tempting as she was by her innocence, beauty, and gentleness, and exposed—without the least shield of law, religion, or public opinion—to the unbridled appetite, I do not say of any lecherous debauchee, but of any polygamous patriarch, amorous youth, or luxurious respectability who might have the fancy or the means to purchase her!

It made my heart grow sick and my brain spin to think of it.

"And then the boy," continued my tormenter. "If you had him as I saw him,—a bright little fellow, just able to speak, full of life and joy, and unable to understand what made his mother cry so,—you might hope to make something of him. He was a child such as nobody need be ashamed of. But what do you suppose he is by this time, with the benefit of a slave education? If, my dear sir, you intended to act the father by him, or the friend by her, you should not have left them all this time in slavery."

I hastened to explain, in general terms, that my leaving them as they were was, at the time of my separation from them, a thing entirely beyond my control—it was not in my power to do otherwise; but that, so soon as I became possessed of the means, I had made every effort to discover and to purchase them; that I had traced them to Augusta, where all clew to them had been lost; but that the clew which he had so unexpectedly and accidentally put into my hands had recalled all the past, and, as I was unmarried, childless, and with nothing else in particular to occupy my thoughts, had inspired me with fresh desire to find them out, and, if possible, to make them free.

"Quite a romantic fellow, I see," rejoined my companion; "quite another Dick Johnson. True enough, the idea is not very agreeable of having one's children kicked, cuffed, and lashed through the world at the discretion of brutal overseers, peevish mistresses, or drunken, cross-grained masters, with no possible opening to rise if they would, and with no chance before them but to propagate a race of slaves. I dare say it seems so to you, with your English education, and especially as you have not any lawful children for your affections to fix upon. But here we don't mind it. A man is expected to sacrifice his own private paternal feelings, if he has any, for the good of the class to which he belongs. I dare say, in the course of time, the only representatives of many of our most distinguished southern statesmen and wealthiest families will be found among their slave descendants.

"The Mississippi planter, to whom the girl and her child were sold, was named Thomas. I have seen him several times since in my travels. Indeed, some handsome sums of money have before now passed from his pocket to mine. He still lives, or did lately, at no great distance from Vicksburg. I have friends in that town to whom I will give you letters, and by whose assistance you can find him out. Perhaps your girl and her boy are still living in his family."

[...]

As I entered the town of Vicksburg, an appalling prospect met my eyes: five men hanging by the neck, just swung off, as it would seem, from an extempore gallows, and struggling in the agonies of death; a military company drawn up in arms; a band of black musicians playing Yankee Doodle; a crowd of bystanders, of all ages and colors, apparently in the greatest state of excitement; and a frantic woman, with a young child in either hand, addressing herself, with vehement gesticulations, to a man who seemed to have the direction of the proceedings, and whom I took—though I did not perceive that he wore any official dress or badge—to be the high sheriff of the county.

On reaching the hotel, I learnt, however, to my great astonishment, that this was no regular execution by process of law, but entirely an amateur performance, got up by a committee of citizens, headed by the cashier of the Planters' Bank,—one of those institutions whose bonds are not unknown in England, though I believe they bear no particular price at the present moment,—the very person, in fact, whom, from the office he had assumed, I had supposed to be the high sheriff. I learnt all this with astonishment, because the victims had appeared to be white men. Had they been black or colored, their being hung in some paroxysm of popular passion or fear would not in the least have surprised me.

Inquiring a little further into the history of this singular proceeding, I was told that the men who had been hung were gamblers, part of a gang of cheats and desperadoes by whom that town had long been infested; that the citizens, determined to tolerate such a nuisance no longer, had ordered them to depart, and, when they refused to do so, had proceeded to force their houses and destroy their gambling tools—an operation which the gamblers resisted by force, firing upon their assailants, and having actually shot dead a leading and very estimable citizen, in the act of forcing his way into one of the houses.

The gamblers, however, had all been taken, except two or three, who had managed to escape. The blood of the company was up. The sight of their slaughtered leader, copious draughts of brandy, the recollection of their own losses at the gaming table, and the dread of being challenged and shot, or shot without being challenged by the gamblers, two or three of whom were known as very desperate fellows,—all these motives coöperating, and it being very doubtful whether, if the matter was referred to the legal tribunals, those who had riotously broken into the houses of other people, even with the professed object of destroying roulette tables, might not run quite as much risk of condemnation as those who had fired, even with fatal effect, upon their burglarious assailants,—all these things considered, it had finally been determined, as the shortest and most expedient method of settling the business, to take the gamblers to the skirts of the town, and to hang them there on the instant.

To those, indeed, accustomed to the curt proceedings of the slave code, under which suspicion serves for evidence, and power usurps the place of judicial discrimination, all the delays and formalities of the ordinary administration of penal jurisprudence must seem tedious and absurd; and hence the constantly increasing tendency in the south to substitute, in the place of that administration, in the case of white men as well as of slaves, the summary process of Lynch law. It is vain, indeed, to expect that men constantly hardened and brutalized in the struggle to extort from their slaves the utmost driblet of unwilling labor, and accustomed freely to indulge, as against these unresisting victims, every caprice of brutal fury, should retain any very delicate sense of the proprieties of justice as among themselves.

Before I had yet learnt more than a general outline of the story, the principal actors in this affair, finding it necessary to sustain their dignity and to recruit their self-reliance by fresh draughts of brandy, reached the hotel at which I was stopping. They were followed by the woman, with the two little children, whom I had noticed as I passed the place of execution, and whom I now found to be the wife of one of the victims. It was in vain that she besought permission to take down and to bury the body of her husband. This was denied, with brutal threats that any person who dared to cut them down till they had hung there twenty-four hours, by way of example, should be made to share their fate. Such, indeed, was the passionate fury of the multitude, that the poor woman, in alarm for her own life, fled to the river bank, and, placing her two children in a skiff, entered herself, and pushed off, thinking this a safer course than to remain longer at Vicksburg.

After the tumult had subsided a little, I showed the bar-keeper the direction of the letter of introduction I had brought, and inquired if he knew such a person.

No sooner had he read the name than his face assumed an expression of horror and alarm. "Do you know that person?" he eagerly inquired.

I told him I did not. This way my first visit to this part of the country. The letter had been given me by a gentleman whom I had met at Augusta.

"Pray don't mention the name," he replied; "say nothing of it to any body. This letter is addressed to one of the persons whom you saw hung as you came into the town. He kept a roulette table, no doubt, and understood a thing or two; but was a generous-hearted soul for all that; and every way quite as much a gentleman as half those concerned in hanging him. Should you mention his name, you might yourself be seized as one of the gang, and hung with the rest."

Congratulating myself on this lucky escape, I then ventured to inquire of the bar-keeper if he knew a planter in that vicinity of the name of Thomas.

There had been, he told me, a planter of that name,—and from the account he gave of him, I was satisfied it was the one of whom I was in search,—who lived formerly a few miles off; but within two or three years past he had moved to a distance of some fifty miles, in Madison county, up the Big Black.

The friendly bar-keeper aided me the next day in procuring a horse, and I set out for Madison county, again passing, as I left the town, the five murdered gamblers still swinging from the gallows.

From *Hatchie, The Guardian Slave; or, The Heiress of Bellevue*

WARREN T. ASHTON (REV. WILLIAM TAYLOR ADAMS)

"Warren T. Ashton" was one of a number of pseudonyms employed by the Reverend William Taylor Adams. Adams was best known to nineteenth-century readers as "Oliver Optic," one of the nineteenth century's most successful and influential authors of books for children. As Sarah Wadsworth has noted, Adams's "most popular books sold at a rate of more than 100,000 a year [. . .] By the time of his death, an estimated two million copies of his books had been sold" (21). Adams's first book, from which the following extract is taken, was directed at a more mature audience. Published in 1853, it was one of the many books to enter into the slavery debate in the wake of *Uncle Tom's Cabin* (1852). Adams claims in a preface that the book "was not designed to illustrate the evils or the blessings of slavery" (5), but the central figure of Hatchie is reminiscent of other "loyal slave" characters appearing in proslavery fiction of the time. In this extract, Hatchie foils the plans of Vernon—a "notorious gambler"—and Maxwell, an unwanted suitor of his mistress Emily, in their attempts to swindle heroic Henry Carroll. For further information on Adams's career as Oliver Optic, see Sarah A. Wadsworth, "Louisa May Alcott, William T. Adams, and the Rise of Gender-Specific Series Books," *The Lion and the Unicorn* 25.1 (January 2001): 17–46.

On board the Chalmetta, Maxwell discovered an old acquaintance in the person of a notorious gambler,—a class of persons who congregate on Mississippi steamers, and practise their arts upon the unwary traveller. This person, who went by the name of Vernon, was well known at the faro and roulette boards in New Orleans. He was an accomplished swindler. In the winter season, when the city is crowded with the élite of the state, and with strangers from all parts of the Union, Vernon found abundant exercise for his professional ability at the hells of the city, in the employment of their proprietors, acting the part of banker, or anything else that offered him the means of gratifying his luxurious habits. A twinge of conscience never prevented him from adopting any means of emptying the pockets of his victims, even without the formality of dice or cards.

In the summer season he beguiled his time on the river, or migrated with the fashionables to Pascagoula, or a more northern watering-place,—in fine, to any sphere which afforded him a theatre for the exercise of his talents as a blackleg. Wherever he was, he never passed by an opportunity to obtain possession of his neighbor's valuables. If the monied man would accept a hand at euchre or poker, why, he was so much the easier cleaned out; if not, false keys, pick-locks, or sleight-of-hand, soon relieved the unfortunate victim of his superfluous possessions.

Early in his career of fashionable dissipation, Maxwell had made the acquaintance of this notorious individual. Indeed, he had sufficient cause to remember him, for he had made a deep inroad into his patrimony. Maxwell was too great a rascal himself to be long duped by a greater one. A kind of business intimacy had grown up between them, and continued to exist at the time of our story. This connection was not, however, publicly acknowledged by Maxwell; it would have been the ruin of his fine prospects but he used him whenever a scheme of profit or revenge required an unscrupulous confederate. Yet this Vernon was by no means a dependent creature of Maxwell's, for he was bold, reckless, and independent to the last degree. Whether acting as the paid devil of another, or on his own responsibility, he bowed to no power but his own will. His physical courage was well known to be of the most obstinate character. When the coward dandy had an enemy to punish, Vernon, for a hundred dollars, would first insult and then fight the luckless individual. This had formerly been a lucrative part of his trade; but latterly his claims to the distinction of *gentleman* and *man of honor* had been of such a questionable character, that the man who refused to meet him did not lose caste among the bloods of the city.

Vernon was now on his way to a wider sphere of action than New Orleans, with its yellow fever season at hand, afforded him. As usual, he practised his arts on board the Chalmetta, which, however, afforded him but a narrow field, the passengers being mostly officers, who had left their pay in the cabarets of Mexico.

By some means he had ascertained that Henry Carroll was in possession of a considerable sum of money. By all the arts in his power he had endeavored to lure him to the gambling-table, which was constantly spread in the cabin, and surrounded by unfortunate victims, vainly striving against the coolness and trickery of professional blacklegs, to recruit their exhausted finances, or retrieve the ruin to which an unlucky hour had enticed them. Henry obstinately refused to take a hand; but Vernon's heart was set upon the bag of gold he knew was in Henry's trunk, and he resolved to possess it,—a feat not easy to accomplish on board a crowded steamer.

After Maxwell had recovered from the blow which had felled him to the deck, and while Henry was soothing the distress of Emily, he met Vernon, who was in the act of reconnoitring the young officer's state-room. Vernon was just the person to serve him in this extremity. The protector of Emily must be removed from his charge, as her uncle had been by De Guy. He resolved upon a consultation with the blackleg. Accordingly he expressed his desire, to which the gambler replied by requesting him to give notice of the approach of any one, while he did a little business in the state-room.

Maxwell vainly remonstrated, but was obliged to comply with the wishes of the robber, or lose his services.

Vernon, thus protected from intrusion, entered the room, and by the aid of a pick-lock soon succeeded in obtaining possession of all poor Henry's earthly wealth. Beckoning Maxwell to follow, he descended to the main deck, where, procuring a lantern, they proceeded aft.

[. . .]

"Now, is the coast clear?" said Vernon, who carried a lantern he had borrowed from the mate.

"All clear; but put out that light,—the engineers will notice us," replied Maxwell.

"But I can't find my way into the hold without it. There is no danger of the engineers, They are all asleep on the forward deck."

"What do you want in the hold?" asked Maxwell, in an irritable tone.

"I want to hide this bag of money," replied Vernon, in a whisper. "As soon as the covey finds he has been picked, they will search the boat; and my character is not likely to save me from the indignity of being obliged to open my trunk, and turn out my pockets."

"It is bad business, and I wish you had not done this thing. As I told you before, *I* have nothing to do with it. I feel myself rather above common robbery."

"Self-esteem! But you came down on your own business, not on mine. You can return, and not trouble yourself any further," growled Vernon.

"I need your help, and will pay you for it."

"Very well, then, wait till *this* job is finished."

"Go on! I will follow," replied Maxwell, finding remonstrance vain.

After a careful scrutiny of the premises, Vernon concealed his lantern under his coat, and leaped into the hold, followed by Maxwell.

"Now," said Vernon, "I must put this bag into one of these boxes, to be guarded by the spirits of the brave men whose bones repose in them."

"Are you mad, man? Would you open the coffins of the dead to hide your ill-gotten gold?" exclaimed Maxwell, alarmed at the purpose of his confederate.

"Why not? We need not disturb the bodies,—only open the outside box."

"Very well," said Maxwell, who felt how useless it was to oppose his companion. "But remember, I have nothing to do with the robbery."

"Of course not, and nothing to do with sharing the proceeds; but sit down, if you have anything to say to me. We are perfectly safe from interruption here"; and Vernon seated himself on the box which was occupied by the mulatto.

"My words need not be many. In the first place, I have been insulted, and must have satisfaction; and, in the second, there is a girl in the cabin to whom I am much attached, and she will not give me the smallest sign of encouragement. Have her I must, by fair means or foul. I would marry her. You understand?"

"Certainly; but what's the plan?" asked Vernon, indifferently.

"Rather a difficult one, and may require some nerve to execute it," replied Maxwell, who proceeded to develop his schemes, both in respect to Henry Carroll and to Emily.

Although the conspirators spoke in a low tone, Hatchie heard and understood the whole plot. The voice of Maxwell he recognized, and, although the name of the lady against whom his designs were meditated was not mentioned, he comprehended who she was.

The confederated scoundrels having finished their conference, Vernon drew from his pocket a small screw-driver, and proceeded to remove the screws from one of the boxes, which, to Hatchie's great relief, was not the one occupied by himself. After much labor, for the boxes were carefully constructed, to bear the rough usage of transportation, he succeeded in removing the lid, and deposited the bag of money between the coffin and the case which enclosed it.

Having effected the object which brought them to the hold, the two ascended again, and made their way to the cabin.

[. . .]

Hatchie explained the plan of Vernon, which had been rendered futile by his precaution.

"The scoundrel! but how knew you this, and how happens it that I escaped while he is wounded?" said Henry.

"I overheard the plot when I did the other. Vernon is a common robber. He came into the hold to conceal a bag of money he had stolen."

"A bag of money!" interrupted Henry, his thoughts diverted from the subject.

"Ay, a bag of money."

"Do you know where they hid it?"

"I do; but why do you ask?" and Hatchie was much pained to discover in Henry what he mistook for a feeling of rapacity. He wanted and expected the perfection of an angel in the man who sustained the relation of lover and protector to his mistress.

"Because I have been robbed of all I had in the world," replied Henry, seeing the shade upon Hatchie's brow.

"Indeed!" exclaimed the mulatto, his doubts removed, and pleased in being able to restore his money.

"The money is undoubtedly mine. Your noble devotion to your mistress has thus proved a fortunate thing for me. But about the pistols?"

Hatchie related the means he had used to derange Maxwell's plan.

"I shall never be able to repay the debt I owe you," said Henry, warmly, as the mulatto finished his story.

"I did it for my mistress' sake. I learned that you were her friend."

"And she will bless you for the act."

"Now, what shall be done to insure her safety to-night? for they will attempt her abduction, I doubt not."

It was arranged that Henry should watch in the vicinity of Emily's stateroom, while Uncle Nathan, Hatchie and Pat Fegan, should occupy the lower deck. Emily was not to be informed of the danger; it would distress her to no purpose.

They had no doubt of their ability to protect her. Accustomed as Henry was to danger, perhaps he did not fully appreciate that which was now gathering around Emily. He felt that, in knowing the particulars of the nefarious scheme, he was abundantly able, even single-handed, to prevent its success.

Obtaining a screw-driver and a lantern from one of the engineers, he succeeded in obtaining possession of his stolen bag of gold. On his return to the cabin, he observed Vernon standing at the bar, and the temptation to give his moral faculties a start could not be resisted. Purchasing a dozen cigars, he remarked that he had no change, and coolly pulled the bag of gold from his pocket. Vernon's astonishment and consternation could not be entirely concealed, as he recognized the bag he had securely deposited in the box with the dead. Henry took no notice of him, though he heard him say, in a suppressed tone, "The devil is in this boat!"

The Pilot's Story

WILLIAM DEAN HOWELLS

William Dean Howells may not be renowned for tales of life on the river frontier, but years before his friend Mark Twain put his imaginative copyright on the Mississippi, he published this poetic account of a tragic episode of riverboat gambling. Though touching on the classic antebellum themes of the tragic mulatta and the slave lost at the card table, Howells's poem manages to breathe new life into these conventions on the brink of the Civil War. That Howells should turn to the theme of riverboat gambling is not as unexpected as it might seem, since his uncles were involved in the steamboat trade. In his own account of the poem, Howells remembered: "I had attempted to treat in it a phase of the national tragedy of slavery, as I had imagined it on a Mississippi steamboat. A young planter has gambled away the slave-girl who is the mother of his child" (*Literary Friends and Acquaintance,* 34). Edwin Cady has argued that the publication of this poem was an important moment in Howells' early career, ensuring him "a hearty welcome when he got to Boston" (73). For further information, see William Dean Howells, *Literary Friends and Acquaintance: A Personal Retrospect of American Authorship* (1900; Bloomington: Indiana University Press, 1968); and Edwin H. Cady, *Young Howells & John Brown: Episodes in a Radical Education* (Columbus: Ohio State University Press, 1985).

I.

It was a story the pilot told, with his back to his hearers,—
Keeping his hand on the wheel and his eye on the globe of the jack-staff,
Holding the boat to the shore and out of the sweep of the current,
Lightly turning aside for the heavy logs of the drift-wood,
Widely shunning the snags that made us sardonic obeisance.

II.

All the soft, damp air was full of delicate perfume
From the young willows in bloom on either bank of the river,—
Faint, delicious fragrance, trancing the indolent senses
In a luxurious dream of the river and land of the lotus.

Not yet out of the west the roses of sunset were withered;
In the deep blue above light clouds of gold and of crimson
Floated in slumber serene, and the restless river beneath them
Rushed away to the sea with a vision of rest in its bosom.
Far on the eastern shore lay dimly the swamps of the cypress
Dimly before us the islands grew from the river's expanses,—
Beautiful, wood-grown isles,—with the gleam of the swart inundation
Seen through the swaying boughs and slender trunks of their willows;
And on the shore beside us the cotton-trees rose in the evening,
Phantom-like, yearningly, wearily, with the inscrutable sadness
Of the mute races of trees. While hoarsely the steam from her 'scape-pipes
Shouted, then whispered a moment, then shouted again to the silence,
Trembling through all her frame with the mighty pulse of her engines,
Slowly the boat ascended the swollen and broad Mississippi,
Bank-full, sweeping on, with nearing masses of drift-wood,
Daintily breathed about with hazes of silvery vapor,
Where in his arrowy flight the twittering swallow alighted,
And the belated blackbird paused on the way to its nestlings.

III.

It was the pilot's story:—"They both came aboard there, at Cairo,
From a New Orleans boat, and took passage with us for Saint Louis.
She was a beautiful woman, with just enough blood from her mother,
Darkening her eyes and her hair, to make her race known to a trader:
You would have thought she was white. The man that was with her,—you
    see such,—
Weakly good-natured and kind, and weakly good-natured and vicious,
Slender of body and soul, fit neither for loving nor hating.
I was a youngster then, and only learning the river,—
Not over-fond of the wheel. I used to watch them at *monte*,
Down in the cabin at night, and learned to know all of the gamblers.
So when I saw this weak one staking his money against them,
Betting upon the turn of the cards, I knew what was coming:
They never left their pigeons a single feather to fly with.
Next day I saw them together,—the stranger and one of the gamblers:
Picturesque rascal he was, with long black hair and moustaches,
Black slouch hat drawn down to his eyes from his villanous forehead:

On together they moved, still earnestly talking in whispers,
On toward the forecastle, where sat the woman alone by the gangway.
Roused by the fall of feet, she turned, and, beholding her master,
Greeted him with a smile that was more like a wife's than another's,
Rose to meet him fondly, and then, with the dread apprehension
Always haunting the slave, fell her eye on the face of the gambler,
Dark and lustful and fierce and full of merciless cunning.
Something was spoken so low that I could not hear what the words were;
Only the woman started, and looked from one to the other,
With imploring eyes, bewildered hands, and a tremor
All through her frame: I saw her from where I was standing, she shook so.
'Say! is it so?' she cried. On the weak, white lips of her master
Died a sickly smile, and he said,—'Louise, I have sold you.'
God is my judge! May I never see such a look of despairing,
Desolate anguish, as that which the woman cast on her master,
Griping her breast with her little hands, as if he had stabbed her,
Standing in silence a space, as fixed as the Indian woman,
Carved out of wood, on the pilot-house of the old Pocahontas!
Then, with a gurgling moan, like the sound in the throat of the dying,
Came back her voice, that, rising, fluttered, through wild incoherence,
Into a terrible shriek that stopped my heart while she answered:—
'Sold me? sold me? sold—And you promised to give me my freedom!—
Promised me, for the sake of our little boy in Saint Louis!
What will you say to our boy, when he cries for me there in Saint Louis?
What will you say to our God?—Ah, you have been joking! I see it!—
No? God! God! He shall hear it,—and all of the angels in heaven,—
Even the devils in hell!—and none will believe when they hear it!
Sold me !'—Fell her voice with a thrilling wail, and in silence
Down she sank on the deck, and covered her face with her fingers."

IV.

In his story a moment the pilot paused, while we listened
To the salute of a boat, that, rounding the point of an island,
Flamed toward us with fires that seemed to burn from the waters,—
Stately and vast and swift, and borne on the heart of the current.
Then, with the mighty voice of a giant challenged to battle,

Rose the responsive whistle, and all the echoes of island,
Swamp-land, glade, and brake replied with a myriad clamor,
Like wild birds that are suddenly startled from slumber at midnight;
Then were at peace once more, and we heard the harsh cries of the peacocks
Perched on a tree by a cabin-door, where the white-headed settler's
White-headed children stood to look at the boat as it passed them,
Passed them so near that we heard their happy talk and their laughter.
Softly the sunset had faded, and now on the eastern horizon
Hung, like a tear in the sky, the beautiful star of the evening.

V.

Still with his back to us standing, the pilot went on with his story—
"Instantly, all the people, with looks of reproach and compassion,
Flocked round the prostrate woman. The children cried, and their mothers
Hugged them tight to their breasts; but the gambler said to the captain,—
'Put me off there at the town that lies round the bend of the river.
Here, you! rise at once, and be ready now to go with me.'
Roughly he seized the woman's arm and strove to uplift her.
She—she seemed not to heed him, but rose like one that is dreaming,
Slid from his grasp, and fleetly mounted the steps of the gangway,
Up to the hurricane-deck, in silence, without lamentation.
Straight to the stern of the boat, where the wheel was, she ran, and the
    people
Followed her fast till she turned and stood at bay for a moment,
Looking them in the face, and in the face of the gambler.
Not one to save her,—not one of all the compassionate people!
Not one to save her, of all the pitying angels in heaven!
Not one bolt of God to strike him dead there before her!
Wildly she waved him back, we waiting in silence and horror.
Over the swarthy face of the gambler a pallor of passion
Passed, like a gleam of lightning over the west in the night-time.
White, she stood, and mute, till he put forth his hand to secure her;
Then she turned and leaped,—in mid air fluttered a moment,—
Down, there, whirling, fell, like a broken-winged bird from a tree-top,
Down on the cruel wheel, that caught her, and hurled her, and crushed her,
And in the foaming water plunged her, and hid her forever."

VI.

Still with his back to us all the pilot stood, but we heard him
Swallowing hard, as he pulled the bell-rope to stop her. Then, turning,—
"This is the place where it happened," brokenly whispered the pilot.
"Somehow, I never like to go by here alone in the night-time."
Darkly the Mississippi flowed by the town that lay in the starlight,
Cheerful with lamps. Below we could hear them reversing the engines,
And the great boat glided up to the shore like a giant exhausted.
Heavily sighed her pipes. Broad over the swamps to the eastward
Shone the full moon, and turned our far-trembling wake into silver.
All was serene and calm, but the odorous breath of the willows
Smote like the subtile breath of an infinite sorrow upon us.

Gilded Age Memories

"I will make money rain"

From *The End of the World: A Love Story*

EDWARD EGGLESTON

Though little read now, Edward Eggleston secured his place in history with the publication of *The Hoosier Schoolmaster* in 1871, a hugely popular and pioneering account of antebellum life in Indiana. As Frank Luther Mott has noted, "It sold twenty thousand copies in its first year, was pirated by English publishers, and soon translated into French" (200). His second novel, *The End of the World* (1872), contained a long account of steamboat life on the Mississippi, which hinged on the activities of a gang of gamblers. As one of the first literary uses of steamboat gambling in the postbellum period, Eggleston's text is highly expressive of its time and place: while he happily exploits the gambling storyline for its essential melodrama, as others had done in the antebellum years, different artistic concerns are also in evidence. Reviewing the novel in the *Atlantic,* William Dean Howells singled out what he felt to be the "great reality" in Eggleston's portrait of "the gamblers on the river-steamboat" ("End of the World" 747). Indeed, Eggleston's realist tendencies can also be seen in the denouement of this section of the novel. While the novel's hero, August Wahle, manages to save his sweetheart's thuggish brother (who nearly lynched Wahle's father) from ruin at the hands of a gambler (who also happens to be August's love rival), he receives no reward for his good deed. Instead, the boat's captain fires him. For further information on Eggleston and his writings, see Frank Luther Mott, *Golden Multitudes: The Story of Best Sellers in the United States* (New York: Macmillan, 1947); William Dean Howells, "The End of the World," *Atlantic Monthly* 30.182 (December 1872): 746–47; and William Randel, *Edward Eggleston* (New York: Twayne, 1963).

It was natural enough that the "mud-clerk" on the old steamboat Iatan should take a fancy to the "striker," as the engineer's apprentice was called. Especially since the striker knew so much more than the mud-clerk, and was able to advise him about many things. A striker with so much general information was rather a novelty, and all the officers fancied him, except Sam Munson, the second engineer, who had a natural jealousy of a striker that knew more than he did.

The striker had learned rapidly, and was trusted to stand a regular watch. The first engineer and the third were together, and the second engineer and the striker took the other watch. The boat in this way got the services of a competent engineer while paying him only a striker's wage.

About the time the heavily-laden Iatan turned out of the Mississippi into the Ohio at Cairo at six in the evening, the striker went off watch, and he ought to have gone to bed to prepare himself for the second watch of the night, especially as he would only have the dog-watch between that and the forenoon. But a passenger had got aboard at Cairo, whose face was familiar. The sight of it had aroused a throng of old associations, pleasant and unpleasant, and a throng of emotions the most tender and the most wrathful the striker had ever felt. Sleep he could not, and so, knowing that the mud-clerk was on watch, he sought the office after nine o'clock, and stood outside the bar talking to his friend, who had little to do, since most of the freight had been shipped through, and his bills for Paducah were all ready. The striker talked with the mud-clerk, but watched the throng of passengers who drank with each other at the bar, smoked in the "social hall," read and wrote at the tables in the gentlemen's cabin, or sat with doffed hats and chatted gallantly in the ladies' cabin, which was visible as a distant background, seen over a long row of tables with green covers and under a long row of gilded wooden stalactites, which were intended to be ornamental. The little pendent prisms beneath the chandeliers rattled gayly as the boat trembled at each stroke of her wheels, and gaping backwoodsmen, abroad for the first time, looked at all the rusty gingerbread-work, and wondered if kings were able to afford anything half so fine as the cabin of the "palatial steamer Iatan," as she was described on the bills. The confused murmur of many voices, mixed with the merry tinkling of the glass pendants, gave the whole an air of excitement.

But the striker did not see the man he was looking for. "Who got on at Cairo? I think I saw a man from our part of the country," he said.

"I declare, I don't know," said the mud-clerk, who drawled his words in a cold-blooded way. "Let me look. Here's A. Robertson, and T. Le Fevre, and L. B. Sykes, and N. Anderson."

"Where is Anderson going?"

"Paid through to Louisville. Do you know him?"

But just then Norman Anderson himself walked in, and went up to the bar with a new acquaintance. They did not smoke the pipe of peace, like red Americans, but, like white Americans, they had a mysterious liquid carefully compounded, and by swallowing this they solemnly sealed their new-made friendship after the curious and unexplained rite in use among their people.

Norman had been dispatched on a collecting trip, and having nine hundred and fifty dollars in his pocket, he felt as much elated as if it had been his own money. The gentleman with whom he drank, had a band of crape around his white hat. He seemed very nearsighted.

"If that greeny is a friend of yours, Gus, I declare you'd better tell him not to tie to the serious-looking young fellow in the white hat and gold specs, unless he means to part with all his loose change before bed-time."

That is what the mud-clerk drawled to August the striker, but the striker seemed to hear the words as something spoken afar off. For just then he was seeing a vision of a drunken mob, and a rope, and a pleading woman, and a brave old man threatened with death. Just then he heard harsh and muddled voices, rude oaths, and jeering laughter, and above it all the sweet pleading of a little girl begging for a father's life. And the quick blood came into his fair German face, and he felt that he could not save this Norman Anderson from the toils of the gambler, though he might, if provoked, pitch him over the guard of the boat. For was not Andrew's letter, which described the mob, in his pocket, and burning a hole in his pocket as it had been ever since he received it?

But then this was Julia's brother, and there was nothing he would not do for Julia. So, sometime after the mud-clerk had ceased to speak, the striker gave utterance to both impulses by replying, "He's no friend of mine," a little crisply, and then softly adding, "Though I shouldn't like to see him fleeced."

By this time a new actor had appeared on the scene in the person of a man with a black mustache and side-whiskers, who took a seat behind a card-table near the bar.

"H'llo!" said the mud-clerk in a low and lazy voice, "Parkins is back again. After his scrape at Paducah last February, he disappeared, and he's been shady ever since. He's growed whiskers since, so's not to be recognized. But he'll be skeerce enough when we get to Paducah. Now, see how quick he'll catch the greenies, won't you?" The prospect was so charming as almost to stimulate the mud-clerk to speak with some animation.

But August Wehle, the striker on the Iatan, had an uncomfortable feeling that he had seen that face before, and that the long mustache and side-whiskers had grown in a remarkably short space of time. Could it be that there were two men who could spread a smile over the lower half of their faces in that automatic way, while the spider-eyes had no sort of sympathy with it? Surely, this man with black whiskers and mustache was not just like the singing-master at Sugar-Grove school-house, who had "red-top hay on to his upper lip," and yet—and yet—

"Gentlemen," said Parkins—his Dickensian name would be Smirkins—

"I want to play a little game just for the fun of the thing. It is a trick with three cards. I put down three cards, face up. Here is six of diamonds, eight of spades, and the ace of hearts. Now, I will turn them over so quickly that I will defy any of you to tell which is the ace. Do you see? Now, I would like to bet the wine for the company that no gentleman here can turn up the ace. All I want is a little sport. Something to pass away the evening and amuse the company. Who will bet the wine? The Scripture says that the hand is quicker than the eye, and I warn you that if you bet, you will probably lose." And here he turned the cards back, with their faces up, and the card which everybody felt sure was the ace proved apparently to be that card. Most of the on-lookers regretted that they had not bet, seeing that they would certainly have won. Again the cards were put face down, and the company was bantered to bet the wine. Nobody would bet.

After a good deal of fluent talk, and much dexterous handling of the cards, in a way that seemed clear enough to everybody, and that showed that everybody's guess was right as to the place of the ace, the near-sighted gentleman, who had drunk with Norman, offered to bet five dollars.

"Five dollars!" returned Parkins, laughing in derision, "five dollars! Do you think I'm a gambler? I don't want any gentleman's money. I've got all the money I need. However, if you would like to bet the wine with me, I am agreed."

The near-sighted gentleman declined to wager anything but just the five dollars, and Parkins spurned his proposition with the scorn of a gentleman who would on no account bet a cent of money. But he grew excited, and bantered the whole crowd. Was there no *gentleman* in the crowd who would lay a wager of wine for the company on this interesting little trick? It was strange to him that no gentleman had spirit enough to make the bet. But no gentleman had spirit enough to bet the wine. Evidently there were no gentlemen in the company.

However, the near-sighted man with the white hat adorned with crape now proposed in a crusty tone to bet ten dollars that he could lift the ace. He even took out a ten-dollar bill, and, after examining it, in holding it close to his nose as a penurious man might, extended his hand with, "If you're in earnest, let's know it. I'll bet you ten."

At this Parkins grew furious. He had never been so persistently badgered in all his life. He'd have the gentleman know that he was not a gambler. He had all the money he wanted, and as for betting ten dollars, he shouldn't think of it. But now that the gentleman—he said *gentleman* with an emphasis—now that the gentleman seemed determined to bet money, he would show him that he was not to be backed down. If the young man would like to wager a hundred dollars, he would cheerfully bet with him. If the gentleman did not feel able to bet a hundred dollars, he hoped he would not say any more about it. He hadn't intended to bet money at all. But he wouldn't bet less than a hundred dollars with anybody. A man who couldn't afford to lose a hundred dollars, ought not to bet.

"Who is this fellow in the white hat with spectacles?" August asked of the mud-clerk.

"That is Smith, Parkins's partner. He is only splurging round to start up the greenies." And the mud-clerk spoke with an indifference and yet a sort of *dilettante* interest in the game that shocked his friend, the striker.

"Why don't they set these blacklegs ashore?" said August, whose love of justice was strong.

"*You* tell," drawled the mud-clerk. "The first clerk's tried it, but the old man protects 'em, and" (in a whisper) "get's his share, I guess. He can set them off whenever he wants to." (I must explain that there is only one "old man" on a steamboat—that is, the captain.)

By this time Parkins had turned and thrown his cards so that everybody knew or thought he knew where the ace was. Smith, the man with the white hat, now rose five dollars more and offered to bet fifteen. But Parkins was more indignant than ever. He told Smith to go away. He thrust his hand into his pocket and drew out a handful of twenty-dollar gold-pieces. "If any gentleman wants to bet a hundred dollars, let him come on. A man who couldn't lose a hundred would better keep still."

Smith now made a big jump. He'd go fifty. Parkins wouldn't listen to fifty. He had said that he wouldn't bet less than a hundred, and he wouldn't. He now pulled out handful after handful of gold, and piled the double-eagles up like a fortification in front of him, while the crowd surged with excitement.

At last Mr. Smith, the near-sighted gentleman in spectacles, the gentleman who wore black crape on a white hat, concluded to bet a hundred dollars. He took out his little porte-monnaie and lifted thence a hundred-dollar bill.

"Well," said he angrily, "I'll bet you a hundred." And he laid down the bill. Parkins piled five twenty-dollar gold-pieces atop it. Each man felt that he could lift the ace in a moment. That card at the dealer's right was certainly the ace. Norman was sure of it. He wished it had been his wager instead of Smith's. But Parkins stopped Smith a moment.

"Now, young man," he said, "if you don't feel perfectly able to lose that hundred dollars, you'd better take it back."

"I am just as able to lose it as you are," said Smith snappishly, and to everybody's disappointment he lifted not the card everybody had fixed on, but the middle one, and so lost his money.

"Why didn't you take the other?" said Norman boastfully. "I knew it was the ace."

"Why didn't you bet, then?" said Smith, grinning a little. Norman wished he had. But he had not a hundred dollars of his own, and he had scruples—faint, and yet scruples, or rather alarms—at the thought of risking his employer's money on a wager. While he was weighing motive against motive, Smith bet again, and again, to Norman's vexation, selected a card that was so obviously wrong that Norman thought it a pity that so near-sighted a man should bet and lose. He wished he had a hundred dollars of his own and—

There, Smith was betting again. This time he consulted Norman before making his selection, and of course turned up the right card, remarking that he wished his eyes were so keen! He would win a thousand dollars before bedtime if his eyes were so good! Then he took Norman into partnership, and Norman found himself suddenly in possession of fifty dollars, gotten without trouble. This turned his brain. Nothing is so intoxicating to a weak man as money acquired without toil. So Norman continued to bet, sometimes independently, sometimes in partnership with, the gentlemanly Smith. He was borne on by the excitement of varying fortune, a varying fortune absolutely under control of the dealer, whose sleight-of-hand was perfect. And the varying fortune had an unvarying tendency in the long run—to put three stakes out of five into the pockets of the gamblers, who found the little game very interesting amusement for gentlemen.

[. . .]

But when nearly a third of Norman's employer's money had gone into the gamblers' heap, and when August began to understand that it was another man's money that Norman was losing, and that the victim was threatened by no half-way ruin, he determined to do something, even at the risk of making himself known to Norman and to Parkins—was he Humphreys in disguise?—and at the risk of arrest for house-breaking. August acted with his eyes open to all the perils from gamblers' pistols and gamblers' malice; and after he had started to interfere, the mud-clerk called him back, and said, in his half-indifferent way:

"Looky here, Gus, don't be a blamed fool. That's a purty little game. That greeny's got to learn to let blacklegs alone, and he don't look like one that'll take advice. Let him scorch a little; it'll do him good. It's healthy for young men. That's the reason the old man don't forbid it, I s'pose. And these fellows carry good shooting-irons with hair-triggers, and I declare I don't want to be bothered writing home to your mother, and explaining to her that you got killed in a fight with blacklegs. I declare I don't, you see. And then you'll get the 'old man' down on you, if you let a bird out of the trap in which he goes snucks; you will, I declare. And you'll get walking-papers at Louisville. Let the game alone. You haven't got any hand to play against Parkins, nohow; and I reckon the greenhorns are his lawful prey. Cats couldn't live without mice. You'll lose your place, I declare you will, if you say a word."

August stopped long enough to take in the full measure of his sacrifice. So far from being deterred by it, he was more than ever determined to act. Not the love of Julia, so much, now, but the farewell prayer and benediction and the whole life and spirit of the sweet Moravian mother in her child-full house at home were in his mind at this moment. Things which a man will not do for the love of woman he may do for the love of God—and it was with a sense of moral exaltation that August entered into the lofty spirit of self-sacrifice he had seen in his mother, and caught himself saying, in his heart, as he had heard her say, "Let us do anything for the Father's sake!" Some will call this cant. So much the worse for them. This motive, too little felt in our day—too little felt in any day—is the great impulse that has enabled men to do the bravest things that have been done. The sublimest self-sacrifice is only possible to a man by the aid of some strong moral tonic. God's love is the chief support of the strongest spirits.

August touched Norman on the arm. The face of the latter expressed anything but pleasure at meeting him, now that he felt guilty. But this was not the uppermost feeling with Norman. He noticed that August's clothes were spotted with engine-grease, and his first fear was of compromising his respectability.

In a hurried way August began to explain to him that he was betting with gamblers, but Smith stood close to them, looking at August in such a contemptuous way as to make Norman feel very uncomfortable, and Parkins seeing the crowd attracted by August's explanations—which he made in some detail, by way of adapting himself to Norman—of the trick by which the upper card is thrown out first, Parkins said, "I see you understand the game, young man. If you do, why don't you bet?"

At this the crowd laughed, and Norman drew away from the striker's greasy clothes, and said that he didn't want to speak any further to a burglar, he believed. But August followed, determined to warn him against Smith. Smith was ahead of him, however, saying to Norman, "Look out for your pockets—that greasy fellow will rob you."

And Norman, who was nothing if not highly respectable, resolved to shake off the troublesome "Dutchman" at once. "I don't know what you are up to now, but at home you are known as a thief. So please let me alone, will you?" This Norman tried to say in an annihilating way.

The crowd looked for a fight. August said loud enough to be heard, "You know very well that you lie. I wanted to save you from being a thief, but you are betting money now that is not yours."

The company, of course, sympathized with the gentleman and against the machine-oil on the striker's clothes, so that there arose quickly a murmur, started by Smith, "Put the bully out," and August was "hustled." It is well that he was not shot.

It was quite time for him to go on watch now; for the loud-ticking marine-clock over the window of the clerk's office pointed to three minutes past twelve, and the striker hurried to his post at the starboard engine, with the bitterness of defeat and the shame of insult in his heart. He had sacrificed his place, doubtless, and risked much beside, and all for nothing. The third engineer complained of his tardiness in not having relieved him three minutes before, and August went to his duties with a bitter heart. To a man who is persistent, as August was, defeat of any sort is humiliating.

As for Norman, he bet after this just to show his independence and to show that the money was his own, as well as in the vain hope of winning back what he had lost. He bet every cent. Then he lost his watch, and at half-past one o'clock he went to his state-room, stripped of all loose valuables, and sweating great drops. And the mud-clerk, who was still in the office, remarked to himself, with a pleasant chuckle, that it was good for him; he declared it was; teach the fellow to let monte alone, and keep his eyes peeled when he traveled. It would so!

The idea was a good one, and he went down to the starboard engine and told the result of the nice little game to his friend the striker, drawling it out in a relishful way, how the blamed idiot never stopped till they'd got his watch, and then looked like as if he'd a notion to jump into the "drink." But 'twould cure him of meddlin' with monte. It would so!

He walked away, and August was just reflecting on the heartlessness of his friend, when the mud-clerk came back again, and began drawling his words out as before, just as though each distinct word were of a delightful flavor and he regretted that he must part with it.

"I've got you even with Parkins, old fellow. He'll be strung up on a lamppost at Paducah, I reckon. I saw a Paducah man aboard, and I put a flea in his ear. We've got to lay there an hour or two to put off a hundred barrels of molasses and two hundred sacks of coffee and two lots of plunder. There'll be a hot time for Parkins. He let on to marry a girl and fooled her. They'll teach him a lesson. You'll be off watch, and we'll have some fun looking on." And the mud-clerk evidently thought that it would be even funnier to see Parkins hanged than it had been to see him fleece Norman. Gus the striker did not see how either scene could be very entertaining. But he was sick at heart, and one could not expect him to show much interest in manly sports.

The steady beat of the wheels and the incessant clank of the engines went on as usual. The boat was loaded almost to her guards, and did not make much speed. The wheels kept their persistent beat upon the water, and the engines kept their rhythmical clangor going, until August found himself getting drowsy. Trouble, with forced inaction, nearly always has a soporific tendency, and a continuous noise is favorable to sleep. Once or twice August roused himself to a sense of his responsibility and battled with his heaviness. It was nearing the end of his watch, for the dog-watch of two hours set in at four o'clock. But it seemed to him that four o'clock would never come.

An incident occurred just at this moment that helped him to keep his eyes open. A man went aft through the engine-room with a red handkerchief tied round his forehead. In spite of this partial disguise August perceived that it was Parkins. He passed through to the place where the steerage or deck passengers are, and then disappeared from August's sight. He had meant to disembark at a wood-yard just below Paducah, but for some reason the boat did not stop, and now, as August guessed, he was hiding himself from Paducah eyes. He was not much too soon, for the great bell on the hurricane-deck was already ringing for Paducah, and the summer dawn was showing itself faintly through the river fog.

[. . .]

August strolled back through the now quiet engine-room to the deck-passengers' quarter. It was about half an hour before six o'clock, when the dog-watch would expire and he must go on duty again. In one of the uppermost of the filthy bunks, in the darkest corner, near the wheel, he discovered what he thought to be his man. The deck-passengers were still asleep, lying around stupidly. August paused a moment, checked by a sense of the danger-ousness of his undertaking. Then he picked up a stick of wood and touched the gambler, who could not have been very sound asleep, lying in hearing of the curses of the mob on the shore. At first Parkins did not move, but August gave him a still more vigorous thrust. Then he peered out between the blan-ket and the handkerchief over his forehead.

"I will take that money you won last night from that young man, if you please."

Parkins saw that it was useless to deny his identity. "Do you want to be shot?" he asked fiercely.

"Not any more than you want to be hung," said August. "The one would follow the other in five minutes. Give back that money and I will go away."

The gambler trembled a minute. He was fairly at bay. He took out a roll of bills and handed it to August. There was but five hundred. Smith had the other four hundred and fifty, he said. But August had a quiet German steadi-ness of nerve. He said that unless the other four hundred and fifty were paid at once he should call in the sheriff or the crowd.

Parkins knew that every minute August stood there increased his peril, and human nature is now very much like human nature in the days of Job. The devil understood the subject very well when he said that all that a man hath will he give for his life. Parkins paid the four hundred and fifty in gold-pieces. He would have paid twice that if August had demanded it.

[. . .]

When the first-engineer and a new man took the engines at noon, Gus was advised by the former to get some sleep, but there was no sleep for him until he had found Norman, who trembled at the sight of him.

"Where is your state-room?" said August sternly, for he couldn't bring himself to speak kindly to the poor fellow, even in his misery.

Norman turned pale. He had been thinking of suicide all the morning, but he was a coward, and now he evidently felt sure that he was to be killed by August. He did not dare disobey, but led the way, stopping to try to apolo-gize two or three times, but never getting any further than "I—I—"

Once in the state-room, he sat down on the berth and gasped, "I—I—"

"Here is your money," said August, handing it to him. "I made the gam-bler give it up."

"I—I—" said the astonished and bewildered Norman.

"You needn't say a word. You are a cowardly scoundrel, and if you say anything, I'll knock you down for treating my father as you did. Only for—for—well, I didn't want to see you fleeced."

Norman was ashamed for once, and hung his head. It touched the heart of August a little, but the remembrance of the attack of the mob on his father made him feel hard again, and so his generous act was performed ungraciously.

[. . .]

August Wehle the striker, just when he was to be made an engineer, when he thought he had smooth sailing, suddenly and provokingly found himself fast aground, with no spar or capstan by which he might help himself off, with no friendly craft alongside to throw him a hawser and pull him off.

It seems that when the captain promised him promotion, he did not know anything of August's interference with the gamblers. But when Parkins filed his complaint, it touched the captain. It was generally believed among the *employés* of the boat that a percentage of gamblers' gains was one of the "old man's" perquisites, and he was not the only steamboat captain who profited by the nice little games in the cabin upon which he closed both eyes. And this retrieved nine hundred and fifty dollars was a dead loss of—well, it does not matter how much, to the virtuous and highly honorable captain. His proportion would have been large enough at least to pay his wife's pew-rent in St. James's Church, with a little something over for charitable purposes. For the captain did not mind giving a disinterested twenty-five dollars occasionally to those charities that were willing to show their gratitude by posting his name as director, or his wife's as "Lady Manageress." In this case his right hand never knew what his left hand did—how it got the money, for instance.

So when August drew his pay he was informed that he was discharged. No reason was given. He tried to see the captain. But the captain was in the bosom of his family, kissing his own well-dressed little boys, and enjoying the respect which only exemplary and provident fathers enjoy. And never asking down in his heart if these boys might become gamblers' victims, or gamblers, indeed. The captain could not see August the striker, for he was at home, and must not be interfered with by any of his subordinates. Besides, it was Sunday, and he could not be intruded upon—the rector of St. James's was dining with him on his wife's invitation, and it behooved him to walk circumspectly, not with eye-service as a man-pleaser, but serving the Lord.

So he refuted to see the anxious striker, and turned to compliment the rector on his admirable sermon on the sin of Judas, who sold his master for thirty pieces of silver. And August Wehle had nothing left to do. The river was falling fast, the large boats above the Falls were, in steamboat-man's phrase, "laying up" in the mouths of the tributaries and other convenient harbors, there were plenty of engineers unemployed, and there were no vacancies.

From *Wanderings of a Vagabond: An Autobiography*

JOHN MORRIS (JOHN O'CONNOR)

John O'Connor's vagabond wanderings stand in contrast to the antigambling narratives of the antebellum years. Indeed, O'Connor had little time for the likes of Jonathan Harrington Green and his campaigns: "It is wonderful how this low and debased fraud should have deceived some of the brightest intellects in the country" (349). But unlike the proud tales of scamming and cheating that would feature in later gambling narratives (particularly in George Devol's autobiography), O'Connor was also vehemently opposed to the sharp practice employed by many gamblers. Indeed, he was a self-styled honest gambler, and frequently lamented the prevalence of cheating on the western rivers, complaining that "it was only when a party of acquaintances sat down to the card-table, to play among themselves, that anything like a square game could be seen on a steamer." As Jackson Lears rightly notes, "Morris's career, as he presented it, was a constant struggle to run an honest game among the hordes of sharpers and the police who protected them" (126). In the following extract, Morris outlines the history of gambling on the river, describes a variety of crooked gambling practices, and puts forward his solution to the problem. For more information on Morris, see Jackson Lears, *Something for Nothing: Luck in America* (New York: Viking, 2003).

A few days after the events recorded in the last chapter, I found myself a passenger on board the "Mediator," gliding along the picturesque banks of the lower Ohio, onward bound for New Orleans. The boat was crowded with passengers—men, women, and children—the greater part of whom were residents of the Crescent City, and who had been wandering in the North during the hot summer months, or perhaps the East or West, wherever business or pleasure led, in order to avoid the myriads of mosquitoes which a kind Providence bestows so bountifully on the denizens of the sunny South during the heated term, and that thrice-dreaded scourge, the yellow fever, about which learned medical men have wrangled and jangled for more than two centuries, without being one whit wiser to-day on the question of where the poison of this terrible disease lies, or from whence it is extracted, than was Père Dutertre when he first saw the fearful malady in the Antilles, in the summer of 1635.

A few minutes' detention at that classic mud-hole denominated Cairo, and I was at length launched on the broad bosom of the great Father of Waters, as American vanity is fond of styling it. The yearning of years was finally gratified; but what a disappointment! The majestic river! The mighty river! The grand river! The father of waters! The very first sight instantly destroyed every vestige of romance engendered by these sounding titles, and many more of the same sort, which, from my earliest youth up, I had heard applied to these turbid and treacherous waters. While steaming down its swift and dingy current, not a single beautiful object in all the landscape met my eye. All was dreary monotony.

[...]

Day and night during our voyage on the "Mediator," from Louisville to New Orleans, were the card-tables surrounded by the votaries of chance, and often as many as five or six of these tables could be seen scattered from the ladies' cabin to the social hall of the boat, with games going forward at each.

The games which were mostly played in those days on river steamers were poker, brag, whist, Boston, and old sledge; and if banking games were set up in the social hall, they were usually vingt-et-un, chuck, and sometimes faro. According to the rules of these steamers, all gambling was prohibited after ten o'clock in the evening; but in many instances these rules were a dead letter, and the morning sun frequently found one or more parties at the card-table engaged at their favorite games. In these jolly times the steamboat officers mingled with the passengers in the cabin as equals, and it was no uncommon thing to see uncouth pilots, mates, and greasy engineers engaged at the card-tables with well-dressed travelers. Passengers were privileged to amuse themselves just as they pleased, so long as they did not infringe upon the rights of others, or interfere in any respect with the duties of the officers or crew. This latitude sometimes led to some rather strong contrasts; for instance, there might frequently be seen in the ladies' cabin a group of the godly praying and singing psalms, while in the dining-saloon, from which the tables had been removed, another party were dancing merrily to the music of a fiddle, while farther along, in the social hall, might be heard the loud laughter of jolly carousers around the drinking bar, and occasionally chiming in with the sound of the revelry, the rattling of money and checks, and the sound of voices at the card-tables.

Previous to the appearance of the card-sharper and his newly invented schemes for cheating, on the river the card-tables of a steamer were free to all persons of gentlemanly habits and manners. The gambler was not excluded from a seat there on account of his superior skill at play; or, at least, it was an exceedingly rare thing for one person to object to another on these grounds. Pride would not permit the humiliating confession. Neither would men holding real or equivocal positions in society, and who, by the arbitrary laws of that society, felt themselves compelled to shun a professional gambler on the street, think their reputation compromised by meeting him as an equal on board a steamer at the card-tables.

The votaries of chance were not yet aroused to the fact that they could be insidiously robbed at the card-table when everything seemed perfectly fair and above-board; but when that enlightening took place, the gambler was immediately classed with the sharper, because the verdant were unable to understand where the gambler left off and the thief began. Thimbleriggers, dice-coggers, trigger-wheel players, strop-players, and card-sharpers of every description, were classed as gamblers.

These river sharpers, for their mutual advantage, traveled in small companies, but while on board a steamer, feigned to be total strangers to each other. Their number was always sufficient to make up a card party whenever they could induce one or two "gulls" to "join them in a small game, merely for amusement." Whenever one of their number could manage to obtain a seat among a poker or brag party that would not stand any rough nonsense in the way of "stocking," or "holding out," his confederates would seat themselves in such a position that they could see the cards held by his adversaries, and "item" the strength of their hands to him by signs. This was done variously, sometimes with the fingers, one held out denoting a pair, two, two pairs, three, threes, four fingers, fours, and five, a flush or full hand. Hands were sometimes telegraphed by twirling the head of a cane in various directions; and men had systems of signs which were perfectly intelligible, consisting in peculiar ways of puffing out cigar smoke.

The early sharpers depended on fleecing their adversaries at poker, brag, euchre, and all-fours, and similar games, while engaged with them at play, by "holding out" one or more cards on them. These would be hidden in their laps or behind the neck, and sometimes in the joint of the knees, and "rung in" whenever a favorable opportunity occurred for doing so. These methods of cheating, as well as "iteming" hands, are time honored institutions among the sharper tribe, and were probably practiced by their European brethren a century before the paddle of a steamboat made its first revolution in the turbid waters of the Mississippi.

Playing marked cards was a specialty with a few sharpers. They marked their own cards on the backs, nearly every sharper having his own secret cipher for doing so. While playing with a single adversary, marked cards could be used most advantageously; the more persons engaged with them in a game of brag or poker, the more difficult was their labor and the more they had to contend with. In a card party consisting of four or five players, the marked-card player can only manage to read the cards of one of his adversaries hands. I have heard that some of them could keep the run of two hands at once with perfect ease, but having never known of such an instance, I beg leave to doubt the assertion.

There are plenty of stamped-card players who can keep the run of two hands correctly in a game of poker where four or more persons are engaged, but it seems to me beyond the range of probability for any one to accomplish the same feat with what is known in sharper's parlance as "scratched paper." The marked-card player could accomplish nothing on a steamer, except by the connivance of the bar-tender, to whom he was obliged to give a certain share in his profits as the price of his assistance and silence, and for ringing in his cards upon whatever party upon whom they thought they could be made profitable. These worthies seldom wasted their talents and their "scratched paper" on any except those who were likely to reward them handsomely for their time and trouble.

The "tricky tribe," while playing all-fours, ecarte, euchre, etc., with verdant adversaries too far advanced to stand a "halfstock," or the "palm," would resort to marking the most advantageous cards with the thumb-nail by scratching them on their edges, generally on their sides near the corners. Sometimes they would "blaze" with their finger-nails, or otherwise mark the aces and kings on their backs, in order to know them at poker, or the braggers and aces at brag; at the latter game the advantage was very considerable, while with the former it amounted to little. The marking of certain cards in a pack, while engaged at a game, is not only a tedious operation, but decidedly a dangerous undertaking if not skillfully done. Persons with whom such tricks are generally tried on are those whose suspicions have been aroused; and parties of this kind are hard to cheat, or rather are on the alert to prevent any frauds from being practiced upon them. None of the tribe that I ever heard of ever succeeded in gaining any prominence among the members of their own profession for successfully marking cards while playing, and making them tell advantageously at a game.

Les chevaliers d'industrie of Europe are far ahead of our own in this art. Many of them, while playing at whist, ecarte, cribbage, and similar games, mark with their thumb-nails in an incredibly short space of time all the important cards in the pack, and play them equally as well as the best stamped-card player. In the year 1860 I met one of these gentlemen in Paris, a Frenchman by birth, of the most suave and agreeable manners and gentlemanly deportment. I had the honor of making his acquaintance, and one evening, while seated in my room discussing with me the various fine arts as practiced at cards, he offered to bet me a napoleon that while we were playing four games of ecarte, he would mark twelve cards in the pack. At any time during the playing of the four games, if I could detect him marking a single card by showing the spot on which it was marked, I won the wager; or if, when the four games were finished, and I had shuffled the pack to my satisfaction, he could not then take up the pack, and running the cards off its back one at a time and turning them over on the table, face up, as he came to it, any card which he had marked, naming its suit and size before doing so, or if he made a single mistake, he lost. I accepted his wager, and we played the four games of ecarte without my being able to detect him marking a single card. When we had finished the games I shuffled the pack and handed it to him; he turned over fourteen cards as he came to them, naming their suit and size as he did so without a single halt. While we were playing our games, he had handled his cards rather awkwardly for an adept, but there was nothing in his actions that would in the least arouse suspicion, and it was only when I held the cards which he had marked, up to the light, and let its glare fall directly upon the marks, which were done near the corner by a fine blaze that was made by the thumb-nail, and in various ciphers, that I was able to detect the fraud.

Who was the inventor of stamped cards I am unable to say, but that they originated in this country is nearly unquestionable. No mention is made of them in any of the gambling works published in Europe; nor among the multitude of tricks which have been exposed, both by writers on the subject and those that have been at various times ventilated before tribunals of justice, have I ever seen or heard of any mention being made of stamped cards. Even at the present day, European sharpers know but little about them, when they might be so serviceably used at the various short-card games played in those countries.

Unlike our own free and enlightened country, the despotic laws of Europe will not permit card manufacturers to fabricate unfair cards and flood the continent with their printed circulars informing whom it may concern that they are ready to supply all varieties of stamped cards of different ciphers, diagrams, and patterns. The European manufacturer who ventured to commit so flagrant and public a breach of honesty would not only find his business broken up, but himself incarcerated in a prison. In this country we have plenty of manufacturers of stamped cards, who send out their circulars to all parts of the country, accompanied by diagrams of the different patterns of cards, and the various ciphers used upon them. A Mr. Bartlett, of the city of New York, has been engaged in this business about forty years, and no law in the smallest degree molests or restrains him. How would the commercial public take it, should some engraver advertise that he was ready to supply counterfeiters with plates on the different banks throughout the country.

Stamped cards were unknown in Mexico previous to our invasion of that country, nor were they known to the people of South America, so far as I have been able to ascertain, and I took great pains to do so, and had many favorable opportunities during more than a year spent in rambling through Peru, Ecuador, and Chili, besides having made in California, in the early days of gold, the acquaintance of gamblers from nearly every country of South America. Not one of these have I ever yet met who had any idea of stamped cards, beyond what they had learned in California. This non-manufacture among the Spanish racers of this hemisphere convinces me that they were unknown to the Spaniards, otherwise they would have introduced them into their colonies; for in no games could they have been made so heavily advantageous and profitable to the sharper, as in the two favorite ones of the Spaniards, viz., the bluff game of "pacao" and the banking game of monte.

Before the Americans invaded their country, the Mexicans knew nothing about stamped cards. When the City of Mexico was captured by General Scott, sharpers from the States flocked there in droves. They were not slow, by any means, in perceiving the immense advantage to be gained from stamped cards when rung in on monte dealers; but where were they to get the monte cards manufactured for this purpose? Some of the brilliant lights of the fraternity started for New York, laid their dilemma before Bartlett, and in a few months the line of travel from Vera Cruz to the city of Mexico was flooded with American manufactured monte cards, *all stamped.* This attempt, however, proved a failure, for neither American nor Mexican gamblers would use the cards; as, though much finer than any before manufactured here, they were very coarse, compared with those made in the City of Mexico. The Mexican government had sold the monopoly of card manufacturing to certain individuals in each State in the Republic, and a single company in the City of Mexico possessed the whole right of doing so in that State, and their cards were in use by all the gamblers on Taylor's and Scott's line of occupation. But one resource was now left to the sharpers, which was to bribe the owners of this establishment. They succeeded in doing so, by paying the manufacturers five thousand dollars for one hundred gross of cards, of patterns similar to the square cards in use, stipulating for an equal amount of each pattern. The sharpers were to furnish the necessary plates, which they were obliged to have made in New York, and brought from thence to the manufacturers in the City of Mexico. This statement I give in substance just as I received it from the lips of a worthy member of the fraternity, now dead, by name Mr. William Clemmens, who was one of the committee of sharpers who negotiated for the manufacture of the stamped cards. But unfortunately for the enterprising movers of this scheme, so much time was consumed in getting the cards ready, that about the period that their speculation was ripe, peace was suddenly declared, and the American troops evacuated the country.

But following close on the heels of the war came the discovery of the golden fields of California, and in the early days of that excitement monte was the only banking game patronized by the shoals who flocked from all parts of the world to the golden State. These cards now came into good play, and during the summer of 1849 were extensively used, many of the sharpers having made fortunes by them. In the following winter they returned to the City of Mexico, and caused two hundred gross more to be made, and brought them back with them to California. But in some manner suspicion was raised against these cards, which finally led to their detection. And no sooner did it become a fixed fact that one pattern of these cards was stamped, and therefore dishonest, than all the cards manufactured in the Republic of Mexico were entirely discarded and repudiated, and those manufactured in Barcelona, Spain, were used instead. These cards have never been tampered with, and retain their popularity to the present day.

Stamped cards first appeared in this country between the years 1834 and 1835. When first discovered the secret was so precious as to be carefully guarded and monopolized by a few sharpers. As is usual with all new inventions of the kind, gamblers first fell victims to them, and continued to be so for many years. At first they were manufactured, like counterfeit money, with great secrecy, in unlikely places; but when, they became more fully known, Bartlett, of New York, and many others, found in their manufacture a profitable business.

In 1837 a man known by the name of Doctor Cross commenced the manufacturing of stamped cards in the city of New Orleans, and continued it up to as late as 1854, and it is more than probable that he was the first who carried on the business in this country. He procured his cards in an unfinished state from the New York manufacturers, and stamped them with plates of his own invention, or said to be such, at least. It was after his manufactory became perfectly well known that his cards were introduced on steamers, and rung in on the passengers by the bar-keepers, who "stood in" for a share of the plunder thus obtained by the sharpers for whom they operated.

At the present time none but the most verdant will stand "bottom-dealing"; but, like all new frauds, it had its day, with many kindred devices for robbing the unsuspecting. From 1834 to 1840 many gamblers who considered themselves *"par excellence"* in their profession, have stood it nobly while imagining themselves, no doubt, the victims of very bad luck. Almost any person, with a little practice, can deal from the bottom; but to perform the feat while several pairs of keen eyes are concentrating their gaze on your fingers and the pack held by them, without being detected, requires an amount of coolness and nerve, not to mention practice, which is possessed perhaps by not one man in a million. Thirty years ago a No. 1 bottom-dealer was a king among sharpers. He was dependent on no outside assistance for fleecing his victims, and if he had a partner, it was only for the purpose of skinning his dupe more expeditiously, by dealing him a large hand from the bottom, while his partner would raise from his lap or from the joints of his knee one yet larger, with which to beat it.

It is said that bottom-dealing was first brought to perfection by a man named Wilson. This desirable consummation was reached in 1834, and about this time first made its appearance on the western rivers, where it was rendered, in the course of a few years, entirely useless, through the blunders of bungling operators, and the verdant learned to protect themselves against the fraud.

Means swifter and more sure were gradually brought into requisition, for robbing the votaries of chance of their money. It is a strong advantage undoubtedly to know the strength of your adversary's hand at poker; but the work was too tedious for your fast sharper. Luck would sometimes protect a "sucker" against "iteming," stamped cards, and bottom-dealing. In the good old times, before draw-poker became fashionable, straight poker was the favorite brag game. At this game the cards were dealt by the winner of the pool, who could, of course, keep on dealing as often as he could win. This rule enabled the bottom-dealer to help himself to good cards as often as he dealt; but he might win twenty pools in succession without securing scarcely any money, should his adversaries hold poor hands, and in the meantime one of them might get, by good luck, better cards than those he held, and thus win from him a large stake. True, if he had a partner who was posted in the game he could give the "sucker" a big hand from the bottom, while his partner raised from his lap a bigger one to beat it with, but it was rather dangerous to attempt such a thing too often, and the least bungling was sure to lead to detection.

Young men perfected themselves in the science of false cutting and shuffling "running-up" hands, "palming out" cards, and "ringing them in," ringing in cold packs, double discarding, etc., etc. These ambitious tyros were taken under the fostering care of some patriarch of the sharper tribe, who assisted them in getting up their games and furnished them with money when that article was needed, which, with this kind of sharpers, was generally the case, when a trip on the river was in prospect.

The popular game of draw-poker, which has entirely superseded straight poker and brag, was the invention of river sharpers, and was first put in practice on the Mississippi steamboats. This game offers to the manipulator a hundred-fold better facilities for fleecing the unwary than either of the old games. The skillful operator can give his victim, with perfect ease, as many big hands as he chooses, and at the same time arm himself or his partner with better ones to beat them. But a shrewd swindler seldom gives a sucker more than an ace-full. He first tempts his appetite with two large pairs; then threes of various kinds; after these are expended, he hoists him up a flush or a full hand of a small denomination, and gradually increases them in size till he beats an ace-full for him; beyond this he is not likely to go. Whenever they find customers who will not stand running up hands, false shuffling and cutting, double discarding is practiced upon them; an advantage peculiar to draw-poker, and not applicable to any other game. Scores of those who have grown gray in the service of the fickle goddess, and who were the most wary among her votaries, have come to grief through the following artful piece of chicanery: Two partners being seated next each other, one attends to the betting department, while the latter manipulates the cards. He goes out with three aces, we will say for example, which he conceals in the joint of his knee until it comes his turn to deal. The cards having been dealt, he is ready to help the discarded hands, and he now conveys from their hiding place the stolen cards, in the palm of his hand, and places them upon the top of the pack while in the act of lifting it from the table. These cards are now drawn by his partner, who is informed, by a secret "item," of their denomination, and discards his hand accordingly for their reception. As he has the first "say" or "age," and the other players may perhaps not chip in for the pool, it is not necessary to bring out the hidden cards; that is, if any of the players chip in, then he tries, by making a large brag, to run them out; but should any of them prove obstinate and stand the raise, then the three aces are brought into action. The persons who can perform this trick well are by no means numerous.

The rough handling frequently received by sharpers, at the hands of their victims, during their various pilgrimages up and down the river, finally caused them to be a little more wary, and it was only when the steamer was about to make a wood-pile or some port that they would venture to put the finishing-stroke to their nefarious work, by dealing a big hand to their victim and then beating it for him.

When they had accomplished this they would leave the boat as quickly as convenient, and get upon the next steamer which stopped at their place of sojourn, whether going up or down mattered very little to them; and having leeched what "suckers" they found on her, abandoned her, in turn, for another which offered them subjects for plunder.

The gambling talents of short-card sharpers rest exclusively in their fingers; scarcely one of them being capable of playing any square game with even ordinary ability; and the non-professionals in the country, who are greatly their superiors in all short-card games played on the square, may be numbered by thousands. It is in fact a rare thing to find a short-card sharp who has sufficient confidence to risk his money on the square at anything except bucking the tiger,[1] which ravenous animal swallows up most of their ill-gotten plunder. When square faro, a two-card box, women, or kindred articles of commerce have depleted their pockets of their stolen funds, they are ready for another trip on the river, and probably are obliged to fall back on the paternal sharper, who fattens on their skill and industry in their nefarious business, for the "sinews of war."

These thieves became so formidable in their numbers, and so bold in their

1. Faro. [O'Connor's note.]

depredations, as to drive almost everything in the shape of square gambling from the river; and it was only when a party of acquaintances sat down to the card-table, to play among themselves, that anything like a square game could be seen on a steamer. As they were all called professional gamblers, the honest and straightforward of that community had to father their crimes and share their odium. Their rascalities even, bad as they were, were made the themes of marvelous romantic stories by the penny-a-liners and story-tellers of every description. Then the wonderful yarns that have been circulated from time to time by the lovers of the marvelous, relating to the outwitting of gamblers at their own games by determined heroes, who have forced them to disgorge their ill-gotten plunder and make restitution to every one whom they had duped, and many more tales, all equally improbable and without foundation, is all clap-trap. Sharpers are birds of prey, and cannot be outwitted in their line of business. They practice their arts on none but those whom they know will stand them, and can discern at a single glance whether the person seated before them can be cheated at play or otherwise. Should they chance on a tough customer, they drop him immediately, and seek others more suitable to their purpose.

About thirty years ago the following story circulated freely through the public press of this country. I have chosen it out of many of the same kind of delicious morsels which the news papers have, for forty years, delighted to dish up to their readers, and with which marvelous story-tellers have amused their hearers. The tale, on its own merits, will compare most favorably with those of that wonderful hero, Baron Munchausen.

"The news having reached the ears of a party of gamblers that a New Orleans bank was about to send to Vicksburg an agent having in his possession $95,000 to discharge a claim in that city, they followed him on board the New Orleans and Vicksburg packet with the intention of robbing him. During the trip he was induced by them to take part in a game of poker, and furnished with a large betting hand; but they did not omit, at the same time, to generously give a member of their own gang one with which to beat it. Several small brags were made by the contestants for the pool, when the agent went $250 better than his opponent, which was all the money belonging to himself which he had about him. This was seen, and a brag of $5,000 more was made by his adversary. The agent claimed a sight for his $250, stating that it was all the money he had; but it was refused. The object of the scoundrels being to induce him to break into the package belonging to the bank, which they knew to be in his possession, shrewdly thinking if he once did so they would not only obtain the $5,000 on the brag, but all the rest of its contents. On the refusal of his adversary to allow him a sight, he had appealed to the other members of the party, who decided that he must call the $5,000 or forfeit all claims to the pool. He again appealed to his opponent for a sight, but was informed by that inexorable gentleman that if he did not call the $5,000 brag within five minutes he should take down the pool. The five minutes were fast ebbing away, amid the breathless stillness of both the actors in the game and the spectators, when the agent, as a "*dernier resort*," determined to save his money from the clutches of the swindlers, took from his bosom the package belonging to the bank and threw it on the table, saying, 'I'll see your five thousand and go you ninety thousand better, and if you don't call the bet in five minutes I shall take down the pool.' The ruse was so unexpected that it completely upset their calculations, and not having sufficient money to call the brag they were compelled to forfeit all claims to the pool, according to their own ruling, and the agent swept it into his pockets, amidst the cheers of the bystanders."

This foolish tale was swallowed with avidity by the credulous, and every word was implicitly believed as if it were holy writ, and the imaginary bank-agent became a public hero. No law except that of might denies to a player at a poker-table a sight for what money he has before him, and it is rather improbable that a set of sharpers would dream of perpetrating such a robbery in so public a place, when they knew it would be impossible for them to escape with their plunder. Sharpers are much too shrewd for such bungling work. They take no chances to lose six or seven thousand dollars, nor two or three hundred dollars, nor even twenty dollars, at a hand of cards. As for the tales regarding the fabulous sums bet at poker-tables on our western rivers, they are all pure humbug. I have grave doubts whether a brag of two thousand dollars has ever been lost and won at a card-table on the Mississippi River, since the steamer Pennsylvania descended that stream in 1813.

Though railways have diverted a large portion of the travel from our western waters, and consequently thinned out some what the horde of sharpers who formerly infested the river steamers, they are still numerous, and still find fools to prey upon; for the crop, unlike more useful harvests, never fails. But the exploits of the noble army of "*chevaliers d'industrie*" are by no means confined to water navigation. Not at all! They are to be found in every city, town, and village, where short-card playing for gain makes up a portion of the pastime of the few or the many, and sufficient money is hazarded to attract their cupidity. Some are satisfied with quick gains and small profits, while others of the class are willing to wait months, in anticipation of taking in a big pile. They can be found of all degrees, from the lowest and most vicious, up to the most enlightened circles of card-players, plying their calling, and among every class find plenty of fools to batten on. Among these short-card sharpers are shrewd and discerning men of persuasive powers and agreeable manners, who, having finished their education on the river, and becoming older and more settled in character, they seek more respectable and profitable fields for their labor, among the upper classes whose card circles are held in private club-rooms or apartments in first-class hotels. Into those hallowed precincts, where none bearing the name of gambler are allowed to enter, designing men who are identified with mercantile pursuits, or some of the professions, easily obtain admittance. Many of these worthy and immaculate gentlemen have been carefully brought up in the paths of morality; some are highly cultured and refined; but in life's breathless struggle for possessions, their perceptions of right and wrong have become so distorted that they look upon the fleecing of a verdant at a card-table as an admirable piece of finesse. When their own skill has become worn out upon their unsuspecting adversaries of the green table, they manage to foist upon them some one of the more skillful experts of their acquaintance; perhaps under some military title, or perhaps will tack to their names the handle of Professor, Doctor, or Honorable. These latter, having once obtained a foothold in the ranks of respectability, endeavor to sustain it by every means in their power, and are most careful to commit no act which might draw upon them the slightest suspicion. Being unable, from their very composition, to support the pangs of a losing, one of them is seldom seen within the doors of a gambling-house, nor under any circumstances would they countenance a professional gambler, or speak to him on the street, and never fail to warn their verdant gulls against the association of such disreputable characters.

The question will naturally arise, Is there any cure for this crying evil? My answer is emphatically, *Yes!* Make cheating at the card-table a felony, punishable by the laws of the land, and card-sharpers and their insidious accomplices will disappear like hoar-frost before the morning sun. So long as the legislatures refuse to make stringent laws for shielding verdant card-players, so long will they be the legitimate prey of sharpers.

Three-card monte players are the worst Pariahs who prey upon society under the cloak of gambling. During the last five and twenty years they have infested our steamers and railways, and every place of public gathering, for the purpose of practicing their arts upon the unsuspecting and the unwary.

These pests outnumber the short-card sharpers on our western waters four to one. The latter claim with the former no affinity, and say they have destroyed all short-card playing on the rivers by their three-card operations. Socially, they look down upon them much as a first-class burglar might look down on some petty thief, at the same time claiming that their own vocation is legitimate, and based upon the true principles of science. For the life of me I cannot see where this nice discrimination comes in. To attain pre-eminence as a three-card monte thrower, seems to me as difficult as to become a first-class short-card sharp, and about equally meritorious. In order to attain pre-eminence in either of these roles, one must possess a self-possession nothing can shake, nerves of iron, dexterity of hand, quickness of perception, and cool judgment; should he lack a single one of these qualities, he would be a bungler, and entirely unfit for his calling. Viewing both these professions in a moral light, they stand on about the same footing, and we must conclude that both are legitimate in the eyes of the law, since none of our legislatures have made any efforts towards their suppression or punishment.

The Professor's Yarn

MARK TWAIN

No anthology of Mississippi writings can be complete without the presence of Mark Twain. That said, it is also true that Twain actually wrote very little about the presence of gambling on the river. Nowhere in his work are the stories of rich planters and nefarious blacklegs that dominated other accounts of life on the Mississippi. In an account of a meeting between Twain and Charlie Almes, a newspaper columnist, which is probably apocryphal, Almes asks, "Mr Twain, you must know a lot about gambling, from your experiences up and down the Mississippi [. . .] Which do you think is the best way to deal with this problem[?]" Even with such prompting, Twain responds with a story of gambling on Lake Michigan—and the adage, "once a sucker, always a sucker" (Read 30). Not that Twain was averse to telling tales of other types of criminality along the river: in *Huckleberry Finn* (1884), the Duke and the King are confidence-men; in *Tom Sawyer* (1876) and other works, the history of river outlaws like John Murrell are important imaginative elements. And, as Dixon Wecter described, Twain did like to relate one youthful tale of gambling that involved the Mississippi in an unexpected way: Twain and his childhood friend Will Bowen "had almost been surprised playing euchre and had hidden the deck in the sleeves of a preacher's 'baptising robe' hanging in the closet [. . .] a few days later when its owner was immersing converts in the river, the cards began to float out upon the water" (88–89). But nowhere is there real mention of gambling on the river. Whether this omission was due to Victorian propriety on Twain's part or testimony that the tall tales of gambling on the river were far removed from reality is uncertain. The following, however, is the closest that Twain comes to telling a story of riverboat gambling. Though set on a boat bound for California, "The Professor's Yarn" is told on a Mississippi steamboat and inspired by "talk about the lynching of the gamblers in Vicksburg half a century ago." See Opie Read, *Mark Twain and I* (Chicago: Reilly & Lee, 1940), and Dixon Wecter, *Sam Clemens of Hannibal* (Boston: Houghton Mifflin, 1961).

Here is a story which I picked up on board the boat that night. I insert it in this place merely because it is a good story, not because it belongs here—for it doesn't. It was told by a passenger—a college professor—and was called to the surface in the course of a general conversation which began with talk about horses, drifted into talk about astronomy, then into talk about the lynching of the gamblers in Vicksburg half a century ago, then into talk about dreams and superstitions; and ended, after midnight, in a dispute over free trade and protection.

It was in the early days. I was not a college professor then. I was a humble-minded young land-surveyor, with the world before me—to survey, in case anybody wanted it done. I had a contract to survey a route for a great mining-ditch in California, and I was on my way thither, by sea—a three or four weeks' voyage. There were a good many passengers, but I had very little to say to them; reading and dreaming were my passions, and I avoided conversation in order to indulge these appetites. There were three professional gamblers on board—rough, repulsive fellows. I never had any talk with them, yet I could not help seeing them with some frequency, for they gambled in an upper-deck state-room every day and night, and in my promenades I often had glimpses of them through their door, which stood a little ajar to let out the surplus tobacco smoke and profanity. They were an evil and hateful presence, but I had to put up with it, of course.

There was one other passenger who fell under my eye a good deal, for he seemed determined to be friendly with me, and I could not have gotten rid of him without running some chance of hurting his feelings, and I was far from wishing to do that. Besides, there was something engaging in his countrified simplicity and his beaming good-nature. The first time I saw this Mr. John Backus, I guessed, from his clothes and his looks, that he was a grazier or farmer from the back woods of some western State—doubtless Ohio—and afterward when he dropped into his personal history and I discovered that he *was* a cattle-raiser from interior Ohio, I was so pleased with my own penetration that I warmed toward him for verifying my instinct.

He got to dropping alongside me every day, after breakfast, to help me make my promenade; and so, in the course of time, his easy-working jaw had told me everything about his business, his prospects, his family, his relatives, his politics—in fact everything that concerned a Backus, living or dead. And meantime I think he had managed to get out of me everything I know about my trade, my tribe, my purposes, my prospects, and myself. He was a gentle and persuasive genius, and this thing showed it; for I was not given to talking about my matters. I said something about triangulation, once; the stately word pleased his ear; he inquired what it meant; I explained; after that he quietly and inoffensively ignored my name, and always called me Triangle.

What an enthusiast he was in cattle! At the bare name of a bull or a cow,

his eye would light and his eloquent tongue would turn itself loose. As long
as I would walk and listen, he would walk and talk; he knew all breeds, he
loved all breeds, he caressed them all with his affectionate tongue. I tramped
along in voiceless misery whilst the cattle question was up; when I could endure it no longer, I used to deftly insert a scientific topic into the conversation; then my eye fired and his faded; my tongue fluttered, his stopped; life
was a joy to me, and a sadness to him.

One day he said, a little hesitatingly, and with somewhat of diffidence:—

"Triangle, would you mind coming down to my state-room a minute, and
have a little talk on a certain matter?"

I went with him at once. Arrived there, he put his head out, glanced up
and down the saloon warily, then closed the door and locked it. We sat down
on the sofa, and he said:—

"I'm a-going to make a little proposition to you, and if it strikes you favorable, it'll be a middling good thing for both of us. You ain't a-going out
to Californy for fun, nuther am I—it's *business,* ain't that so? Well, you can
do me a good turn, and so can I you, if we see fit. I've raked and scraped and
saved, a considerable many years, and I've got it all here." He unlocked an old
hair trunk, tumbled a chaos of shabby clothes aside, and drew a short stout
bag into view for a moment, then buried it again and relocked the trunk.
Dropping his voice to a cautious low tone, he continued, "She's all there—a
round ten thousand dollars in yellow-boys; now this is my little idea: What I
don't know about raising cattle, ain't worth knowing. There's mints of money
in it, in Californy. Well, I know, and you know, that all along a line that's
being surveyed, there's little dabs of land that they call 'gores,' that fall to the
surveyor free gratis for nothing. All you've got to do, on your side, is to survey in such a way that the 'gores' will fall on good fat land, then you turn 'em
over to me, I stock 'em with cattle, *in* rolls the cash, I plank out your share of
the dollars regular, right along, and—"

I was sorry to wither his blooming enthusiasm, but it could not be helped,
I interrupted, and said severely,—

"I am not that kind of a surveyor. Let us change the subject, Mr.
Backus."

It was pitiful to see his confusion and hear his awkward and shamefaced
apologies. I was as much distressed as he was—especially as he seemed so far
from having suspected that there was anything improper in his proposition.
So I hastened to console him and lead him on to forget his mishap in a con-
versational orgy about cattle and butchery. We were lying at Acapulco; and,

as we went on deck, it happened luckily that the crew were just beginning to hoist some beeves aboard in slings. Backus' melancholy vanished instantly, and with it the memory of his late mistake.

"Now only look at that!" cried he. "My goodness, Triangle, what *would* they say to it in *Ohio?* Wouldn't their eyes bug out, to see 'em handled like that?—wouldn't they, though?"

All the passengers were on deck to look—even the gamblers—and Backus knew them all, and had afflicted them all with his pet topic. As I moved away, I saw one of the gamblers approach and accost him; then another of them; then the third. I halted; waited; watched; the conversation continued between the four men; it grew earnest; Backus drew gradually away; the gamblers followed, and kept at his elbow. I was uncomfortable. However, as they passed me presently, I heard Backus say, with a tone of persecuted annoyance:—

"But it ain't any use, gentlemen; I tell you again, as I've told you a half a dozen times before, I warn't raised to it, and I ain't a-going to resk it."

I felt relieved. "His level head will be his sufficient protection," I said to myself.

During the fortnight's run from Acapulco to San Francisco I several times saw the gamblers talking earnestly with Backus, and once I threw out a gentle warning to him. He chuckled comfortably and said,—

"Oh, yes! they tag around after me considerable—want me to play a little, just for amusement, they say—but laws-a-me, if my folks have told me once to took out for that sort of livestock, they've told me a thousand times, I reckon."

By and by, in due course, we were approaching San Francisco. It was an ugly black night, with a strong wind blowing, but there was not much sea. I was on deck, alone. Toward ten I started below. A figure issued from the gamblers' den, and disappeared in the darkness. I experienced a shock, for I was sure it was Backus. I flew down the companion-way, looked about for him, could not find him, then returned to the deck just in time to catch a glimpse of him as he re-entered that confounded nest of rascality. Had he yielded at last? I feared it. What had he gone below for?—His bag of coin? Possibly. I drew near the door, full of bodings. It was a-crack, and I glanced in and saw a sight that made me bitterly wish I had given my attention to saving my poor cattle-friend, instead of reading and dreaming my foolish time away. He was gambling. Worse still, he was being plied with champagne, and was already showing some effect from it. He praised the "cider," as he called it, and said now that he had got a taste of it he almost believed he would drink it if it was spirits, it was so good and so ahead of anything he had ever run across before. Surreptitious smiles, at this, passed from one rascal to another, and they filled all the glasses, and whilst Backus honestly drained his to the bottom they pretended to do the same, but threw the wine over their shoulders.

I could not bear the scene, so I wandered forward and tried to interest myself in the sea and the voices of the wind. But no, my uneasy spirit kept dragging me back at quarter-hour intervals; and always I saw Backus drinking his wine—fairly and squarely, and the others throwing theirs away. It was the painfulest night I ever spent.

The only hope I had was that we might reach our anchorage with speed—that would break up the game. I helped the ship along all I could with my prayers. At last we went booming through the Golden Gate, and my pulses leaped for joy. I hurried back to that door and glanced in. Alas, there was small room for hope—Backus's eyes were heavy and bloodshot, his sweaty face was crimson, his speech maudlin and thick, his body sawed drunkenly about with the weaving motion of the ship. He drained another glass to the dregs, whilst the cards were being dealt.

He took his hand, glanced at it, and his dull eyes lit up for a moment. The gamblers observed it, and showed their gratification by hardly perceptible signs.

"How many cards?"

"None!" said Backus.

One villain—named Hank Wiley—discarded one card, the others three each. The betting began. Heretofore the bets had been trifling—a dollar or two; but Backus started off with an eagle now, Wiley hesitated a moment, then "saw it" and "went ten dollars better." The other two threw up their hands.

Backus went twenty better. Wiley said,—

"I see that, and go you a *hundred* better!" then smiled and reached for the money.

"Let it alone," said Backus, with drunken gravity.

"What! you mean to say you're going to cover it?"

"Cover it? Well I reckon I am—and lay another hundred on top of it, too."

He reached down inside his overcoat and produced the required sum.

"Oh, that's your little game, is it? I see your raise, and raise it five hundred!" said Wiley.

"Five hundred *better!*" said the foolish bull-driver, and pulled out the amount and showered it on the pile. The three conspirators hardly tried to conceal their exultation. All diplomacy and pretence were dropped now, and the sharp exclamations came thick and fast, and the yellow pyramid grew higher and higher. At last ten thousand dollars lay in view. Wiley cast a bag of coin on the table, and said with mocking gentleness,—

"Five thousand dollars better, my friend from the rural districts—what do you say *now?*"

"I *call* you!" said Backus, heaving his golden shot-bag on the pile. "What have you got?"

"Four kings, you d——d fool!" and Wiley threw down his cards and surrounded the stakes with his arms.

"Four *aces,* you ass!" thundered Backus, covering his man with a cocked revolver. "*I'm a professional gambler myself, and I've been laying for you duffers all this voyage!*"

Down went the anchor, rumbledy-dum-dum! and the long trip was ended.

Well—well, it is a sad world. One of the three gamblers was Backus's "pal." It was he that dealt the fateful hands.

According to an understanding with the two victims, he was to have given Backus four queens, but alas, he didn't.

A week later, I stumbled upon Backus—arrayed in the height of fashion— in Montgomery Street. He said, cheerily, as we were parting,—

"Ah, by-the-way, you needn't mind about those gores. I don't really know anything about cattle, except what I was able to pick up in a week's apprenticeship over in Jersey just before we sailed. My cattle-culture and cattle-enthusiasm have served their turn—I shan't need them any more."

From *Old Times on the Upper Mississippi*

GEORGE BYRON MERRICK

George Byron Merrick's memories of piloting on the river provide an interesting counterpoint to Mark Twain's more famous works. Though heavily influenced by Twain, Merrick had his own stories to tell about life on the Mississippi, a river that he knew in a variety of capacities until he left it to join the Union army in 1863. In contrast to Twain, Merrick certainly acknowledged the existence of gambling on the western rivers. Even though Merrick is adamant that "a small fraction of truth is diluted with a great deal of fiction" in most riverboat gambling narratives, he still paints a fascinating picture of the antebellum gamblers that he knew on the steamboat *Fanny Harris*.

Volumes have been written, first and last, on the subject of gambling on the Mississippi. In them a small fraction of truth is diluted with a deal of fiction. The scene is invariably laid upon a steamboat on the lower Mississippi. The infatuated planter, who always does duty as the plucked goose, invariably stakes his faithful body servant, or a beautiful quadroon girl, against the gambler's pile of gold, and as invariably loses his stake. Possibly that may occasionally have happened on the lower river in ante-bellum days. I never travelled the lower river, and cannot therefore speak from actual observation.

On the upper river, in early times, there were no nabobs travelling with body servants and pretty quadroons. Most of the travellers had broad belts around their waists, filled with good honest twenty-dollar gold pieces. It was these belts which the professional gamblers sought to lighten. Occasionally they did strike a fool who thought he knew more about cards than the man who made the game, and who would, after a generous baiting with mixed drinks, "set in" and try his fortune. There was, of course, but one result—the belt was lightened, more or less, according to the temper and judgment of the victim.

So far as I know, gambling was permitted on all boats. On some, there was a cautionary sign displayed, stating that gentlemen who played cards for money did so at their own risk. The professionals who travelled the river for the purpose of "skinning suckers" were usually the "gentlemen" who displayed the greatest concern in regard to the meaning of this caution, and who freely expressed themselves in the hearing of all to the effect that they seldom played cards at all, still less for money; but if they did feel inclined to have a little social game it was not the business of the boat to question their right to do so, and if they lost their money they certainly would not call on the boat to restore it.

After the expression of such manly sentiments, it was surprising if they did not soon find others who shared with them this independence. In order to convey a merited reproof to "the boat," for its unwarranted interference with the pleasure or habits of its patrons, they bought a pack of cards at the bar and "set in" to a "friendly game." In the posting of this inconspicuous little placard, "the boat" no doubt absolved itself from all responsibility in what might, and surely did follow in the "friendly games" sooner or later started in the forward cabin. Whether the placard likewise absolved the officers of the boat from all responsibility in the matter, is a question for the logicians. I cannot recollect that I had a conscience in those days; and if a "sucker" chose to invest his money in draw poker rather than in corner lots, it was none of my business. In that respect, indeed, there was little choice between "Bill" Mallen on the boat with his marked cards, and Ingenuous Doemly at Nininger, with his city lots on paper selling at a thousand dollars each, which to-day, after half a century, are possibly worth twenty-five dollars an acre as farming land.

Ordinarily, the play was not high on the upper river. The passengers were not great planters, with sacks of money, and "niggers" on the side to fall back upon in case of a bluff. The operators, also, were not so greedy as their real or fictitious fellows of the lower river. If they could pick up two or three hundred dollars a week by honest endeavor they were satisfied, and gave thanks accordingly.

Probably by some understanding among themselves, the fraternity divided themselves among the different boats running regularly in the passenger trade, and only upon agreement did they change their boats; nor did they intrude upon the particular hunting ground of others.

The "Fanny Harris" was favored with the presence, more or less intermittently, of "Bill" Mallen, "Bill" and "Sam" Dove, and "Boney" Trader. "Boney" was short for Napoleon Bonaparte. These worthies usually travelled in pairs, the two Dove brothers faithfully and fraternally standing by each other, while Mallen and "Boney" campaigned in partnership. These men were consummate actors. They never came aboard the boat together, and they never recognized each other until introduced—generally through the good offices of their intended victims. In the preliminary stages of the game, they cheerfully lost large sums of money to each other; and after the hunt was up, one usually went ashore at Prescott, Hastings, or Stillwater, while the other continued on to St. Paul. At different times they represented all sorts and conditions of men—settlers, prospectors, Indian agents, merchants, lumbermen, and even lumber-jacks; and they always dressed their part, and talked it, too. To do this required some education, keen powers of observation, and an all-around knowledge of men and things. They were gentlemanly at all times—courteous to men and chivalrous to women. While pretending to drink large quantities of very strong liquors, they did in fact make away with many pint measures of quite innocent river water, tinted with the mildest liquid distillation of burned peaches. A clear head and steady nerves were prerequisites to success; and when engaged in business, these men knew that neither one nor the other came by way of "Patsey" Donnelly's "Choice wines and liquors." They kept their private bottles of colored water on tap in the bar, and with the uninitiated passed for heavy drinkers.

The play was generally for light stakes, but it sometimes ran high. Five dollars ante, and no limit, afforded ample scope for big play, provided the players had the money and the nerve. The tables were always surrounded by a crowd of lookers-on, most of whom knew enough of the game to follow it understandingly. It is possible that some of the bystanders may have had a good understanding with the professionals, and have materially assisted them by signs and signals.

The chief reliance of the gamblers, however, lay in the marked cards with which they played. No pack of cards left the bar until it had passed through the hands of the gambler who patronized the particular boat that he "worked." The marking was called "stripping." This was done by placing the high cards—ace, king, queen, jack, and ten-spot—between two thin sheets of metal, the edges of which were very slightly concaved. Both edges of the cards were trimmed to these edges with a razor; the cards so "stripped" were thus a shade narrower in the middle than those not operated upon; they were left full width at each end. The acutely sensitive fingers of the gamblers could distinguish between the marked and the unmarked cards, while the other players could detect nothing out of the way in them. "Bill" Mallen would take a gross of cards from the bar to his stateroom and spend hours in thus trimming them, after which they were returned to the original wrappers, which were carefully folded and sealed, and replaced in the bar for sale.

A "new pack" was often called for by the victim when "luck" ran against him; and Mallen himself would ostentatiously demand a fresh pack if he lost a hand or two, as he always did at the beginning of the play.

I never saw any shooting over a game, and but once saw pistols drawn. That was when the two Doves were holding up a "tenderfoot." There was a big pile of gold on the table—several hundred dollars in ten and twenty dollar pieces. The losers raised a row and would have smashed the two operators but for the soothing influence of a cocked Derringer in the hands of one of them. The table was upset and the money rolled in all directions. The outsiders decided where the money justly belonged, in their opinion, by promptly pocketing all they could reach while the principals were fighting. I found a twenty myself the next morning.

I saw "Bill" Mallen for the last time under rather peculiar and unlooked-for circumstances. It was down in Virginia, in the early spring of 1865. There was a review of troops near Petersburg, preparatory to the advance on Lee's lines. General O. B. Wilcox and General Sam. Harriman had sent for their wives to come down to the front and witness the display. I was an orderly at headquarters of the First Brigade, First Division, Ninth Army Corps, and was detailed to accompany the ladies, who had an ambulance placed at their disposal. I was mounted, and coming alongside the vehicle began to instruct the driver where to go to get the best view of the parade. The fellow, who was quite under the influence of liquor, identified himself as Mallen, and sought to renew acquaintance with me.

It went against the grain to go back on an old messmate, but the situation demanded prompt action. "Bill" was ordered to attend closely to his driving or he would get into the guardhouse, with the displeasure of the division commander hanging over him, which would not be a pleasant experience. He knew enough about usages at the front, at that time, to understand this, and finished his drive in moody silence. After the review was over he went back to the corral with his team, and I to headquarters. I never saw or heard of him again, the stirring incidents of the latter days of March, 1865, eclipsing everything else. I presume he was following the army, nominally as a mule driver, while he "skinned" the boys at poker as a matter of business. The whiskey had him down for the time being, however, otherwise I would have been glad to talk over former times on the river.

From *Flush Fred's Full Hand; or, Life and Strife in Louisiana*

EDWARD WILLETT

In the character of Flush Fred, Edward Willett created the definitive dime-novel riverboat gambler. Though trained as a lawyer, Willett turned to journalism in the years before the Civil War and began his notable career as a dime-novelist in 1864. Since Willett moved to St. Louis in the late 1850s and remained there until the 1880s, it is highly possible that Flush Fred was modeled on gamblers of Willett's acquaintance. Wherever the inspiration came from, the character demonstrated a compelling combination of attributes, and Fred was a model for the literary hero-gamblers who followed him. Far removed from the villainous and cowardly blackleg of the antebellum years, Fred is honest, brave, and attractive—and his proficiency at gambling is a vital dimension of his masculinity. As one character puts it, he is one of the "fine specimens" of American manhood. He was also popular enough with readers to sustain four separate adventures. In the following extract, Fred acts in typically heroic fashion, winning a hand of cards before piloting a steamboat to safety. For more information on Willett, see Albert Johannsen, *The House of Beadle and Adams and Its Dime and Nickel Novels,* 2 vols. (Norman: University of Oklahoma Press, 1950), 2:305–10.

The good steamer Sabine, Captain Spillers, was slowly making her way down the lower Mississippi.

Slowly, because the river was at an uncertain stage.

There had been a big rise, accompanied by an extensive inundation, and while it lasted the largest boats had been free to go wherever they pleased, as long as they kept between the two banks; for the channel was everywhere, and there was no danger of getting out of it.

But when the water began to decline, it fell very rapidly, and the chutes or short cuts that could have been taken a few days previous to the present trip of the Sabine were not then practicable.

The channel, too, had suffered many and great changes, and was still changing continually, as it always does on a falling river, so that pilots who had known it "like a book" before the "fresh" were disposed to feel their way dubiously, and indisposed to rely upon their previous knowledge.

Darkness also added to their difficulties, the night being moonless and starless, and the jack-staff scarcely visible from the pilot-house.

Down below all was light and jollity, and the passengers who had gathered in the Social Hall gave no thought to the perplexities of the pilots over their heads.

Several of them were playing cards, and at one table a game that had been in progress between four men of gentlemanly appearance and manners had been brought to a close.

All had risen from the table, and one of them, a tall and handsome young man, with dark eyes and hair, was emptying into his pocket a good-sized "pot" which he had just won.

"If you should happen to want your revenge at any time, gentlemen," said he, "you will find me always ready to accommodate you."

He slightly lifted his hat, and went out forward.

He was followed by the glance of one of the party—an elderly gentleman, with white hair and ruddy complexion, whose attire and bearing bespoke him a person of wealth and consideration.

"Who is that young man?" inquired the old gentleman.

"Thought you knew him, Mr. Delarosse," replied another of the party.

"I have been about so little of late years—that is, in my own country—that I hardly know anybody. Who is he, Peters?"

"His name is Fred Henning, and he is known on the river as Flush Fred. He is a professional gambler; but you wanted a lively game, and nobody could give you better satisfaction in that way than he could."

"That is all right. I am not ashamed of my company. Gamblers should not be choosers, anyway, and a professional ought to be as good as an amateur, if not a little better. I like the young fellow's looks, and I like his style, and I was quite willing that he should win my money. Will you join me, gentlemen, in drinking the health of the man who got the best of us?"

The subject of this conversation, after a glance from the guards at the blackness of the night, had mounted to the hurricane roof, from which elevation he surveyed the surroundings of the Sabine more carefully.

Then he mounted the texas, and ascended the stair that led to the pilot house.

It was Sam Byrne's watch as pilot, his partner being not only off duty, but suffering with a severe chill.

Sam and his cub, Joe Pettus, were the only persons in the pilot house when Flush Fred entered, and both were gazing intently into the darkness ahead, as if they could see anything there.

"Glad to see you, Fred," said the pilot as he glanced hastily at the new-comer. "This is better luck than I had looked for."

"I have been busy raking in some ducats, or I would have come up before," answered Fred Henning. "Sha'n't I order something for us, Sam!—something cool with a straw in it."

"Not just now. I've got a sweetener of a job before me—all I can attend to. I say, Fred, I want to test that memory of yours you brag of. You were with me that last time I ran Paddy White's chute. Do you remember how I raised the towhead?"

"By a patch of cloud under the moon, right ahead of the jackstaff!" promptly replied Fred.

"Right you are. There's no moon tonight, and the patch of cloud was top of a big sycamore; but it's there yet. Can you see it?"

"What are you giving me, Sam Byrne?" demanded Fred. "Do you mean to say that we are near to Paddy White's?"

"We are just at the head of the chute. Use your eyes."

"And are you going to run the chute this dark night, and on a falling river?"

"You may bet your bottom dollar that I am. It is a big cut-off, and when we are through it I can trust Joe Pettus or any other baby to steer the Sabine."

"I suppose you know what you are doing, Sam Byrne! What are your marks?"

"After we pass the towhead, as you know, the chute is straight and easy enough until we reach the bar, and I have learned from an upriver boat that the bar is now just opposite the old tree on the false point at the right. There ought to be seven feet now. If there's less than that I must shove her over for all she's worth. After we pass the bar and the bend the bottom drops out of the chute."

Fred Henning lighted a cigar. He had the most serene and implicit confidence in Sam Byrne.

That was exactly the kind of confidence that pilot had in himself, and he was as calm and placid as a May morning, though he was about to enter on the performance of a pretty risky exploit.

He rung the bell to slow, and then to stop, and the motion of the boat was scarcely perceptible at that lofty elevation.

She was simply drifting with the swift current of the river—drifting steadily into a bank of blackness, where it would seem that more than human eyes were needed to distinguish as much as an outline of anything.

Suddenly the pilot whirled the spokes of the big wheel to the right, and put his weight upon them.

The boat answered admirably, and her head swung around as if she would thrust the bank of blackness to one side.

Fred Henning stood behind Byrne, and said nothing, as he gazed intently ahead, his eyes gradually adapting themselves to the surroundings.

On each side the blackness became, if possible, denser, and it was evident to an experienced person that the Sabine had passed the towhead, and fairly entered the chute. The young cub pilot stood with his hands in his pockets, staring blankly and uselessly, as to his vision there was nothing but utter darkness in any direction.

Under the direction of the pilot-house bell, the wheels began to churn the water again, and the big boat moved more rapidly down the chute, steadily shoving the bank of blackness ahead, but leaving it fairly *caked* at each side.

The pilot pulled the big bell forward, and a deck-hand came out below, and began to throw the lead.

Again the bell was struck, and another man went forward with the larboard lead.

They were not visible; but their sing-song was clearly audible in the night air at the pilot-house.

Plenty of water was what they reported at first; but it soon began to shoal.

"Now we're coming to it, Fred," said Byrne, in a whisper, as he rung the stopping bell.

"Can I help you?" asked Fred.

There was no answer.

Suddenly the grasp of the pilot's hands on the wheel relaxed, and he gasped audibly.

Then he fell backward heavily upon the floor.

Flush Fred stepped upon the bench instantly, and seized the wheel.

He could not stop to discover what was the matter with Byrne—to learn whether he was living or dead.

The lives of a boat-load of passengers were to be considered, rather than the life of any one man.

It was to be supposed that Byrne was dead, as he did not move after he struck the floor.

Fred Henning was no pilot.

In the mere act of steering he was sufficiently an adept, having practiced it on many boats and in the company of various pilots.

He had, moreover, an excellent memory, and the amount of river lore he had accumulated was something remarkable.

But he was no pilot.

Yet at the moment the entire responsibility for the safety of the Sabine and her passengers and crew and cargo was thrown upon him.

Everything depended on his head and his hands; but he did not flinch.

The best that could be done by a man in his position he would do, and it would not be his fault if he should fail.

He was glad that he had asked Byrne how he intended to run the chute, and he strained his eyes to catch a glimpse of the dead tree on the false point.

It was like looking through the wall of a house; but he meant to find that tree.

In this he was assisted by the headsmen, who reported the water shoaling as the steamer floated down the chute, and this meant that she was nearing the bar.

Young Joe Pettus, quite off his head, had run out of the pilot house as soon as Fred Henning grabbed the wheel.

His first impulse was to seek the captain, and he met him coming up to the hurricane roof.

"That you, Joe?" demanded Captain Spillers. "Where are we? What is Mr. Byrne doing?"

"In Paddy White's chute, and Mr. Byrne is dead or in a fit."

"Hell's delight!" exclaimed the frightened captain, as he brushed by the boy, and gained the hurricane deck. "Hell's delight! Who's got the wheel?"

"Flush Fred," answered Joe. Captain Spillers drew a long breath of relief.

It was at least better than nothing that somebody was there, and Fred Henning was a cool and clear-headed man.

The captain cast a quick glance up at the pilot-house, and walked forward.

He could only wait and hope.

Fred was sure that he had his eyes glued to the dead tree on the false point, and he coolly listened to the cry of the leadsmen.

"Eight and a half!"

"Eight feet!"

Fred rung the go-ahead bell, and spoke to the engineer through the speaking-tube.

"Seven and a half!"

"Seven feet!"

"Crack onto her, Jim!" shouted Fred down the tube. "Give her oceans of it!"

"Six and a—"

The cry was drowned by the roaring of the steam as it rushed out of the escape-pipes in great white clouds, and the boat stopped with a shock that sent a shiver all through her.

She had struck on the bar.

Just then the other pilot, who had been roused by Joe Pettus, came staggering up into the texas, without hat or coat or shoes, his face so white that it fairly shone in the darkness.

He was dazed by what he saw and could guess, and was as helpless as a baby.

But the big wheels of the Sabine were churning the chute like mad, and she "humped herself," and fairly crawled over the bar until she slid into the deepening water beyond.

"Eight feet!" cheerily cried the leadsman.

"All right, Jim!" shouted Fred through the speaking-tube.

"Quarter less twain!"

Fred struck the big bell, and the leadsman's song ceased.

The danger was over, and the bend was successfully rounded, and the Sabine steamed gaily down the chute and into the broad river.

Captain Spillers came up, and the pilot-house was soon crowded with men from below, including a physician who happened to be among the passengers.

But there was nothing that could be done for Sam Byrne.

Heart disease was announced as the cause of his death, and he was supposed to have been dead when he struck the floor.

"Poor Sam Byrne!" exclaimed the captain. "This will be sad news to send back to his wife and babies."

The dead pilot was carried below, and praises were poured in upon the man who had taken his place.

"Go back to your berth, Mr. Saunders," said Fred Henning to the remaining pilot. "You are not fit to be on duty now. I will whirl this wheel until morning, with Joe Pettus to help me, and then you may be well enough to get about."

The next day, when Flush Fred had got up and stirring about, he discovered that he was the lion of the hour in the cabin.

The tragic fate of the pilot had of course made a great sensation on the Sabine, and with it had naturally been connected the exploit of the man who had jumped into his tracks and performed the difficult task that death had prevented him from executing.

It was not alone the daring of the act, but the coolness and quite unexpected skill that had entered into the exploit, and, above all, the fact that the hero of the occasion had saved boat, and possibly many lives.

On the spur of the moment a purse was raised by the passengers to show their appreciation of Fred Henning's courage and skill; but he accepted it only on the condition that he should be allowed to turn it over to the family of the dead pilot.

This increased his popularity, and the Sam Byrne fund, thus started, was speedily raised to a very pretty sum.

Captain Spillers, who fully understood and admitted the nature and value of Fred Henning's service, was not at all backwards in giving him the credit that was his due. Among those who praised and congratulated the temporary pilot no person was more enthusiastic than Mr. Delarosse, the Louisiana gentleman who had lost money to him at cards the night before.

"I am glad to know you, Mr. Hemming," said the old gentleman. "Begad, sir, I am proud to have made you acquaintance, and it is not every man that Leon Delarosse considers worth knowing. I wish I had your nerve and you pluck, and I wish I had your youth and spirit, and, begad, sir, I wish I could play poker with your dash and spirit. I want to introduce my nephew to you, if you are willing. Here, Paul!"

A young man who was about the age of Fred Henning stepped forward gracefully, but with a frown on his face.

He was not a young man of prepossessing appearance, though he was faultlessly dressed, and his style, at least on the outside, was that of a well-bred gentleman.

His dark eyes were small and restless, and his brow was low, and his black mustache gave his face a sinister look, perhaps due to the sneer that usually lurked under it.

Flush Fred was prepared to dislike him as soon as he saw him, and this feeling was doubtless reciprocated by the other.

"This is my nephew, Paul Delarosse," said the old gentleman. "As he has been educated abroad, he is not very well acquainted with his native country, and I want him to see what fine specimens of manhood America can produce. This gentleman, Paul, is Mr. Fred Henning, who saved the boat and her passengers, last night, when the pilot was struck dead at his post. We can well boast of our young men here, when they can do such daring and skilful deeds as that."

Paul Delarosse spoke with a slightly Frenchified accent, and his sneer was quite perceptible.

"Mr. Henning will hardly thank you, uncle Leon," he said, "for your extravagant praise, as it seems that he is something of a pilot, and he only did what any pilot would have done in his place. Besides, he put at risk the lives of all the people on the boat."

"If you put it in that way, my boy, I must say that his own life was worth more to him than a good many other lives, and he risked that."

"After all, uncle, there is not a vast amount of peril in a mud-bank, and I suppose that Mr. Henning is accustomed to games of bluff."

"Why, you supercilious young dog, I wonder if anything on this earth will ever please you. Mr. Henning, you must overlook Paul's little queerishness as I do. He is the only son of my dead brother, and I am taking him home to my place to put a little life into the old plantation."

"And to make him your heir," thought Fred. He did not speak, however, but smiled pleasantly, being amused by what looked like an absurd jealousy on the part of the young man.

"Now I shall want you to come and see me, Mr. Henning," said the old gentleman. "You have plenty of leisure, or can have if you want to, and I shall insist upon a visit. It is easy to find my place—Gravelly Bayou, a few miles from Martigny—and everything I have shall be at your disposal when you come. You can make expenses by playing poker with me, if nothing else will suit you; but I do hope that you will come and give me a long visit."

Fred thanked the hearty old gentleman for his kind invitation, and said that he hoped to be able to avail himself of it.

Paul Delarosse frowned more darkly than usual, but did not openly express his displeasure until he walked away with his uncle.

"How could you invite that man to your house, uncle Leon?" he asked. "Don't you know that he is a professional gambler?"

"I think I know as much about it as you do," crustily answered the old gentleman.

"Do you wish me to associate with that class of people?"

"Now, Paul, you ought not to get to be too high-minded quite so suddenly. It is my opinion that the people I choose to associate with are quite good enough for you. What were you but a card-sharper when I picked you up in Paris?"

Fred Henning looked after the couple rather critically.

"The old gentleman is a good and well-preserved specimen of the Louisiana planter," he muttered; "but the young fellow has got something on his mind that ought not to be there."

From *Forty Years a Gambler on the Mississippi*

GEORGE DEVOL

For Bernard De Voto, "To read the autobiography of George Devol is to perceive at once that the river as it was is not the river of Mark Twain" (110). For
those looking for a corrective to the dearth of gambling stories in Twain's
work, Devol is certainly a gold mine. No other riverboat character left such
a complete record of his gambling career. Devol's unique account of his experiences has proven to be a constant source of inspiration for writers who
followed him; most of the popular stories of riverboat gambling are trace-
able to his reminiscences. Certainly, many readers will fervently disagree
with Louis Hunter's assertion that "despite the heavy coating of adventure
and excitement with which his tales are varnished they make dull reading"
(409). On the contrary, Devol's biography presents a panorama of river gambling. Throughout, he is at pains to develop his particular viewpoint of the
gambling world. On one hand, he presents his development as a gambler as a
conscious rejection of the world of manual labor. Pushing his caulking tools
in the river, he declares "it was the last lick of work I would ever do." Alongside the self-aggrandizing rhetoric, Devol was also certain that his confidence tricks had a moral imperative: "It is a good lesson for a dishonest man
to be caught by some trick, and I always did like to teach it." See Bernard De
Voto, *Mark Twain's America* (1932; Lincoln: University of Nebraska Press,
1997; and Louis Hunter, *Steamboats on the Western Rivers: An Economic and
Technological History* (1949; New York: Dover, 1993).

My Dear Reader: I first saw the light of day in a little town called Marietta, at
the mouth of the Muskingum River in the State of Ohio, on the first day of
August, 1829. I was the youngest of six children, and was the pet of the family. My father was a ship carpenter, and worked at boat-building in the beginning of the present century. I had good opportunities to secure an early education, as we had good schools in the West at that time. I had very little liking
for books, and much less for school. When my parents thought me at school,
I was playing "hookey" with other boys, running about the river, kicking
foot-ball, playing "shinny on your own side," and having a fight nearly every
day. I hardly ever went home that I did not have my face all scratched up
from having been in a fight, which innocent amusement I loved much better than school. When I was hardly ten years of age, I would carry stones in
my pocket and tackle the school teachers if they attempted to whip me. My

father was away from home at his work most of the time, and my mother (God bless her dear old soul) could not manage me. She has often called in some passer-by to help her punish me. I can now see I richly deserved all the punishment I ever received, and more too. When there was company at our house, and my mother would be busy preparing a meal, I would get my bow and arrows and shoot the cups off from the table, and then run away. I guess I was about the worst boy of my age west of the Allegheny Mountains that was born of good Christian parents. I have often heard the good old church members say: "That boy will be hung if he lives to be twenty years old." But I have fooled them, and am still on the turf, although I have had some pretty close calls, as you will see by reading this book.

LEAVING HOME.

In the year 1839, while at the river one day, I saw a steamer lying at the wharf-boat by the name of *Wacousta*. The first steward said I could ship as a cabin boy at $4 per month. I thought this a great opportunity, so when the boat backed out I was on board without saying anything to my parents or any one else. My first duty was to scour knives. I knew they would stand no foolish-ness, so at it I went, and worked like a little trooper, and by so doing I gained the good will of the steward. At night I was told to get a mattress and sleep on the floor of the cabin; this I was very glad to do, as I was tired.

About four o'clock in the morning the second steward came up to me and gave me a pretty hard kick in the side that hurt me, and called out: "Get up here, and put your mattress away." I did get up and put away my bed, and then I went to the steward who kicked me and said: "Look here! Don't kick me that way again, for you hurt me." He let go and hit me a slap in the face that made my ears ring; so into him I pitched. I was a big boy for only ten years old; but I struck the wrong man that time, for he hit me another lick in the nose that came very near sending me to grass, but I rallied and came again. This time I had a piece of stone coal that I grabbed out of a bucket; I let it fly, and it caught him on the side of the head and brought him to his knees. By this time the passengers were getting up to see what was the mat-ter; the pilot and first steward soon put a stop to the fight. I told my story to the boss, and he took sides with me. He told the officers of the boat that I was the best boy to work that he had; so they discharged the second steward at Cincinnati, and you can bet I was glad. I remained on the *Wacousta* for some time, and thought myself a good steamboat man. I knew it all, for I had been there.

The next boat I shipped on was the *Walnut Hills,* at $7 per month. You could hear her "scape" (whistle) for a distance of twenty miles on a clear day or night. I would get up early in the morning and make some "five-cent pieces" (there were no nickels in those days) by blacking boots.

PUT ASHORE FOR FIGHTING.

I quit the *Walnut Hills* after three months, and shipped with Captain Patterson on the *Cicero,* bound for Nashville. The first trip up the Cumberland River the boat was full of passengers, and I had a fight with the pantryman. The Captain said I should go ashore. They brought me up to the office, and the clerk was told to pay me my wages, which amounted to the large sum of one dollar and fifty cents. I was told to get my baggage; but as two blue cotton shirts and what I had on my back was all I possessed, it did not take me long to pack. My trunk was a piece of brown paper with a pin lock. They landed me at a point where the bank was about one hundred feet high, and so steep that a goat could not climb it. They commenced to pull in the plank, when the steward yelled out to the Captain, "that he could not get along without that boy," and asked him to let me go as far as Nashville. I was told to come aboard, which I did, and I remained on that boat for one year, during which time I learned to play "seven-up," and to "steal card," so that I could cheat the boys, and I felt as if I was fixed for life. I quit the *Cicero,* and shipped with Captain Mason on the steamer *Tiago.* Bill Campbell, afterward the first captain of the *Robert E. Lee,* was a cabin boy on the same boat. He is now a captain in the Vicksburg Packet Line. During the time I was on the *Tiago* the Mexican War broke out.

WAR WITH MEXICO.

"Lands intersected by a narrow frith
Abhor each other. Mountains interposed
Make enemies of nations who had else,
Like kindred drops, been mingled into one."

When the Mexican War broke out, our boat was lying at Pittsburg. The Government bought a new boat called the *Corvette,* that had just been built at Brownsville. A cousin of mine was engaged to pilot her on the Rio Grande. His name was Press Devol. He was a good pilot on the Ohio, from Cincinnati to Pittsburg, but had never seen the Rio Grande, except on the map. I thought I would like to go to war, and to Mexico. My cousin got me the position as barkeeper, so I quit our boat, and shipped on the *Corvette,* for the war.

Jack McCourtney, of Wheeling, was the owner of the bar. There was a man aboard, on our way down, who took a great liking to me. He was well posted on cards, and taught me to "stock a deck," so I could give a man a big hand; so I was a second time "fixed for life."

When we got down to New Orleans they took the boat over to Algiers, took her guards off, and part of her cabin, and we started across the Gulf; and you bet my hair stood up at times, when those big swells would go clear over her in a storm. But finally we landed at Bagdad, and commenced to load her with supplies for the army.

I soon got tired of the Rio Grande, and after cheating all the soldiers that I could at cards (as there was no one else to rob), I took a vessel, and came back to New Orleans. When I landed there, I was very comfortably fixed, as I had about $2,700, and was not quite seventeen years old. Here I was in a big city, and knew no one; so I went and got a boarding house, and left all my cash, but what I might need, in the care of an old gentleman that looked something like my father. I thought he must be honest, as he looked like him, and he proved himself so.

I then picked up courage, and said to myself, "I believe that I will go home." But to pay passage was all foolishness, as I was such a good hand on a boat, so I shipped on the steamboat *Montgomery,* Captain Montgomery, and Windy Marshall (as they called him) Mate. I shipped as second steward, at twenty dollars per month.

The boat was full of people, and the card tables were going every night as soon as the supper tables were cleared. We had been out from New Orleans two days and nights before I picked up a game. One afternoon in the texas, I beat my man out of $170; and as there was no "squeal" in those days, I was all right, although they did not allow any of the crew to play with passengers.

We got to Louisville, where the boat laid up and paid off her crew, and I came on to Cincinnati.

HOME AGAIN.

"Be it a weakness, it deserves some praise;
We love the play-place of our early days."

"Well, now I'll go home to the folks," I said, "and see if they will forgive me." I thought I would take home some presents, so I bought about $400 worth of goods, including coffee, sugar, teas, etc., and took the old steamer *Hibernia,* of Pittsburg, Captain Clinefelter, master. You ought to have seen me when I stepped on the wharfboat at Marietta, my birthplace, dressed to death, with my gold watch and chain, and a fine trunk I had bought in New Orleans for $40. I got my groceries off the wharfboat, and hired a wagon, and I took it afoot, as in those days you could not get a hack except at a livery stable.

My mother knew me at first sight. Father was working at the shipyard at Port Homer, on the other side of the Muskingum River, and did not come home until night.

I stopped at home a year, and had a fight nearly every week. I then came to Cincinnati again, where I met my brother Paul, who was working at calking steamboats. He coaxed me to stay with him, saying that he would teach me the trade. I consented, and soon was able to earn $4 per day. We worked together a few years, and made a good deal of money; but every Monday morning I went to work broke. I became infatuated with the game of faro, and it kept me a slave. So I concluded either to quit work or quit gambling. I studied the matter over a long time. At last one day while we were finishing a boat that we had calked, and were working on a float aft of the wheel, I gave my tools a push with my foot, and they all went into the river. My brother called out and asked me what I was doing. I looked up, a little sheepish, and said it was the last lick of work I would ever do. He was surprised to hear me talk that way, and asked me what I intended to do. I told him I intended to live off of fools and suckers. I also said, "I will make money rain"; and I did come near doing as I said.

THE GAME OF RONDO.

After shoving my calking tools into the river, I went to keeping a "Rondo" game for Daniel and Joseph Smith, up on Fifth Street, at $18 per week. Hundreds of dollars changed hands every hour, both day and night. At the end of six months I was taken in as a partner, and at that time the receipts of the game were about $600 every day. I had money to sell (or throw away), and, for a boy, I made it fly. In a short time the police began to raid us, and we would be fined fifty dollars each about once a month. Then they raised it to $100, and next to $500. This was too much, so we had heavy oak and iron doors put up; but the police would batter them down, and get us just the same. One night they surrounded the house, broke down the door, and arrested my two partners; but I escaped by the roof. The next day I went up to the jail to take the boys something to eat, when they nabbed and locked me up also. They put me in the same cell with Kissane, of the steamer *Martha Washington* notoriety, who was living in great style at the jail. They fined us $500 each and let us go, and that broke up "Rondo."

After retiring from the "Rondo" business, I took passage with Captain Riddle on the steamer *Ann Livington* bound for the Wabash River, to visit a sister, who lived near Bloomfield, Edgar County, Ills. There were no rail-roads in that part of the country in those days. My sister's husband bought 3,000 acres of land near Paris, at $1.25 per acre, and the same land is now worth $300 per acre. During my trip up the river I formed the acquaintance of Sam Burges, who was a great circus man. Captain Riddle and Burges got to playing poker, and the Captain "bested" him for about $200. I told Burges that I could make him win if he could get me into the game. So, after sup-per, they sat down to play, and I was a looker-on. Burges asked me to take a hand, which I did, and on my deal I would "fill" his hand, so that he soon had the Captain badly rattled, and he lost about $900. The old Captain was get-ting "full," and I looked for a fight sooner or later. Burges invited all to take a drink, when the Captain refused, and told Burges that he was a "d——d gambler." Burges called him a liar, so at it they went. The Captain was getting the best of it when we parted them, and it was all we could do to keep Burges from shooting. I got one-half of the $900, and no one called me a gambler ei-ther.

As the boat was going through the "draw," at Terre Haute, she took a "shear" on the pilot, and knocked down her chimneys. The Captain went up on deck, cursed the pilot, went down on the lower deck, knocked down two deck-hands, and raised cain generally. Burges expected he would tackle him again, but the Captain did not want any of that gun. When we arrived at the landing, I got off, and went to my sister's. I remained there about one month, and had a good time shooting wild turkeys and chickens. On my return trip I got into a game of poker, and took in a few hundred. I stopped off at Louis-ville a short time, and then shipped for Cincinnati, where I remained until I was very near broke.

NOW A GAMBLER.

"If yet you love game at so dear a rate,
Learn this, that hath old gamesters dearly cost;

> Dost lose? rise up. Dost win? rise in that state.
> Who strives to sit out losing hands are lost."

I left Cincinnati for St. Louis; and when I landed there, I had just $40 left. I secured a boarding house, and started to take in the town. I made inquiries for a faro bank, and at last found one; and I bolted in as if I was an old sport. I stepped up to the table, and asked the dealer for $40 worth of checks. I then commenced to play, and won; and, pressing my good luck, in two hours had $780 in checks in front of me. I told the dealer to cash my checks, and I walked out.

The next day I was on my way to St. Paul, as at that time there was a great emigration in that direction. I took passage on a steamer that had nearly 300 people on board, going there to buy homes, and, of course, they had plenty of money with them. After the supper tables were cleared, a game of poker was commenced; then another, then another, until there were five tables going. I sat at one of the tables looking on for a long time, until at length one of the gentlemen said to me, "Do you ever indulge?" I said, "Hardly ever, but I do not care if I play a while." The bar was open, and they all appeared to enjoy a good drink, but I never cared for anything stronger than a lemonade. The result was that they all got full, and I thought I might as well have some of their money as to let the barkeeper have it, and I commenced to try some of the tricks I had learned. I found they worked finely, and at daybreak the bar and I had all the money. I got about $1,300, which made me $2,000 strong.

When we arrived at St. Paul I struck another bank, and to my sorrow. I found one conducted by Cole Martin and "King Cole," two old sports, who soon relieved me of my $2,000. I then was without a cent, and too game to let the gamblers know I was broke. After I had been there about a week, one of them stopped me on the street, and asked me why I did not come around and see them. He said: "I don't ask you to play, but come and dine with us." I accepted his invitation, and went around that evening, and had as fine a bird supper as I ever sat down to.

CAUGHT A SLEEPER.

I was playing poker once on the steamer *General Quitman*. The party were all full of grape juice. Along about morning the game was reduced to single-handed, and that man I was playing with was fast asleep, so I picked up the deck and took four aces and four kings out, with an odd card to each. I gave him the kings and I took the aces. I gave him a hunch, and told him to wake up and look at his hand. He partly raised his hand, but laid it down again and I knew he had not seen it. I gave him a push and shook him up pretty lively, and he opened his eyes. I said: "Come, look at your hand, or I will quit." He got a glimpse of it, and I never saw such a change in a man's countenance. He made a dive for his money and said: "I will bet you $100, for I want to show you I am not asleep." I told him I thought he was "bluffing." I said in a joking way: "I will raise you $1,000." So he pulled out all his money and laid it on the table, and said: "I will only call you, but I know I have you beat." I showed down four big live aces, and he was awake sure enough after that. He never went into any more of those fits, and we played until they wanted the table for breakfast. I used to make it a point to "cold deck" a sucker on his own deal, as they then had great confidence in their hands. My old paw is large enough to hold out a compressed bale of cotton or a whole deck of cards, and it comes in very handy to do the work. I could hold one deck in the palm of my hand and shuffle up another, and then come the change on his deal. It requires a great deal of cheek and gall, and I was always endowed with both—that is, they used to say so down South.

TEN THOUSAND IN COUNTERFEIT MONEY.

We had a great "graft," before the war, on the Upper Mississippi, between St. Louis and St. Charles. We would go up on a boat and back by rail. One night going up we had done a good business in our line, and were just putting up the shutters, when a man stepped up and said "he could turn the right card." My partner, Posey Jeffers, was doing the honors that night, and he said, "I will bet from $1 to $10,000 that no man can pick out the winning ticket." The man pulled out a roll nearly as large as a pillow, and put up $5,000. Posey put up the same amount, and over the card went for $5,000; but it was not the winner. "Mix them up again," said the man, and he put up the same sum as before. He turned, and Posey put the second $5,000 in his pocket. The man then went away as if to lose $10,000 was an every-day thing with him. We then closed up our "banking house," well pleased with ourselves. The next day we were counting our cash, and we found we had on hand $10,000 in nice new bills on the State Bank of Missouri, but it was counterfeit. We deposited it in the (fire) bank, as we had no immediate use for it.

BLOWING UP OF THE PRINCESS.

I was on board of the steamer *Princess* on a down trip when she was carrying a large number of passengers, and there were fourteen preachers among
them, on their way to New Orleans to attend a conference. The boat was
making the fastest time she had ever made. I had a big game of "roulette"
in the barber shop, which ran all Saturday night; and on Sunday morning,
just after leaving Baton Rouge, I opened up again, and had thirty-five persons in the shop, all putting down their money as fast as they could get up to
the table. I was doing a land-office business, when all of a sudden there was
a terrific noise, followed by the hissing of escaping steam, mingled with the
screams and groans of the wounded and dying. The boat had blown up, and
was almost a total wreck. There was but very little left, and that consisted
mostly of the barber shop, which was at the time full of gamblers, and not
one of them was hurt. The steamers *Peerless* and *McRay* came to our aid; one
boat looked after the dead and wounded, and the other took us lucky fellows
out of the barber shop. One hundred souls were landed into eternity without
a moment's warning, and among them were the fourteen preachers. It was
a horrible sight; the bodies were so mangled and scalded that one could not
have recognized his own brother or sister. Captain William Campbell (now
of the Vicksburg Packet line) was steward of the *Princess* at the time of the
explosion, and there was not a man on the boat that worked harder to save
life and relieve the wounded. He richly deserved his promotion, and is now
one of the best captains on the river.

A WOMAN WITH A GUN.

I was on a boat coming from Memphis one night, when my partner beat a
man out of $600, playing poker. After the game broke up, the man went into
the ladies' cabin and told his wife. She ran into his room and got his pistol,
and said, "I will have that money back, or kill the man." I saw her coming,
pistol in hand, and stepped up to the bar and told the barkeeper to hand me
that old gun he had in the drawer, which I knew had no loads in it. She came
on, frothing at the mouth, with blood in her eyes. I saw she was very much
excited, and I said to her: "Madame, you are perfectly right. You would do
right in shooting that fellow, for he is nothing but a gambler. I don't believe
your pistol will go off; you had better take my pistol, for I am a government

detective, and have to keep the best of arms." So I handed her the pistol, and took hers. Just a moment later out stepped the man who had won the money, and she bolted up to him and said: "You won my husband's money, and I will just give you one minute to hand it to me, or I will blow your brains out in this cabin." Well, you ought to have seen the passengers getting out of the cabin when she pulled down on him; but he knew the joke and stood pat, and showed what a game fellow he was. He told the woman her husband lost the money gambling, and he could not get a cent back. Then she let go; but the pistol failed to go off, and he got her to go back into the cabin, and pacified her by giving her $100. After taking the charge out of her pistol, I returned it to her. So, reader, you can see what a gay life there is in gambling.

LEAP FOR LIFE.

Another time I was coming up on the steamer *Fairchild* with Captain Faw-cett, of Louisville. When we landed at Napoleon there were about twenty-five of the "Arkansas Killers" came on board, and I just opened out and cleaned the party of money, watches, and all their valuables. Things went along smoothly for a while, until they commenced to drink pretty freely. Finally one of them said: "Jake, Sam, Ike, get Bill, and let us kill that d——d gam-bler who got our money." "All right," said the party, and they broke for their rooms to get their guns. I stepped out of the side door, and got under the pi-lot-house, as it was my favorite hiding place. I could hear every word down stairs, and could whisper to the pilot. Well, they hunted the boat from stem to stern—even took lights and went down into the hold—and finally gave up the chase, as one man said I had jumped overboard. I slipped the pilot $100 in gold, as I had both pockets filled with gold and watches, and told him at the first point that stood out a good ways to run her as close as he could and I would jump. He whispered, "Get ready," and I slipped out and walked back, and stood on the top of the wheelhouse until she came, as I thought, near enough to jump, and away I went; but it was farther than I expected, so I went down about thirty feet into the river and struck into the soft mud clear up to my waist. Some parties who were standing on the stern of the boat saw me and gave the alarm, when the "killers" all rushed back and commenced firing at me, and the bullets went splashing all around me. The pilot threw her into the bend as quick as he could, and then let on she took a sheer on him and nearly went to the other side. The shooting brought the niggers from the fields to the bank of the river. I hallooed to them to get a long pole and pull me out, for I was stuck in the mud. They did so, and I got up on the bank and waited for another boat.

I was always very stubborn about giving up money if any one wanted to compel me to do it, but I wish I had one-quarter of what I have given back to people that did need it. I have seen many a man lose all he had, and then go back into the ladies' cabin and get his wife's diamonds, and lose them, thinking he might get even. But that was always a good cap for me, for I would walk back into the cabin, find the lady, and hand her jewels back; and I never beat a man out of his money that I did not find out from the clerk if his passage was paid. If not, I would pay it, and give the man some of his money to assist him to his destination. By so doing I was looked upon as being a pretty good robber—that is, if you call it robbing; but I tell you that a man that will bet on such a game as monte is a bigger robber than the man who does the playing, for he thinks he is robbing you, and you know you are robbing him.

THE BLACK DECK-HAND.

Charlie Clark and I left New Orleans one night on the steamer *Duke of Orleans*. There were ten or twelve rough looking fellows on board, who did their drinking out of private bottles. Charlie opened up shop in the cabin, and soon had a great crowd around him. I saw that the devils had been drinking too much, so I gave Charlie the wink, and he soon closed up, claiming to be broke. Then we arranged that I should do the playing, and he would be on the lookout. I soon got about all the money and some watches out of the roughs, besides I beat seven or eight of the other passengers. They all appeared to take it good-naturedly at the time; but it was not long before their loss, and the bad whisky, began to work on them. I saw there was going to be trouble, so I made a sneak for my room, changed my clothes, and then slipped down the back stairs into the kitchen. I sent word for Clark to come down. I then blackened my face and hands, and made myself look like a deckhand. I had hardly finished my disguise, when a terrible rumpus upstairs warned me that the ball was open. The whisky was beginning to do its work. They searched everywhere; kicked in the state-room doors, turned everything upside down, and raised h——l generally. If they could have caught me then, it would have been good bye George. They came down on deck, walked past, and inquired of a roustabout who stood by me if he had seen a well-dressed man on deck. He told them "he had not seen any gemman down on deck afore they came down." They had their guns out, and were swearing vengeance. The boat was plowing her way along up the river; the stevedores were hurrying the darkies to get up some freight, as a landing was soon to be made. The whistle blew, and the boat was headed for shore. Those devils knew I would attempt to leave the boat, so as soon as the plank was put out they ran over on the bank, and closely scanned the face of every one who got off. There was a lot of plows to be discharged, so I watched my chance, shouldered a plow, followed by a long line of coons, and I fairly flew past the mob. I kept on up the high bank and threw my plow on to the pile, and then I made for the cotton fields. I lay down on my back until the boat was out of sight, and then I came out, washed myself white, and took a boat for Vicksburg, where I met Clark the next day, and we divided the boodle that he had brought with him. He told me that after I had left the boat they got lights and went down into the hold, looking for me, as they were sure I was still on the boat. It was a pretty close call, but they were looking for a well-dressed man, and not a black deck-hand.

GENERAL REMARKS.

When a sucker sees a corner turned up, or a little spot on a card in three-card monte, he does not know that it was done for the purpose of making him think he has the advantage. He thinks, of course, the player does not see it, and he is in such a hurry to get out his money that he often cuts or tears his clothes. He feels like he is going to steal the money from a blind man, but he does not care. He will win it, and say nothing about how he did it. After they have put up their money and turned the card, they see that the mark was put there for a purpose. Then they are mad, because they are beat at their own game. They begin to kick, and want their money back, but they would not have thought of such a thing had they won the money from a blind man, for they did think he must be nearly blind, or he could have seen the mark on the winning card. They expected to rob a blind man, and got left. I never had any sympathy for them, and I would fight before I would give them back one cent. It is a good lesson for a dishonest man to be caught by some trick, and I always did like to teach it. I have had the right card turned on me for big money by suckers, but it was an accident, for they were so much excited that they did not get the card they were after. I have also given a big hand in poker to a sucker, and had him to knock the ginger out of me, but this would make me more careful in the future. I've seen suckers win a small amount, and then run all over the boat, telling how they downed the gambler; but they were almost sure to come back and lose much more than they had won.

I have often given a sucker back his money, and I have seen them lose it with my partner, or at some other game on the same boat. I have won hundreds of thousands from thieves who were making tracks for some other country to keep out of jail and to spend their ill-gotten gains. I enjoyed beating a man that was loaded down with stolen money more than any one else. I always felt as if it was my duty to try and keep the money in our own country.

Young men and boys have often stood around the table and bothered me to bet. I would tell them to go away, that I did not gamble with boys. That would make some of the smart Alecks mad, and they would make a great deal of noise. So, when I was about to close up, I would take in the young chap. He would walk away with a good lesson. But when I had to win money from a boy to keep him quiet, I would always go to him and return the money, after giving him a good talking to.

I meet good business men very often now that take me by the hand and remind me of when I won some money from them when they were boys, and returned it with a good lecture. I have sometimes wished I had one-tenth part of what I have returned to boys and suckers, for then I would have enough to keep me the balance of my life.

I had the niggers all along the coast so trained that they would call me "Massa" when I would get on or off a boat. If I was waiting at a landing I would post some old "nig" what to say when I went on board, so while the passengers were all out on the guards and I was bidding the "coons" good-bye, my "nig" would cry out: "Good-bye, Massa George; I's goin' to take good care of the old plantation till you comes back."

I would go on board, with one of the niggers carrying my saddle-bags, and those sucker passengers would think I was a planter sure enough; so if a game was proposed I had no trouble to get into it, as all who play cards are looking for suckers that they know have money; and who in those old ante-bellum times had more money than a Southern planter? I have often stepped up to the bar as soon as I would get on board and treat every one within call, and when I would pay for the drinks I would pull out a roll that would make everybody look wild. Then I was sure to get into the first game that would be started, for all wanted a part of the planter's roll.

I have downed planters and many good business men, who would come to me afterwards and want to stand in with my play; and many are the thousands I have divided with them; and yet the truly good people never class such men among gamblers. The world is full of such men. They are not brave enough to take the name, but they are always ready for a part of the game. A gambler's word is as good as his bond, and that is more than I can say of many business men who stand very high in a community. I would rather take a true gambler's word than the bond of many business men who are to-day counted worth thousands. The gambler will pay when he has money, which many good church members will not.

Three Portraits of "Canada" Bill Jones

ALLAN PINKERTON, MASON LONG, GEORGE DEVOL

If one figure from the world of riverboat gambling captured the imagination of Gilded Age writers, it was "Canada" Bill Jones. Though leaving no written account of his own, he featured regularly in tales of gambling along the Mississippi and emerged as a transcendent figure—the apotheosis of the gambler as idiot savant, as a moral touchstone in a world of topsy-turvy ethics. Bill adopted the demeanor of a rural simpleton and worked his three-card monte routine on steamboats and railroads. If this was far removed from the kind of gambler heroics attributed to literary figures like Flush Fred, it was no less beguiling. Even those who wrote to condemn his activities were forced into begrudging admiration despite themselves. Allan Pinkerton, the pioneering detective, marvels: "He was certainly different from all other men whom I have been called upon to study. He always had a mellow and old look about him that at once won the looker on and caused a real touch of warmth and kindliness toward him [. . .] Among his kind he was king." Reformed gambler Mason Long describes him as "a most expert operator [. . .] [A]mong his victims were many persons of intelligence and experience." But the greatest encomiums came from his partner George Devol. In Devol's reckoning, "There never lived a better hearted man." Though a gambler and confidence man—indeed, perhaps because he was precisely those things—Canada Bill Jones was "honest to a fault."

From *Criminal Reminiscences and Detective Sketches*

ALLAN PINKERTON

There are some men who naturally choose, or, through a series of unfortunate blunders, drift into the life of social outlaws, who possess so many remarkably original traits of character that they become rather subjects for admiration than condemnation when we review their life and career. On first thought it could hardly be imagined that one who has been all his life, so far as is known, a gambler and a confidence man, whose associates were always of the same or worse class than himself, who had no more regard for law than a wild Indian, and who never in his entire career seemed to have an aspiration above being the vagabond, par excellence, could move us to anything beyond a passing interest, the same as we would have for a wild animal or any unusual character among men and women.

But here is a man who, from his daring, his genuine simplicity, his great aptitude for his nefarious work, his simple, almost childish ways, his unequaled success, and a hundred other marked and remarkable qualities, cannot but cause something more than a common interest, and must always remain as an extraordinarily brilliant type of a very dangerous and unworthy class.

Such was "Canada Bill," whose real name was William Jones. He was born in a little tent under the trees of Yorkshire, in old England. His people were genuine Gypsies, who lived, as all other Gypsies do, by tinkering, dickering, or fortune-telling, and horse-trading. Bill, as he was always called, grew up among the *Romany* like any other Gypsy lad, becoming proficient in the nameless and numberless tricks of the Gypsy life, and particularly adept at handling cards. In fact, this proficiency caused him finally to leave his tribe, as, wherever he went among them, he never failed to beat the shrewdest of his shrewd people on every occasion where it was possible for him to secure an opponent willing to risk any money upon his supposed superiority in that direction.

Having become altogether too keen for his Gypsy friends, he began appearing at fairs and traveling with provincial catchpenny shows in England. Tiring of successes in that field, he eventually came to America, and wandered about Canada for some time in the genuine Gypsy fashion. This was about twenty-five years ago, when Bill was twenty-two or twenty-three years of age, and when thimble-rigging was the great game at the fairs and among travelers.

Bill soon developed a great reputation for playing shortcard games, but finally devoted his talents entirely to three-card monte under the guise of a countryman, and may be said to have been the genuine original of that poor, simple personage who *had* been swindled by sharpers, and who, while bewailing his loss and showing interested people the manner in which he had been robbed, invariably made their natural curiosity and patronizing sympathy cost them dearly.

Himself and another well-known monte-player, named Dick Cady, traveled through Canada for several years, gaining a great notoriety among gamblers and sporting men; and it was here that this singular person secured the *sobriquet* of "Canada Bill," which name clung to him until his death, in the summer of 1877; and he was known by everybody throughout the country who knew him at all by that name, it being generally supposed that he was of Canadian birth.

As a rule, three-card monte men are among the most godless, worthless, unprincipled villains that infest society anywhere; but this strange character, from his simplicity, which was genuine, his cunning, which was most brilliant, his acting, which was inimitable, because it was nature itself, created a lofty niche for himself in all the honor there may be attached to a brilliant and wholly original career as a sharper of this kind; and however many imitators he may have—and he has hundreds—none can ever approach his perfection in the slightest possible degree.

Any deft person, after a certain amount of practice, can do all the trickery there is about the sleight-of-hand in three-card monte; but the game is so common a dodge among swindlers, that unless the *confidence* of the dupe is first fully secured, he seldom bites at the bait offered.

This must either be confidence, on the part of the person being operated on, that he is smarter than the dealer, if his real character is known; or, in case it is not known, a conviction that he is a genuine greenhorn who can easily be beaten the second time.

It was here that Canada Bill's peculiar genius never failed to give him victory; and it is said of him that he never made a mistake and never failed to win money whenever he attempted it.

His personal appearance, which was most ludicrous, undeniably had much to do with his success. He was the veritable country gawky, the ridiculous, ignorant, absurd creature that has been so imperfectly imitated on and off the stage for years, and whose true description can scarcely be written. He was fully six feet high, with dark eyes and hair, and always had a smooth-shaven face, full of seams and wrinkles, that were put to all manner of difficult expressions with a marvelous facility and ease. All this—coupled with long, loose-jointed arms, long, thin, and apparently a trifle unsteady legs, a shambling, shuffling, awkward gait, and this remarkable face and head bent forward and turned a little to one side, like an inquiring and wise old owl, and then an outfit of Granger clothing, the entire cost of which never exceeded fifteen dollars—made a combination that never failed to call a smile to a stranger's face, or awaken a feeling of curiosity and interest wherever he might be seen.

One striking difference between Canada Bill and all the other sharpers of his ilk lay in the fact that he *was* the thing he seemed to be. Old gamblers and sporting-men could never fathom him. He was an enigma to his closest friends. A short study of the awkward, ambling fellow would give one the impression that he was simply supremely clever in his manner and make up; that he was merely one of the most accomplished actors in his profession ever known; and that he only kept up this *appearance* of guilelessness for the purpose of acquiring greater reputation among his fellows. But those who knew him, as far as it was possible to know the wandering vagabond that he was, assert that he was the most unaffected, innocent, and really simple-hearted of human beings, and never had been anything, and never could have been anything, save just what he was.

This would hardly seem possible of even an exceptional person among ordinary people, and I can only reconcile this singular case with consistency when I call to mind many of the interesting old Gypsy tinkers I have myself known, who, with all their wise lore and cunning tricks were the merriest, kindest-hearted, jolliest, and most childlike simple dogs on earth.

It seems almost impossible that any living person waging such a relentless war against society as Canada Bill did, until the day of his death, could have anything generous and simple about him; but he certainly had those two qualities to a remarkable degree. They were uppermost in everything that he did. It almost seemed that this man had no thought but that his vocation in life was of the highest respectability; that skinning a man out of a thousand dollars as neatly as he could do it was an admirable stroke of business, even if it led to that man's ruin; and that every act of his criminal life was one of the most honorable accomplishments; so that this sunny temper and honest face was an outgrowth of a satisfaction in upright living.

He was certainly different from all other men whom I have been called upon to study. He always had a mellow and old look about him that at once won the looker on and caused a real touch of warmth and kindliness toward him. His face was always beaming with a rough good-fellowship and a sturdy friendliness that seemed almost something to cling to and bet on, while every movement of his slouchy, unkempt body was only a new indication of his rustic ingenuousness.

[. . .]

Just after the close of the war Canada Bill, in company with a river gambler, named George Devol, or "Uncle George," as he had a fondness for being called, started for the South, and began operating in and about New Orleans. This George Devol was himself a character, as he had once been a station-agent of some railroad in Minnesota, and on being "braced" and beaten out of his own and considerable of the company's funds, had such an admiration for the manner in which he had been beaten, that he turned out a gambler himself, and became quite well known along the lower Mississippi.

The two men, in company with one Jerry Kendricks, did an immense business in New Orleans, in the city, upon the boats, and on the different railroad lines running out of that place. Here, in New Orleans, Bill was the green, rollicking, back-country planter, and nearly always made his appearance upon a boat or a train as though he had had a narrow escape from a gang of cutthroats, but was in high glee over the fact that they had not stolen quite all of his money, and had left him a fine package of tin-ware, two or three packages of cow-hide shoes, large enough for a Louisiana negro, and a side or two of bacon. Old "Ben" Burnish, a character well known among sporting men in the North, was one of his most accomplished "cappers" during these days, and the gang made vast sums of money.

But finally "Uncle George" Devol hoped to get the best of Bill, he was so careless and really ingenuous among his friends; and, knowing that he carried a twenty-five hundred dollar roll, got a man and arranged things to beat him. Through his wonderful faculty for reading people and character, Bill permitted the play, and when his opponent won, remarked quietly: "George, you sized my pile pretty well, and got things fixed nice. Your friend will find that roll the smallest twenty-five hundred dollar pot he ever grabbed. Good-by, Uncle George!"

Bill having arranged a "road-roll," or a showy pile of bills of small denomination, was willing to expend that much to ascertain definitely that Devol had played him false, and immediately took leave of him forever.

[. . .]

Countless instances are related of the shrewdness and success of this strange man. Among his kind he was king and I have only given this sketch of him as illustrative of a striking type of a dangerous class, still powerful and cunning, which the public would do well to avoid in whatever guise they may appear.

Canada Bill, after an unprecedently successful career of over twenty years in America, died a pauper—as nearly every one of all the criminal classes do—at the Charity Hospital, in Reading, Pennsylvania, in the summer of 1877.

From *The Life of Mason Long, The Converted Gambler*
MASON LONG

During my stay in Utica I was so "light" financially, that I was unable most of the time to attend the races.

The city was crowded with people, and there was much gambling and robbing going on. The confidence men and monte players were in clover, and counted their gains by the thousands. Among them was the most notorious and successful thief who ever operated in this country, "Canada Bill," whose name is familiar to every newspaper reader. He had rented for the week, at an exorbitant figure, a saloon on one of the principal streets of the city. Here he made his headquarters, and he had scores of "ropers" and "decoy ducks" on the streets, in the saloons, at the track, and, in fact, every where capturing "suckers." To these "cappers" he paid fifty per cent, of the amount realized from the "bloaks" they brought in. At the rear of the saloon there was a little room, carefully guarded, in which the robberies were committed. Only one party was allowed in this place at one time, so that the game might not be exposed to prospective dupes.

On the afternoon of the great races at Utica, a well-known Fort Wayne sport, whom I will call "Dan," and myself, found ourselves without sufficient means to attend. Our cash was limited to a small supply of "shinnies," and we concluded to pass away the time in playing dominoes for the beer. While thus engaged, an elderly, well dressed, intelligent looking gentleman entered the saloon and called for a glass of beer. He watched us play for a moment, and asked us to join him in his refreshments, which, it is needless to say, we promptly did. We drank two or three times together, and, getting into conversation, we learned that the stranger was a leading attorney from Albany, who was in Utica trying an important canal case. The old gentleman, being somewhat overcome with the heat, stepped into a barber-shop near by and asked permission to sit in one of the chairs and cool himself off until the arrival of a customer. He sat down and soon fell asleep. I suggested to "Dan" that if we took him to Canada Bill's place, he might drop some money, and we would thus make a raise. "Dan" scouted the idea, saying he was too smart a man to be caught on three-card monte. But I thought not, and we determined at all events to make the effort.

How to get the old gentleman out of the barber's chair was the first problem that presented itself. Just then I saw a poor demoralized looking tramp wandering aimlessly about, and as he evidently needed a dose of the razor,

I handed him money enough to get shaved, instructing him to go into the barber-shop and demand the chair occupied by our Albany friend. He did so, and the lawyer stepped out of the shop. Meeting us, he suggested another glass of beer, whereupon I remarked that the best beer I had found in Utica was at a saloon in the next block, and asked if we should not go there. All were agreed, and we proceeded to "Canada Bill's." While en route there the attorney spoke of the large number of confidence men in the city, and the rich harvest they were reaping. "Dan" and myself exchanged significant glances. This rather discouraged us, but we continued, on our way. Arrived at Bill's establishment, we stepped into the back room, and I motioned for "Dutch Charley," of Chicago, the principal "capper," to come in and work the case, as I didn't understand it. We sat down at the table and were enjoying a glass of beer, when a rustic looking creature entered the room, munching a huge piece of pie, which he ate with palpable relish. He was a large man, dressed in coarse clothes, with a sunburnt countenance, a nose highly illuminated by the joint action of whisky and heat, and an expression of indescribable greenness and "freshness" about him. He at first seemed to notice no one, but sat down quietly at our table, and devoted himself strictly to his pie, until it had disappeared into his capacious stomach.

This strange looking creature naturally attracted our attention. The Albany man was particularly startled by the apparition, and after a careful survey of the new comer, ejaculated, "My God, see what we're coming to."

"Yes," responded I, "and we haven't got far to go unless we stop drinking."

The subject of our remarks, who seemed to be in blissful ignorance of the fact that we were discussing him, at this juncture, looked at us and said: "Gentlemen, wont ye'z huv a drink of suthin' with me?" We all declined the invitation, but continued to study the appearance and actions of the supposed "Hoosier," with much interest and amusement. He took no offense at our refusal, but quietly produced from the recesses of his great-coat pocket, a large roll of money, with a five hundred dollar bill for a wrapper. He noticed that we were watching him closely, and said:

"I done better with this 'ere druv of cattle than I done on t'other trip. This time I cleared five thousand dollars from my druv, but last time afore this them New York chaps skinned me, confound 'em." After a pause he continued: "But I had a little streak o' bad luck comin' down on the train from New York this mornin.' I met some strangers, and we had a little game with tickets like, and they bet me I couldn't turn the ticket, and won thirty-five dollars from me, durn their buttons."

"Why, man, you've been playing three-card monte," said our legal friend. "Don't you know better than that? "

"Thar, thar, that's what they called it; three-card monte, that's it. Wal, if they did get my thirty-five dollars, I took their tickets away from 'em, plague on 'em. I am goin' to larn that 'ere game myself, so I kin git my thirty-five dollars back."

With this remark, Canada Bill (for it was he) produced the cards, or tickets, as he called them, and began throwing them on the table in a very awkward manner. His clumsiness amused the party, and finally he said, "Wal, I want to get even, and I'll bet any man ten dollars he can't turn that 'ere ticket."

"Dutch Charley" was on hand, and promptly took the bet. After winning he said, "I'll bet you twenty, now."

"O, you're too lucky," said Bill, "I won't throw 'em agin for you no how but I'll try you for twenty dollars," continued he, turning to me, "and see how your luck is."

Charley slipped me a twenty dollar bill, and I won the bet. I offered to bet again, but Bill said:

"Thar, thar, I lost again. Wal, did you ever see sich luck. I'm out now nearly one hundred dollars on these durned tickets. I won't bet yer twenty dollars, but I'll just put up five hundred dollars agin any ov ye'z."

With this he turned the cards to win, the old gent from Albany meanwhile watching every movement closely, and evidently wholly engrossed in Bill's words and actions.

"I have only eight dollars, or I'd bet you," remarked he.

"Wal," said Bill, "I'll go yer two hundred dollars agin yer watch and chain."

"How do you know my watch and chain are worth two hundred dollars?"

"Wal, I didn't allow that a man of yer standing wud war one that cost much less; of course I'd have to luk at it afore I'd bet that much agin it."

"It didn't cost me that much," said the gentleman, as Bill examined it.

"I couldn't go yez no more'n one hundred and ninety dollars, stranger, on that 'ere watch and chain."

The cards in the mean time had been lying on the table, and the attorney's eyes had never been removed from them. The bet was taken. Bill put his one hundred and ninety dollars in my hands, and the lawyer covered it with the watch, retaining the chain about his neck. In his excitement and haste to make the winning, which he considered a certainty, he reached to turn the card, when Bill covered the "ticket" with his hands, remarking: "Stranger, yer stake isn't all up yet."

Thereupon the gentleman removed the chain from his neck, handed it to me and then turned a card. Of course he lost, and as quick as a flash of lightning, a complete understanding of the situation dawned upon his mind. He leaned back in his chair, rubbed his eyes, took a careful survey of the gang by which he was surrounded, and propounded the following conundrum:

"Is it possible that I've been beat at three-card monte at last!"

"Yes, you've got beat," quickly answered the shark as I handed him the watch.

"Well boys," said the victim, who cared little for the pecuniary loss, but seemed humiliated at the fact that he had swallowed the bait, "I don't want to part with that watch and chain, because it was a present to me; how much will you take for it?"

"I've taken more than half a bushel of watches this week, and I don't know what to do with them, so I'll return this to you for one hundred dollars," said Bill, as quietly as if he were discussing the most legitimate business transaction.

"I don't think my fun has been worth over fifty dollars to me," responded the attorney, "but I will give you that amount."

"Well, I'll take it, as I didn't have a great deal of trouble with you."

A check was produced, the attorney filled it out for fifty dollars, signed it, and recovered his watch and chain. Bill sent a messenger with him to a business house to get the money. Arriving at the door of the establishment, the gentleman said he was well known there and desired to enter alone to avoid any suspicion. He asked his companion for the check, saying he would go in, get it cashed, and bring out the money. The fellow handed the check over, the lawyer hastily tore it into fragments and dismissed the young man with a kind message to his master. Upon reporting the facts he found himself out of a situation. "Bill," after all, lost his swag, and "Dan" and I failed to get our percentage. This was my first and last experience as "capper" for a confidence man. Canada Bill made many thousands of dollars that year during the races. He was a most expert operator and among his victims were many persons of intelligence and experience. The only way to avoid such sharks is not to bet on anything, and I have described this game in detail, for the purpose of exposing the *modus operandi* of the sharpers who go about in search of victims, thus placing my readers upon their guard. "Bill" squandered his money very lavishly and drank himself to death in about a year after the incident I have related. He died a pauper.

From *Forty Years A Gambler on the Mississippi*
GEORGE DEVOL

Canada Bill was a character one might travel the length and breadth of the land and never find his match, or run across his equal. Imagine a medium-sized, chicken-headed, tow-haired sort of man with mild blue eyes, and a mouth nearly from ear to ear, who walked with a shuffling, half-apologetic sort of a gait, and who, when his countenance was in repose, resembled an idiot. For hours he would sit in his chair, twisting his hair in little ringlets. Then I used to say, "Bill is studying up some new devilment." His clothes were always several sizes too large, and his face was as smooth as a woman's and never had a particle of hair on it. Canada was a slick one. He had a squeaking, boyish voice, and awkward, gawky manners, and a way of asking fool questions and putting on a good natured sort of a grin, that led everybody to believe that he was the rankest kind of a sucker—the greenest sort of a country jake. Woe to the man who picked him up, though. Canada was, under all his hypocritical appearance, a regular card shark, and could turn monte with the best of them. He was my partner for a number of years, and many are the suckers we roped in, and many the huge roll of bills we corralled. He was an arrant coward, though, and would not fight a woman if she said boo. His right name was Jones. When Tom Brown and Holly Chappell traveled with me, the four of us made a quartette that could give most any crowd any sort of monte they wanted. Brown got $240,000 for his share of the profit, and Chappell went North with his portion, and is to-day as poor as myself. Bill never weighed over 130 pounds, and was always complaining of pains in his head. I always found him honest to a fault; and when the poor fellow died, I felt that I had lost one of my truest friends.

[...]

He died in Reading, Penn., about ten years ago, and, poor fellow, he did not leave enough money of all the many thousands he had won to bury him.

The Mayor of Reading had him decently interred, and when his friends in Chicago learned the fact, they raised money enough to pay all the funeral expenses and erect a monument to the memory of one who was, while living, a friend to the poor. I was in New Orleans at the time of his death, and did not hear the sad news for some months after.

I hope the old fellow is happy in a better land. If kind acts and a generous heart can atone for the sin of gambling, and entitle men to a mansion in the skies, Canada Bill surely got one, "where the wicked cease from troubling, and the weary are at rest."

There never lived a better hearted man. He was liberal to a fault. I have known him to turn back when we were on the street and give to some poor object we had passed. Many a time I have seen him walk up to a Sister of Charity and make her a present of as much as $50, and when we would speak of it, he would say:

"Well, George, they do a great deal for the poor, and I think they know better how to use the money than I do."

Once I saw him win $200 from a man, and shortly after his little boy came running down the cabin, Bill called the boy up and handed him the $200 and told him to give it to his mother.

He was a man, take him for all in all, that possessed many laudable traits of character. He often said suckers had no business with money. He had some peculiar traits. While he was a great man at monte, he was a fool at short cards. I have known men who knew this to travel all over the country after Bill, trying to induce him to play cards with them. He would do it, and this is what kept him poor.

Mason Long, the converted gambler, says of William Jones (Canada Bill):

"The confidence men and monte players were in clover. Among them was the most notorious and successful *thief* who ever operated in this country, Canada Bill. He was a *large* man, with a nose *highly illuminated* by the joint action of *whisky* and heat. Bill squandered his money very lavishly, and *drank* himself to death in about a year after the incident I have related. He died a pauper."

> "But by all thy nature's weakness,
> Hidden faults and follies know.
> Be thou, in rebuking evil,
> Conscious of thine own."

Is Mason Long converted? God and himself only know.

Was he fully converted when he wrote "The Converted Gambler"?

If the Bible be true, and it was left for me to decide, I would answer in the language of St. Paul: "Though I speak with the tongues of men and of angels, and have not charity, I am become as sounding brass or a tinkling cymbal." A true Christian will exercise charity toward all offenders, granting a boon of pity to the erring, and cast a glance of mercy upon the faults of his fellows. He will cherish a recollection of his virtues, and bury all his imperfections.

Is Mason Long a true Christian? Read his description of Canada Bill. Then read a true description of Bill's personal appearance in this book. If Mason Long had never seen Canada Bill, I would excuse him, but he said he capped for him once, or at least he tried to do so.

Has he shown any Christian charity in speaking of a man in his grave? Read what he says, and you will see that he or I are mistaken.

Bill was not a thief, he was honest to a fault. He was not a large man, for he never weighed over 130. He did not have a nose highly illuminated by the joint action of whisky and heat. He did not drink himself to death within a year of 1876, for he visited me in New Orleans in 1877. He did not drink whisky at all. His great drink was Christian cider, and it was very seldom I could get him to drink wine. He did die a pauper, and God bless him for it, for he gave more money to the poor than a thousand professed Christians that I know, who make a great parade of their reformation.

The public put all sporting men into one class, called gamblers; likewise they put all church members into classes and call them Christians, etc.

There is as wide a difference between a true gambler and one who styles himself a sport, as there is between a true Christian and one who puts on the cloak of Christianity to serve the devil in.

There is an old saying, "Honor among thieves." I will add a maxim or two: There is honor among gamblers, and dishonor among some business men that stand very high in the community in which they live.

Epilogue

"They were great old times then, and they'll never come back"

From *Poker Stories*

COMPILED BY J. F. B. LILLARD

By the time J. F. B. Lillard collected these accounts of gambling on the Mississippi, those sharpers who had worked the steamboats in the antebellum golden age of river travel were a dying breed. Whether or not the memories contained in Lillard's collection are authentic, they provide a very useful summation of the shifting attitudes toward gambling and gamblers. Taken together, these accounts present a vivid picture of the changing fortunes of the riverboat gambler in popular culture. The first anonymous speaker ("an old man I met on the steamer between Memphis and Helena") presents a romantic tale of gambling and violent retribution on the river that would not have been out of place in an antebellum adventure novel or antigambling work. Next, "Mr. Martin, of St. Louis" is at pains to undercut the glamour of gambling as it was presented in popular culture: "It's very pretty to read about, but the real thing was not so nice." But the star of the show is "Tom Ellison," who, as Lillard describes him, is one of "about twenty real old-time Mississippi River gamblers who linger about Memphis and Vicksburg." Ellison is unapologetic about his gambling past, and elegiac about the lost world that he knew. His luminous re-creation of the now mythical "great old times" and "good fellows" of his youth provides a compelling finale to a century of Mississippi gambling stories.

> Don't wonder if the poker sharp
> Who monkeys with the deck
> Should sometimes overreach the mark,
> And get it in the neck.

"There's many a change up and down the Mississippi since I was a youngster," said an old man whom I met on the steamer between Memphis and Helena. "Before the war, sir, these boats were floating palaces, and the people who travelled on them were able to pay for anything on earth that could be supplied to them; and they expected the best of everything and they got it, too.

"The time to see life then was about the last of the year, when the planters were travelling home from New Orleans after selling their cotton crops. They would have, every man of them, a fortune in his pocket, and not one had the least conception of the value of money. As a matter of course, there were gamblers on the boats. 'Where the carcass is, there will the eagles be gathered together,' the good book tells us, and it is true enough. There was always a game of cards—poker usually—going on in the saloon, and the gamblers seldom got the worst of it. I have seen many a thousand dollars change hands in a single game, for there was no such thing as a limit recognized excepting on the old law that a man had a show for his money. You couldn't make him bet more than he had. Men were very handy with knives and pistols, too, in those days, and more than once I have seen shots fired across the table.

"I never saw but one man killed, though, and in that case I said, as everybody else in the saloon said, 'Served him right.' Nobody thought he was entitled to any show at all, for there was one thing that put a man outside of the reach of human sympathy on the Mississippi when he was caught at it, and that fellow was caught dead to rights.

"There was a mighty stiff game going on that night, and some pretty good players had dropped out one after another when the luck ran too heavily against them, but as fast as one man rose from the table another would take his place, and the game went on steadily till long after midnight. Two men sat all night, but luck was against one and toward the other from the first. The lucky man was watched closely by more than one in the room who knew him for a professional gambler, but although he must have known it he did not flinch. He played on as steady as a machine and took his winnings as calmly as though they were pennies instead of thousands of dollars.

"The other man was a youngster. He couldn't have been more than twenty-two or three, and although he tried to keep from showing his excitement he could not altogether hide it. He grew paler and paler as he kept losing, and those who watched his game saw that he got to playing recklessly and trying to force his luck.

"He lost over $8,000 before he came to the end of his money, but after a time he called for a show, putting a $500 bill on the table and saying, 'That's all I have.'

"I'll never forget the hands that were shown in that deal. Even the other players who lost took no pains to conceal their sympathy with the young fellow for his hard luck. One of them had a small straight, one had three aces and another had a flush. The youngster had four sevens and the lucky player showed down four eights. There was not the faintest show of emotion on his face as he raked in the largest pot of the evening—there was more than $3,000 in it—as coolly as he had done everything else, and picked up the cards, for it happened to be his deal.

"The young man was good grit. He did not say a word in reply to three or four exclamations from the other players and the bystanders, but rose from his chair and turned to leave the table. Pale as he was before, he turned paler yet though, when he faced the man who stood before his chair. This was a stern-looking gentleman some fifty years old, but well preserved, and, as we afterward found out, with the muscles of a giant.

"'Why father,' exclaimed the younger man, 'I didn't know you were on board.'

"'I got on at Natchez,' said the father, briefly. 'How much have you lost?'

"'All I had,' said the son in a low tone.

"'And your sister's money?' said the father, speaking still lower.

"'All gone, too,' faltered the unhappy young man, and he should have passed out of the saloon, but the father said very sternly, 'Don't go away, sir,' and took the vacant chair with a polite question to the other players as to whether he was welcome in the game. It was a form strictly observed, but objections were never made in those days to any gentleman joining in the game when there was an empty chair at the table.

"The son looked on with astonishment. 'Why, father,' he said, 'I thought you never played.' But his father paid no attention. His eyes were fixed on the lucky player opposite and I, who was looking on very attentively, thought I could see a slight change in the latter's face.

"The game went on, but not in the old way. Whether I was right or not about the change of countenance, there was certainly a change in the gambler's play. He was far more cautious, and yet he began to lose. Once or twice he fumbled the cards as he had not done before, but I could detect no other signs of nervousness. One thing soon became evident—that the new comer was playing at one adversary only. He betrayed no anxiety to win money from any of the others, but lost no chance to bet with the gambler. The others saw it, and one by one dropped out, leaving the two to their duel. They all felt that some kind of a story was being acted out, and were all unwilling to interfere with it.

"After they were out the play grew higher, the father forcing it at every opportunity. Twice he called for a fresh pack of cards, and the gambler's face showed his annoyance every time. The luck was against him, but that of itself was not enough to make him nervous. More than one man in the room had seen him play a heavier game than this with worse luck and show no sign of emotion.

"Suddenly the climax came. With a motion so quick that my eyes, at least, could not follow it, the elder man drew a pistol and had it pointed at the other's face.

"'Don't move a hair or I'll blow your brains out, Jim Baisley,' he said, as coolly as he had asked for cards a moment before.

"'I'm not moving,' said the gambler, sullenly. 'You've got the drop on me.'

"'Yes, and I've caught you,' said the other. 'I told you twenty years ago I'd kill you if I ever caught you cheating.'

"'It's a lie,' said the gambler, angrily; but he did not move. The pistol was at his face.

"'A lie, is it?' said the other, coolly, as before. In those days to give a man the lie was to provoke a shot, and we expected to hear the report, but none came. Instead the elder man reached over with his left hand and suddenly snatched the five cards the gambler had dealt to himself and which he held in his hand. He threw them face up on the table. There were three aces among them. Then, with another quick motion, he spread the pack out, and three more aces were shown.

"'You see, gentlemen,' he said to the bystanders, without moving his eyes from those opposite him. A chorus of curses answered him, but nobody lifted a hand. We all felt that justice was about to be done, and a capable man had the matter in charge.

"'Harry,' said the father to his son, 'how much did you lose?'

"'About $9,000,' said the son.

"'How much is there on the table? Will some gentleman please count it?'

"'I will,' said the captain of the boat, who had been looking on for twenty minutes. He did so, and said, 'There's $9,800 here.'

"'A thousand of it is mine, that I began with,' said the elderly man. 'Harry, take it all.' The son did so, and we all waited breathlessly. At length the elder man spoke again: 'I swore I'd kill you, Baisley, but I don't believe I can. You can go, but don't ever try to play cards on the river again.'

"The gambler sat like a statue. 'I suppose I can take my satchel,' he said, 'or are you going to rob me of that, too?' It seemed as if he was trying to provoke a shot. He certainly showed grit.

"'Rob you? No,' said the other, contemptuously. 'Go, and be sure you leave the boat at the next landing.'

"The other stooped as if to pick up the little satchel of money that stood beside his chair, but with a motion as quick as the older man's had been, he drew a bowie knife and sprang to one side.

"The pistol spoke, but the ball went astray, and the gambler sprang forward like a cat, stabbing at the other's heart.

"The blow, however, did not fall. The planter caught his right hand with his own left, and seized him by the throat with his right hand. There was a short struggle, but the planter, without shifting his hold, lifted the gambler as if he were a child and carried him bodily out of the saloon. We all followed, of course, expecting to see what actually did follow. The miserable wretch, half strangled by the other's vise-like grip, was thrown fairly over the low guard rail and fell with a splash into the river.

"Anything done to the planter? Oh, no! It was a fair fight, and they didn't bother a gentleman for anything like that in those days."

Mr. Martin, of St. Louis, tells a story on a planter whose chips were the wrong color. "I read romantic rose-colored accounts of those old days, sometimes," said old Mr. Martin, "when the steamboats that plied between New Orleans and St. Louis were floating gambling dens. Strange odds and ends get into the press and come to me. It's very pretty to read about, but the real thing was not so nice. The black-eyed, black-mustached hero gambler that you read about was anything but a hero. There was no chivalry in his nature, and he was ready for any dark deed that would profit him. Of course, I am speaking of the professional gambler, for every one gambled; if they had not done so the professional's occupation would have been gone.

"The chivalrous ones were the young Southern planters, reckless, but not mean, who would play the full limit and get fleeced. We read now, too, of beautiful octoroon girls, white as their masters, who were put up as stakes representing so much money, and who have been won and carried off by strange men, away from mother, father, husband or sweetheart.

"In the whole course of my experience I never saw an octoroon disposed of in this way. These light-colored negresses, who have been the stakes in stories, are the creation entirely of the writers. The fact is the octoroon and other light-colored negroes are a great deal more common to-day than they were then. But I have seen negro women disposed of in this fashion, but there was no romance to it. They were generally plantation negroes, rough and hard, and fit for the severest work, and were sold at the first market where the winners happened to land.

"Fights were not as common as might be supposed amid such surroundings, and with such lawless characters. The known readiness to shoot and fight of these men was the guarantee of peace. They respected each other's abilities in the fighting line too much to quarrel over trivial affairs, and many of the unprofessional passengers who gambled knew better than to dispute. There is one incident in this connection that is more prominent than any other.

"I was on one of the smaller boats one night on which were some gamblers going down the river to meet a large steamer coming up. I suppose the partners on the big boat had most of their gambling machinery. At any rate, when they saw two or three young plantation men on the boat they could only find one greasy pack of cards and no chips. The boat had a cargo of corn, so one of the party shelled some and it was used for chips.

"About the time this decision was made one of the planters disappeared. He had managed to slip down into the hold where the corn was, and in the dark he took the first ear he found, and, shelling it, put the corn in his pocket. He afterward joined the game, buying some chips, which he placed in another pocket. It was his intention, if he lost the chips he bought, to fall back on the chips he had stolen.

"Luck was against him, and he lost his last honest chip. It was his turn to ante. He plunged his hand down into his pocket, got some grains of corn and slapped them down on the table. When he raised his hand, lo and behold, the grains were red. In an instant every man was on his feet. One held a pistol at his head, while the rest went through his pockets. Of course they brought up a whole lot of red corn. The corn that the dealers had shelled and given out was white. They bound him hand and foot, and were holding a council to determine what to do with him when we heard the whistle of the big steamer.

"They took him on board with them, and I never could learn what they did with him, but I was on the river for many years after that and I never saw him again."

[. . .]

There are about twenty of the real old-time Mississippi River gamblers who linger about Memphis and Vicksburg, and a common delight of theirs is to relate the glories of gambling on "the river" in the good old days before railroads hemmed in the Mississippi up and down each bank from source to mouth. Tom Ellison, now tottering about Vicksburg on warm days, and showing the effects of severe rheumatism and 72 years of age in every movement, is probably the most widely known of any. The tourists from the cold

North in this region every Winter make a favorite of Tom Ellison, and he re-counts to them many a thrilling tale of the time when he made $10,000 and over in one night and lost it all the succeeding night.

"There isn't any more gambling now," said Tom Ellison, the other day, "and no gamblers, either. Look at what they call gamblers now—kids, noth-ing but kids, who haven't got either sense or manners. There ain't many of us old fellows left, and it is hard scratching most of the time to make regu-lar connections with meals. The river used to be the place for gambling, but that's been dead for over twenty years, and I don't guess it'll ever come to life again. But those were the days, my boy—great days for the town, with thirty-six steamboats all at the wharf at once, the levee covered with drays, and every sport with stuff in his pockets and lots of good clothes.

"I guess there was 500 men who worked the boats between here and New Orleans, and there's no telling how much money they did pull off the travel-lers. It was dead easy money, too, all the time. Every one who travelled had lots of stuff, and every one was willing to bet, and bet high; so when a fellow did win he won right out of the hole at once. Those Southern planters used to lose money just like fun, and were skinned right and left. Occasionally they caught on and there was a shooting match, but the boys didn't take much chance on being plugged.

"I've seen forty gamblers on one boat, the John Dickey. That was in '57, when the officers at Natchez cleaned all the gamblers out of town. The whole gang met the boat at the wharf and started to come aboard, but the Captain wouldn't let them on unless they promised not to play a card aboard. They promised, and he took them on, and the boat came on up the river.

"You never saw a tireder-looking lot of gamblers in your life than them. They hadn't anything to do, and some of them looked as if they had just as soon jump overboard as not. They kept their promise not to play a card, but how they did skin passengers on other games.

"George Devoll got a little piece of tinfoil, wrapped it around some salt and, sitting down near the stove, warmed it and put it up against his cheek. He'd hold it there a while, warm it again, and put it back.

"Presently a passenger who got acquainted with one of George's pals ob-served his actions and inquired what he was doing. George said he was cur-ing his neuralgia, and he explained the cure. After he had done so he kept up the thing for a while, and then he left the cure on the stove hearth and went out.

"Then George's pal marked the package, and suggested that it would be a good joke to change the salt for ashes, just to observe what strength De-voll's belief had in curing his neuralgia. The passenger, a planter, fell in and changed the salt for ashes, and left it on the hearth. Devoll comes back and begins his monkey business again, and the planter comes around and guys George about the cure being no good, and finally George is so dead sure he is cured himself that the planter gets hot and says he'll bet there is no salt in the tinfoil.

"George puts him off and his pal shows the planter what a dead sure thing he has got, and works him up for George in great shape. They finally bet—$300 was the money—and, of course, George shifts a duplicate of his first package on the planter and shows up the salt. The planter was clean 'cornered,' but he was working George on a dead sure thing and couldn't squeal.

"Well, sir, those gamblers got all on that boat, and though they didn't touch a card they cleaned out pretty near everybody that had stuff. We landed at a woodpile to take on wood and the passengers all got out on the bank, and the gamblers all got to betting about running jumps, and, of course, the passengers dropped in. So they'd run off the gangplank and up to a tree to jump, when the first gambler would say, 'Hello, what's here?' and stop. Behind the tree one of the gang had begun throwing three-card monte, while the other got up the jumping scheme. The gamblers won just to make the game good, and the way those fellows skinned the passengers was horrible.

"The Captain got on to the scheme, and when the boat started off up stream the whole gang—40 of them—were just marooned there in the woods on a cold night.

"But they took the next boat up or down, and worked their way up this way or down to New Orleans.

"That wasn't gambling—it was robbing; but that's what went as gambling in those times. The fellows had to be pretty slick, I can tell you. When a boat started out of New Orleans, say, a couple of gamblers would be on board. They were often well-educated fellows, and always fine dressers. All they did was just get acquainted with men with money, and size up how much they had. This was easily done, because card playing was the only thing to pass away the time. These cappers wouldn't win any money. They were just to do the gentlemen, but when they got off the boat their pals came on at some point up the river with a full knowledge of how much money there was on the boat, what men had it, and how these men were best approached.

"It wasn't hard to get acquainted, and it wasn't hard to get up a game of euchre after a drink. Once the game was on the thing was smooth; the dealer fixed the deck and dealt out a good poker hand to the mark, but a better one to his own partner, who promptly declared:

"'I've got a good hand I'd like to bet on.'

"'So have I,' replied Mr. Mark, and then they got into betting, and the stranger got skinned right and left. The cards were stacked and marked on the back, so that he didn't have any chance at all to win. All the playing was done with old star backs. I've seen fellows pick every card in a pack and call it without missing once. I've seen them shuffle them one for one all through from top to bottom, so that they were in the same position after a dozen shuffles that they were in at first. They'd just flutter them up like a flock of quail and get the aces, kings, queens, jacks and tens all together as easy as pie.

"A sucker had no more chance against those fellows than a snowball has in a red-hot oven. Every deck was marked.

"When the fellow was roped into the game the gamblers went to the bartender and bought a deck for a dollar. They owned all the decks. The bartender usually stood in, and that's where most of those old river men got their money. A bartender on the river couldn't knock down anything, so his only chance was to stand in with the gang. They divided pretty fair in those times. I have known Captains to stand in and take their share of the plunder like little men.

"The bartender often came in very handy. When the party sat down to play he would first show up with the drinks ordered by the gambler. He'd get there just after the suckers cut the deck, and pass around the drinks on the tray. It wasn't any trouble to just carry a marked deck under the tray and drop it down while picking up the cut deck. The deal went on, and the suckers got skinned. I have seen this shift made often, and a fellow would hardly believe it could be done so quickly.

"Another scheme was to get the sucker to bet on picking out the cards, say the jacks. He'd bet the sharper couldn't pick out the jack of spades, and the sharper would miss it a couple of times and complain that his head was wrong. He managed to go away just then and leave the deck behind him, when his pal would suggest the plan of stealing the jack and then beating his own game. The victim fell in, of course, and they stole the jack and he hid it in his pocket. Then the first man came back and the talk is renewed and the bets get high. The sucker is sure he can't lose, for he has his jack in his pocket, and he is willing to bet on a dead sure thing.

"So they go, and the man with the cards picks out the cards.

"'There's the jack of diamonds,' and up it turns; 'jack of hearts,' and there he is, sure enough. 'Jack of clubs' comes all right, and next he says, 'And here's your card, sir, jack of spades,' and he pulls it out, face down, and pushes it toward the mark, who has his hand on his card in his pocket. He doubles his bet that it isn't the card, and the bet is taken. The third party turns up the card, and to his surprise it is the jack of spades, shifted in out of another deck. I saw a man lose $1,500 on that game to an old gambler named Bill Vose, and he never said a word, but just got his grip and left the boat at the next landing.

"Billy Peoples used to work on the lower river, and he was a dandy. He roped in a Judge from this city one day to a little game, and the Judge, who wasn't very flush, caught on to his game. He went to the bartender and got a lot of wildcat money, wrapped it around with a couple of twenties, and put some fives in the middle. They started on euchre and the Judge got the usual poker hand, and Mr. Peoples played in. The Judge knew Peoples' game was to let him win to make his final skinning all the surer. He lost a couple of times just to flash his roll and skin off fives to Billy. They played till supper, and the Judge quit $185 winner.

"After supper Billy wanted to open up the game, but the Judge wouldn't have it, and Billy kicked. He went ashore and told a friend about the fellow who had done him, and just as he was telling it the Judge came to the rail, and Billy pointed him out to his friend.

"'Why, you sucker,' said the friend, 'that's so-and-so, from St. Louis. He knows every gambler on the river.'

"Billy offered the Judge a $300 suit of clothes not to tell the story, but the Judge wouldn't hear of it, and all New Orleans heard the story when the Judge got off the boat.

"Another old gambler was Glasscock. Starr Davis was a great old boy. Jim McLane's mother allowed him $10,000 a year not to come near her, but he was broke nearly all the time for all that, and he had to gamble to make his way. Hank Johnson was a daisy, a hard player who never wore a pair of boots worth less than $20. Gib Cohern and Tom Mackay were the dressers of the river. All their winnings used to go in clothes. They'd send to Paris for their under-clothing and all that sort of thing. They were great rivals in those days, when dress went for something. Dock Hill was McLane's partner. Then there was Big Alexander, who worked out of Natchez; Jim McDonald, a dead shot with the pistol; Ashlock, who could do more funny work with a deck of cards than I ever saw before or since. I couldn't name them all.

"They were good fellows, free with their money as water, after scheming to bust their heads to get it. A hundred didn't bother them any more than a chew of tobacco would you.

"What drunks they used to get on after they came in off a trip!

"And clothes! They were all dressers. They wore soft black hats, black clothes, high-heeled boots, low-necked shirts, with big loose collars and ties and frilled bosoms. They had a solitaire breastpin and a big solitaire ring, and one of those big, long gold chains going around the neck three or four times and hanging down over their breast. They didn't drink anything but wine, and they would ride across the streets in hacks rather than get mud on their shoes. They were fine fellows, educated men, who could talk to anyone about anything, and as polite as anything you ever saw.

"There used to be some big games on every boat. Poker was mostly the game. They played bluff and brag a great deal, and the betting was high.

"I saw a man from Hopkinsville, Ky., lose his whole tobacco crop in one night and get up and never mind it particularly. Many a time I've seen a game player just skin off his watch and ring and studs and play them in. Men often lost their goods playing in their way bills. I've seen them betting a bale of cotton at a crack, and it wasn't at all uncommon to hear an old planter betting off his negroes on a good hand. Every man who ever ran on the river knows that these old planters used to play in their lady servants, valuing them all the way from $300 to $1,500. I saw a little colored boy stand up at $300 to back his master's faith in a little flush that wasn't any good on earth.

"The niggers didn't seem to care particularly about it, and it was so common that nobody noticed it particularly. Gambling was commoner then.

"Why, it was nothing but gamble from the time the boat left St. Louis till it reached New Orleans. I've seen a faro game, three poker games and monte running in the cabin, and the deckhands playing at chuck-a-luck. The gamblers would come in disguised in hayseed clothes to skin the passengers. Maybe there'd be four or five on a boat, all supposably strangers to each other and playing into each other's hands. Sometimes there'd be a kick and the Captain would get hot.

"When a passenger would squeal the Captain would ask him to pick out the man who robbed him, and the gambler, if nabbed, would have to give up the stuff and get off the boat anywhere the Captain chose to run her in. The boys used to have false whiskers and wigs for these occasions, so that when the kick was made they couldn't be picked out under their disguises. Many a time I have known them to jump off the boat to get away before the kick was made and the victim could look at the passengers to find out his man. I've swam ashore myself many a time.

"There wasn't much prosecuting then if a fellow was caught. The Captain was boss, and he made the man give up, put him off the boat, and that settled it. They didn't jug a man right away.

"They were great old times then, and they'll never come back."

Works Cited

Primary Sources

Aaron, Daniel. *Cincinnati: Queen City of the West, 1819–1838.* Columbus: Ohio State University Press, 1992.

Anderson, John Q. *Louisiana Swamp Doctor: The Writings of Henry Clay Lewis.* Baton Rouge: Louisiana State University Press, 1962.

"Anecdotes of Western Travel." *Spirit of the Times* 15.17 (June 21, 1845): 189–90.

A.W. "The Mississippi Gambler." *New York Times,* January 30, 1953.

Baldwin, Joseph Glover. *The Flush Times of Alabama and Mississippi.* New York: D. Appleton, 1853.

Beecher, Henry Ward. *Lectures to Young Men, On Various Important Subjects.* 1844. London: James Blackwood & Co. [1871].

Bennett, Emerson. "The Gamblers Outwitted." *Wild Scenes on the Frontiers; or, Heroes of the West* (Philadelphia: Hamelin, 1859). 125–34.

———. *Viola, or Adventures in the Far South-West.* Philadelphia: T. B. Peterson, 1852

Bibb, Henry. *Narrative of the Life and Adventures of Henry Bibb, An American Slave.* New York: the author, 1849.

Brown, William Wells. *Clotel; or, The President's Daughter.* London: Partridge & Oakley, 1853.

Cooke, John Esten. *The Last of the Foresters.* New York: Derby & Jackson, 1856.

Cowell, Joseph. *Thirty Years Passed Among the Players in England and America.* New York: Harper & Bros., 1844.

Dana, Richard Henry. *Two Years Before the Mast.* New York: Harper & Bros., 1844.

Devol, George. *Forty Years a Gambler on the Mississippi.* Cincinnati: Devol & Haines, 1887.

Dick, William. *The American Hoyle.* New York: Dick & Fitzgerald, 1894.

Doesticks, Q. K. Philander [Mortimer Thompson]. *Doesticks: What He Says.* New York: Edward Livermore, 1855.

Dowd, Matt. "Suitable Casino Sites in Mississippi: What Are They? Why? What about the Future?" *Gaming Law Review* 9.4 (2005): 325–32.

Drake, Benjamin. "Putting a Black-Leg on Shore." *Tales and Sketches from the Queen City.* Cincinnati: E. Morgan & Co., 1838. 27–37.

Eggleston, Edward. *The End of the World: A Love Story.* New York: Orange Judd and Company, 1872.

Falconbridge. *Dan. Marble: A Biographical Sketch of that Famous and Diverting Humorist*. New York: Dewitt & Davenport, 1851.

Faulkner, William. *Absalom, Absalom!* New York: Random House, 1936.

———. *Big Woods*. New York: Random House, 1955.

———. *The Unvanquished*. 1938. *Novels, 1936–1940*. New York: Library of America, 1990. 317–492.

Ferber, Edna. *Show Boat*. 1926. London: Pan, 1953.

Fitz James, Zilla. *Zilla Fitz James, The Female Bandit of the South-West; or, The Horrible, Mysterious and Awful Disclosures in the Life of the Creole Murderess [. . .]*. Edited by A. Richards. Little Rock: A. R. Orton, 1852.

Flint, Timothy. *Recollections of the Last Ten Years, Passed in Occasional Residences and Journeyings in the Valley of the Mississippi*. Boston: Cummings, Hilliard, and Company, 1826.

"A Game of 'Full Deck Poker.'" *Spirit of the Times* 15.47 (January 17, 1846): 554.

Gay, Sydney. "How We Grow in the Great Northwest." *Atlantic Monthly* 23.168 (April 1869): 438–49.

Gould, Emerson. *Fifty Years on the Mississippi*. St. Louis: Nixon-Jones Printing Co., 1889.

Green, Jonathan. *Gambling Exposed; a Full Exposition of All the Various Arts, Mysteries and Miseries of Gambling*. 1847. Philadelphia: T. B. Peterson, 1857.

Habermehl, John. *Life on the Western Rivers*. Pittsburgh: McNary & Simpson, 1901.

Hall, Abraham Oakey. *The Manhattaner in New Orleans; or, Phases of "Crescent City" Life*. New York: J. S. Redfield, Clinton Hall, 1851.

Hamilton, Thomas. *Men and Manners in America*. 2 vols. Edinburgh: William Blackwood, 1833.

Hildreth, Richard. *Despotism in America: An Inquiry into the Nature, Results, and Legal Basis of the Slave-Holding System in the United States*. Boston: Whipple and Damrell, 1840.

———. *The White Slave; or, Memoirs of a Fugitive*. Boston: Tappan and Whittemore, 1852.

Howells, William Dean. "The Pilot's Story." *Atlantic Monthly* 6.35 (September 1860): 323–26.

Hugunin, Henry Edward. *Life and Adventures of Henry Edward Hugunin; or, Thirty Years a Gambler*. New York: Oliphant, 1879.

Hundley, Daniel R. *Social Relations in Our Southern States*. New York: Henry B. Price, 1860.

Ingraham, Joseph Holt. "The Bivouac; or, A Night at the Mouth of the Ohio, A Sketch of Western Voyaging." *The Spectre Steamer and Other Tales*. Boston: United States Publishing Company, 1846. 71–76.

———. *The South-West. By a Yankee*. 2 vols. New York: Harper & Brothers, 1835.

Klauprecht, Emil. *Cincinnati, or The Mysteries of the West*. Edited by Don Heinrich Tolzman. Translated by Steven Rowan. New York: Peter Lang, 1996.

Lakier, Aleksandr Borisovich. *A Russian Looks at America*. Translated and edited by Arnold Schrier and Joyce Story. Chicago: University of Chicago Press, 1979.

Latrobe, Charles Joseph. *The Rambler in North America*. 2 vols. New York: Harper & Brothers, 1835.

Lewis, M. G. "How Dodge 'Dodged' the Sharpers." *Spirit of the Times* 20.32 (September 28, 1850): 375–76.

Lillard, J. F. B. *Poker Stories: As Told By Statesmen, Soldiers, Lawyers, Commercial Travelers, Bankers, Actors, Editors, Millionaires, Members of the Ananias Club and the Talent, Embracing the Most Remarkable Games 1845–95*. London: Gibbings and Company, 1896.

Little 'Un. "Uncle Abe's 'Winnin' Hand.'" *Spirit of the Times* 19.44 (December 22, 1849): 518.

Long, Mason. *The Life of Mason Long, The Converted Gambler*. 1878. Fort Wayne, Ind.: Mason Long, 1882.

Marryat, Frederick. *A Diary in America, With Remarks on its Institutions: Part Second*. 3 vols. London: Longman, Orme, Brown, Green & Longmans, 1839.

Melville, Herman. *The Confidence-Man: His Masquerade*. New York: Dix, Edwards & Co., 1857.

Merrick, George Byron. *Old Times on the Upper Mississippi: Recollections of a Steamboat Pilot from 1854 to 1863*. 1909. Minneapolis: University of Minnesota Press, 2001.

Mitchell, Margaret. *Gone with the Wind*. 1936. London: Pan, 1974.

Morris, John [John O'Connor]. *Wanderings of a Vagabond. An Autobiography*. New York: the author, 1873.

Mott, Luther. *Golden Multitudes: The Story of Best Sellers in the United States*. New York: Macmillan, 1947.

Nathan, George Jean. "The Old-Time Train Gambler." *Harper's Weekly*, May 21, 1910, 11–12.

New Hampshire Gazette. April 19, 1825.

Nichols, George Ward. "Down the Mississippi." *Harper's New Monthly Magazine* 41.246 (November 1870): 835–45.

Olmsted, Frederick Law. *A Journey in the Seaboard Slave States*. 2 vols. New York: G. P. 1856. Putnam's Sons, 1904.

Pinkerton, Allen. *Criminal Reminiscences and Detective Sketches*. New York: G. W. Dillingham, 1878.

Power, William Grattan Tyrone. *Impressions of America, During the Years 1833, 1834, and 1835*. 2 vols. London: Richard Bentley, 1836.

P.U.T. "A Strong Hand at Poker." *Spirit of the Times* 17.36 (October 30, 1847): 422.

Rekrap. "A Gambling Incident." *Spirit of the Times* 17.27 (August 28, 1847): 314.

Richardson, Albert D. *Beyond the Mississippi.* Hartford: American Publishing Company, 1867.

Rogers, Laura Bibb. "The Hasty Marriage." *Southern Literary Messenger* 34 (April 1862): 239–45.

Sargent, Epes. *Peculiar: A Tale of the Great Transition.* New York: Carleton, 1864.

Schultz, Christian. *Travels on an Inland Voyage.* 2 vols. New York: Isaac Riley, 1810.

[Smith, Richard Penn]. *Col. Crockett's Exploits and Adventures in Texas.* Philadelphia: T. K. & P. G. Collins, 1836.

Smith, Solomon. "Breaking a Bank." *Theatrical Management in the West and South For Thirty Years* (New York: Harper & Brothers, 1868), 189–91.

Tensas, Madison [Henry Clay Lewis]. "Taking Good Advice." *Odd Leaves from the Life of a Louisiana "Swamp Doctor."* Philadelphia: A. Hart, 1850.

Thackeray, William Makepeace. *The Yellowplush Papers.* New York: D. Appleton, 1852.

The Times (London). August 25, 1835.

Trollope, Frances. *Domestic Manners of the Americans.* 2 vols. London: Whittaker, Treacher & Co., 1832.

Twain, Mark. *Life on the Mississippi.* Boston: James R. Osgood and Company, 1883.

———. *Notebooks & Journals.* Vol. 2. Edited by Frederick Anderson, Lin Salamo, and Bernard L. Stein. Berkeley: University of California Press, 1975.

———. *Roughing It.* Hartford: American Publishing Company, 1891.

"The Vicksburg Tragedy." *Niles' Weekly Register,* August 8, 1835.

"The Way an Old One Mistook a Green Case." *Spirit of the Times* 17.10 (May 1, 1847): 109.

Whipple, Edwin Percy. *Essays and Reviews.* 2 vols. New York: D. Appleton, 1849.

Willett, Edward. *Flush Fred's Double.* New York: Beadle & Adams, 1884.

———. *Flush Fred's Full Hand.* New York: Beadle & Adams, 1884.

Secondary Sources

Anthony, Irvin. *Paddle Wheels and Pistols.* Philadelphia: Macrae Smith, 1929.

Asbury, Herbert. *The French Quarter: An Informal History of the New Orleans Underworld.* 1936. New York: Thunder's Mouth, 2003.

Barthelme, Frederick, and Steven Barthelme. *Double Down: Reflections on Gambling and Loss.* New York: Harcourt, 1999.

Berkeley, Edmund, and Dorothy Smith Berkeley. *George William Featherstonhaugh: The First U.S. Government Geologist.* Tuscaloosa: University of Alabama Press, 1988.

Booth, Michael R. *English Melodrama.* London: Herbert Jenkins, 1965.

Brandstadter, Evan. "Uncle Tom and Archy Moore: The Antislavery Novel as Ideological Symbol." *American Quarterly* 26.2 (May 1974): 160–75.

Buchanan, Thomas C. *Black Life on the Mississippi: Slaves, Free Blacks, and the Western Steamboat World.* Chapel Hill: University of North Carolina Press, 2004.

Cady, Edwin H. *Young Howells & John Brown: Episodes in a Radical Education.* Columbus: Ohio State University Press, 1985.

Cash, W. J. *The Mind of the South.* 1941. New York: Vintage, 1961.

Cohen, David. *Chasing the Red, White, and Blue: A Journey in Tocqueville's Footsteps through Contemporary America.* New York: Picador, 2001.

Cook, Jonathan A. *Satirical Apocalypse: An Anatomy of Melville's* The Confidence-Man. Westport, Conn.: Greenwood, 1996.

Crosby, Sara Lynn. "Poisonous Mixtures: Gender, Race, Empire, and Cultural Authority in Antebellum Female Poisoner Literature." Diss. University of Notre Dame, 2005.

De Voto, Bernard. *Mark Twain's America.* 1932. Lincoln: University of Nebraska Press, 1997.

Dowd, Matt. "Suitable Casino Sites in Mississippi: What Are They? Why? What about the Future?" *Gaming Law Review* 9.4 (2005): 325–32.

duCille, Ann. "Where in the World Is William Wells Brown? Thomas Jefferson, Sally Hemings, and the DNA of African-American Literary History." *American Literary History* 12.3 (Autumn 2000): 443–62.

Emerson, Donald E. *Richard Hildreth.* Baltimore: Johns Hopkins Press, 1946.

Fabian, Ann. *Card Sharps, Dream Books, & Bucket Shops: Gambling in Nineteenth-Century America.* 1990. New York: Routledge, 1999.

Findlay, John. *People of Chance: Gambling in American Society from Jamestown to Las Vegas.* New York: Oxford University Press, 1986.

Gillespie, Michael. *Come Hell or High Water: A Lively History of Steamboating on the Mississippi and Ohio Rivers.* Stoddard, Wisc.: Heritage, 2001.

Greenberg, Kenneth S. *Honor & Slavery: Lies, Duels, Noses, Masks, Dressing as a Woman, Gifts, Strangers, Humanitarianism, Death, Slave Rebellions, the Proslavery Argument, Baseball, Hunting, and Gambling in the Old South.* Princeton: Princeton University Press, 1996.

Halttunen, Karen. *Confidence Men and Painted Women: A Study of Middle-Class Culture in America, 1830–1870.* New Haven: Yale University Press, 1982.

Hanners, John. *"It Was Play or Starve": Acting in the Nineteenth-Century American Popular Theatre.* Bowling Green, Ohio: Bowling Green University Press, 1993.

Hargrave, Catherine Perry. *A History of Playing Cards.* 1930. New York: Dover Publications, 2000.

Hite, Roger W. "Voice of a Fugitive: Henry Bibb and Ante-bellum Black Separatism." *Journal of Black Studies* 4.3 (March 1974): 269–84.

Hobson, Fred. *Tell about the South: The Southern Rage to Explain.* Baton Rouge: Louisiana State University Press, 1983.

Hollingsworth, Keith. *The Newgate Novel, 1830–1847: Bulwer, Ainsworth, Dickens & Thackeray.* Detroit: Wayne State University Press, 1963.

Horwitz, Tony. *Confederates in the Attic: Dispatches from the Unfinished Civil War.* New York: Vintage, 1999.

Howells, William Dean. "The End of the World." *Atlantic Monthly* 30.182 (December 1872): 746–47.

———. *Literary Friends and Acquaintance: A Personal Retrospect of American Authorship.* 1900; Bloomington: Indiana University Press, 1968.

Hunter, Louis. *Steamboats on the Western Rivers: An Economic and Technological History.* 1949. New York: Dover, 1993.

Johannsen, Albert. *The House of Beadle and Adams and Its Dime and Nickel Novels.* 2 vols. Norman: University of Oklahoma Press, 1950.

John, Juliet. *Dickens's Villains: Melodrama, Character, Popular Culture.* New York: Oxford University Press, 2003.

Jordan, Philip D. "Ossian Euclid Dodge: Eccentric Troubadour." *Historian* 31.2 (February 1969): 194–210.

Lears, Jackson. *Something for Nothing: Luck in America.* New York: Viking, 2003.

Levine, Robert S., ed. *Clotel; or, The President's Daughter: A Narrative of Slave Live in the United States.* By William Wells Brown. Boston: Bedford/St. Martin's, 2000.

Morris, Christopher. *Becoming Southern: The Evolution of a Way of Life, Warren County and Vicksburg, Mississippi, 1770–1860.* New York: Oxford University Press, 1995.

Penick, James Lal, Jr. *The Great Western Land Pirate: John A. Murrell in Legend and History.* Columbia: University of Missouri Press, 1981.

Randel, William. *Edward Eggleston.* New York: Twayne, 1963.

Read, Opie. *Mark Twain and I.* Chicago: Reilly & Lee, 1940.

Reith, Gerda. *The Age of Chance: Gambling in Western Culture.* London: Routledge, 1999.

Reynolds, David S. *Beneath the American Renaissance: The Subversive Imagination in the Age of Emerson and Melville.* New York: Alfred A. Knopf, 1988.

Rose, Cynthia. *Lottie Deno: Gambling Queen of Hearts.* Santa Fe: Clear Light Publishers, 1994.

Rourke, Constance. *Davy Crockett.* New York: Harcourt, Brace & Company, 1934.

Seelye, John. Introduction. *On to the Alamo: Colonel Crockett's Exploits and Adventures in Texas.* By Richard Penn Smith. New York: Penguin, 2003.

Simms, William Gilmore. *Richard Hurdis: A Tale of Alabama*. 1838. New York: W. J. Widdleton, 1864.

Smith, James F. *Gambling Cultures: Studies in History and Interpretation*. London: Routledge, 1996.

Smith, Thomas Ruys. "Independence Day, 1835: The John A. Murrell Conspiracy and the Lynching of the Vicksburg Gamblers in Literature." *Mississippi Quarterly* 59.1–2 (Winter-Spring 2006): 129–60.

Volberg, Rachel A. *Gambling and Problem Gambling in Mississippi: A Report to the Mississippi Council on Compulsive Gambling*. Starkville: Mississippi State University, 1997.

Wadsworth, Sarah A. "Louisa May Alcott, William T. Adams, and the Rise of Gender-Specific Series Books." *The Lion and the Unicorn* 25.1 (January 2001): 17–46.

Watson, Charles S. *The History of Southern Drama*. Lexington: University Press of Kentucky, 1997.

Wecter, Dixon. *Sam Clemens of Hannibal*. Houghton Mifflin, 1961.

Wilgoren, Jodi. "Midwest Towns Feel Gambling Is a Sure Thing." *New York Times*, May 20, 2002.

Wimsatt, Mary Ann. *The Major Fiction of William Gilmore Simms*. Baton Rouge: Louisiana State University Press, 1989.

Yates, Norris W. *William T. Porter and the* Spirit of the Times: *A Study of the Big Bear School of Humor*. Baton Rouge: Louisiana State University Press, 1957.